Small, Strong Congregations

Creating Strengths and Health for Your Congregation

∞

Kennon L. Callahan

JOSSEY-BASS
A Wiley Company
San Francisco

Jossey-Bass Inc., 350 Sansome Street, San Francisco, California 94104.
Jossey-Bass is a registered trademark of Jossey-Bass Inc., A Wiley Company.

Unless otherwise stated, biblical quotations are from *The Holy Bible,
Revised Standard Version* (copyright © Thomas Nelson & Sons). Also
cited are the *King James Version* and *New English Bible* (KJV and NEB:
Copyright © Christianity Today, Inc., 1965).

Jossey-Bass books and products are available through most book-
stores. To contact Jossey-Bass directly, call (888) 378-2537, fax to
(800) 605-2665, or visit our website at www.josseybass.com.

Substantial discounts on bulk quantities of Jossey-Bass books are
available to corporations, professional associations, and other organizations. For details and discount information, contact the special
sales department at Jossey-Bass.

TCF Manufactured in the United States of America on Lyons Falls Turin
Book. This paper is acid-free and 100 percent totally chlorine-free.

Library of Congress Cataloging-in-Publication Data

Callahan, Kennon L.
    Small, strong congregations : creating strengths and health for your
congregation / Kennon L. Callahan.— 1st ed.
        p. cm.
Includes index.
    ISBN 0-7879-4980-9 (alk. paper)
    1. Small churches.   I. Title.
    BV637.8 .C35 2000
    250—dc21

                                                                00-09569

FIRST EDITION
HB Printing   10 9 8 7 6 5 4 3 2 1

Contents

v

100061

To D'Wayne Roberts and Jane Eubank
Marvin and Murlene Judy
Earl and Ethel Brewer

We are grateful for their gifts in our lives.
We are thankful for their wisdom and compassion,
for their encouragement and hope.

Kennon L. and Julia McCoy Callahan

Preface

This book is for congregations and pastors looking forward to being small, strong congregations.

The twenty-first century is the century of small, strong congregations. In the future, there will be many mega-congregations. There will be even more small, strong congregations. We are seeing the emergence of a vast movement of small, strong congregations across the planet. Indeed, this movement is already well under way.

You will discover, in this book, the qualities that are decisive in shaping a strong, healthy, small congregation. With these qualities well in place, your congregation will be helpful in the lives of many people for years to come.

Small, Strong Congregations encourages you to develop your strengths, not your size. There has been a preoccupation with being bigger. To be bigger is to be bigger, not necessarily better. The art is to advance the distinctive strengths and qualities of a small, strong congregation. Focus on your spirit and strengths.

Being a small, strong congregation is a way of thinking and planning, behaving and acting. This book helps you appreciate the distinctive values and advantages of small, strong congregations. You discover wisdom, clear insights, and practical suggestions. You discover the possibilities for a

healthy, constructive approach with your congregation. The
suggestions in the book invite you to a helpful, effective future.

God invites us to serve in mission. God gives us the
remarkable gifts of compassion and community. God encourages us toward self-reliance and self-sufficiency. God gives us
the amazing gifts of worship and hope. God helps us to be,
together, a team of leaders and congregation. God provides
just enough of a home that we can be God's family together.
God shares extraordinary generosity with us. With God's
help, we live with the spirit of promise.

Have fun with the book. Have fun with your small, strong
congregation.

Acknowledgments

I want to thank the countless small congregations that have
been generous in sharing with me their wisdom and experiences. Their journeys are remarkable. The possibilities they
have discovered along the way are extraordinary. I am grateful to them for helping me understand the qualities that contribute to being a small, strong congregation.

I especially want to express my appreciation to these congregations:

Mountville

Thompson

Brady Lake

Pleasant Valley

Bethel

Mt. Gilead

Turin

Coke's Chapel

Julie and I have had the distinctive privilege of serving these small, strong congregations. We discovered wonderful people in each congregation, and they were gracious to include us in the family.

I want to thank the many congregations with which I have had the privilege of serving as their consultant. In the process of helping them, they have helped me understand, richly and fully, the way of thinking, planning, behaving, and living in a small, strong congregation.

I want to thank Marvin and Murlene Judy. Julie and I met them in 1958. They have served as wonderful leaders across this country, helping small congregations. Marvin taught for many years in the Perkins School of Theology at Southern Methodist University. He and I have worked together on a vast range of projects in the years come and gone. Marvin and Murlene have been a remarkable team, and I am most grateful for all I have learned from them.

I want to thank Earl and Ethel Brewer. Julie and I met them in 1969. They, too, have been pivotal leaders in helping small congregations. Earl taught for many years in the Candler School of Theology at Emory University. Earl and Ethel have contributed much wisdom to me. Their spirit and vision have been extraordinarily helpful to my understanding of small congregations.

Julie and I are blessed to have had the privilege of sharing and working with Marvin and Murlene and with Earl and Ethel. Their wisdom and spirit, their compassion and hope have been profoundly helpful. We are more than friends. We have shared together as family.

I want to thank D'Wayne Roberts and Jane Eubank for their distinctive contributions to the book. D'Wayne is a remarkable person. She did the original typing of the manuscript with accuracy and precision. Moreover, D'Wayne and

Jane, who are sisters, have offered extraordinary editorial suggestions. The book is richer and more helpful because of their major gifts.

I especially appreciate their contributions since Jane had Lou Gehrig's disease. She and D'Wayne were exceptionally gracious to give of their wisdom and time to advance the book, even as time was short for Jane. I am grateful for their participation in the book, even as they were sharing some of their last time together. Jane died during the final editing. I thank them both for their spirit in this book.

I want to thank Julia McCoy Callahan for her wisdom and insight. I thank her especially for sharing in our ministry with the small, strong congregations we have been privileged to serve. She is a remarkable person, and we share an extraordinary life together.

I want to thank Sarah Polster. She is a most remarkable senior editor. This is our fourth book together. I am grateful for her wisdom and many insights in advancing this work. She has a wonderful gift of clarity. Her comprehension of the material is exceptional. Her counsel has advanced the book considerably. It is a stronger, more helpful book because of her wisdom.

I want to thank Joanne Clapp Fullagar. She and her team have done excellent work in bringing this book to publication. I am grateful for her invaluable assistance and her thoughtfulness. The whole production staff at Jossey-Bass is excellent. Production of this book moved forward in a straightforward, timely way because of her leadership.

I encourage you to enjoy the book. You will find it a good fun book. The wisdom and suggestions will benefit you. May God bless you, your mission, and your congregation in this extraordinary time.

KENNON L. CALLAHAN
August 2000

1

Small Is Strong

O my Strength, I will sing praises to thee,
for thou, O God, are my fortress,
the God who shows me steadfast love.

—PSALMS 59:17 (RSV)

Be at peace, John," I said. "You are doing well. They cannot compete with you."

John and I were standing on a small patch of grass that passes for the front lawn of his congregation. We were looking across the street at one of the largest mega-congregations on the planet.

John has been pastor of his congregation for five years now. In that time, the congregation has become legendary for its mission with preschool children, its shepherding in people's lives, its leadership team, and its generosity with worthwhile projects in the community and around the world. It has been a solid five years. The congregation has done well.

John is of average height, slightly balding, quiet, and shy. People admire his gentle spirit, the twinkle in his eye, the remarkable compassion he shares with them. He is good with children, has the compassion of a good shepherd, and gives leadership with wisdom and encouragement.

The congregation is a small, strong congregation. They think, plan, and work together like a small, strong congregation. In earlier times, they behaved like a small, weak congregation. There was also a brief period of time during which they were a small, dying congregation. In recent years, they have become a small, strong congregation.

I had come to help John and his congregation look to their future for the coming three to five years. For some time, we had been standing on that small patch of grass looking across the street at the people and the cars coming and going from the vast buildings and parking lots of that megachurch. It was a weekday afternoon, and there were lots of programs and activities happening there. Many people were coming to participate.

I said, "John, they do well what their church does. They are a healthy mega-congregation. You do well what your church does. You are a small, strong congregation.

"So long as you focus on what you do well and think and act in that way, they cannot compete with you. However, the minute you try to become a 'mini' mega-congregation, you will be done in. If you do that, you will have moved to their way of doing church, rather than the solid, creative, and successful way you are now doing church."

A quiet kind of peace came over John's face. He relaxed. He became less preoccupied with all the things his church was not doing that mega-congregations do well. He began to see more clearly all the things his church is doing that small, strong congregations do well.

Four Futures

In the century before us, God gives us four futures for congregations:

1. Small, strong congregations

2. Middle-sized congregations

3. Large, regional congregations

4. Mega-congregations

Each of these is a distinctive way of thinking, planning, and acting as a church. The result is a congregation of a certain size.

Bill is happy. He was not always as peaceful and content as he is now. He had come to his current congregation eight years earlier. Years before, while in seminary, he had served as pastor of two rural congregations. They were joined together as a circuit, and, on Sunday morning, he would preach in one at nine o'clock and in the other at eleven o'clock. During the week, he would attend seminary and, with good spirit and deep love, pastor the people of the two congregations. He and his wife had married just before they went to serve the two congregations. While there, they had a wonderful time. They loved the people, and the people loved them. It was hard to leave.

At the time of graduation, he moved to serve three congregations on a circuit, one in a small town and the other two out in the country. Each Sunday morning, he would preach in the town congregation at nine-thirty, and on alternating Sundays in one of the country congregations at eleven. During the week, now that he was out of seminary, he would share his compassion, wisdom, and encouragement with the families in all three congregations.

Their first child was born soon after they arrived. Their second child came three years later. While they were there, they had a grand time. The three small, strong congregations flourished.

Since he had been so successful, he was asked to be the pastor of a midsized congregation. It would be a move to the city. They said he was the person for the job. When he arrived he found a weak, declining, middle congregation, without much future. It was on the verge of becoming a dying congregation.

He began to put in place the behavior patterns of a healthy medium-sized congregation. He helped his people think, plan, and behave like a healthy middle congregation. They started to build on their strengths, and to put in place, with excellence and wisdom, nine of the twelve central character-istics of an effective church (which I list later in this chapter).

They developed a superb linkage of mission and program that is the best in the city. Their mission with children is leg-endary. Their program of vacation Bible school is the most competent in the community. Over these eight years, they have developed a number of healthy new groups. They are no longer two groups, old-timers and newcomers. (Well, the newcomers are not that new. They came thirty years before. But, from the standpoint of the old-timers, they are new.) Now, with the development of several new groups, the con-gregation is no longer two groups who fuss and feud with each other.

With the help of several wise persons, Bill developed a team of talented, compassionate leaders and staff who work together as a mission team. Their competencies and their long-term continuity have meant much to advancing the health of the congregation.

The congregation quit trying to do everything. They gave up trying to be the church that had something for everyone. They developed their capacity to keep focused on the few "20 percenters" that, for them, deliver 80 percent of the results. They created the flexibility of a mission-driven, rather than a survival-driven, structure. They paid off the debt so they would no longer be preoccupied with it. They advanced their mission with children.

In his early years of ministry, Bill learned how to serve as the pastor of small, strong congregations. With this congregation, he learned how to think, plan, and act as the pastor of a healthy middle-sized congregation. It was not always easy. There were troubling, difficult times. In the fourth year, he almost called it quits. Nonetheless, he persevered. Now, he is happy and content. He and his wife are looking forward to raising their three children (the third was born two years after they came to the congregation). Bill is glad that he and the congregation have together come into their own.

David is the pastor of a large, regional congregation. He has been there for a total of fifteen years. Actually, as David and I visited, we discovered he served "three pastorates" with his people. The first three years he was the "interim" pastor, cleaning up the messes left by his two predecessors. His immediate predecessor (with the help of the church bookkeeper) had used church funds in inappropriate ways. Both were asked to leave. The congregation never did find the missing $40,000.

The minister before that left on his own. The difficulty was that the choir director went with him, slipping away one dark October night without saying anything to anyone. Both of them were married to other partners. The two divorces that ensued, the custody issues surrounding the children, the battles over property—all these took their toll on the families and on the congregation.

When David arrived, there was still much heat and fire, grieving and confusion over this series of events. It took three years to deal with all of it. In his fourth year, he began his second pastorate. He and his leaders intentionally began learning how to think, plan, and act like a large, regional congregation. It was clear to them, simply by looking at their current strengths and the community around them, that God was inviting them to serve a large, regional mission. For about five years, from his fourth through ninth years, he and his leaders advanced their understanding of how to lead in such a mission.

Beginning in the tenth year, they came into their own and David began his third pastorate. By then, the congregation was delivering nine of the twelve central characteristics of an effective church. They were doing so in strong ways. They developed an extended regional mission outreach, serving people within an average trip time from their location. (Average trip time is the amount of time people invest in driving to work, to major shopping, and to major social and recreational activities. In David's community, that is twenty-five minutes one way.)

They advanced their capacity to serve many in the community. They put in place excellent mission and service projects with children, youths, and senior adults. They do these things better than anyone else in the community. They have built the continuity of an extremely competent team of key leaders and staff. They function together, in a holistic, unified spirit. Each leader and staff person brings considerable gifts and competencies to the team. They now have three healthy worship services. Each has its own integrity and identity. Each serves a distinctive, important purpose in helping people with their lives. There are many groupings, with new groupings starting each year.

David is glad he and his congregation have emerged as a strong, healthy regional church. As we talked, he shared that he could have moved to several churches and had several pastorates at various times during the fifteen years. I suggested to him that in fact he had. In a real way, he served three different pastorates across the years. He did so without packing and unpacking, without moving boxes in and out of communities. He loves his congregation and community. They love him, and they look ahead to many years together.

Jim is the pastor of a mega-congregation. He never thought he would be. He was surprised when the call came. He was happy where he was and having fun doing solid work. They said, "That is precisely why we want you to consider coming. We know you will be happy here, and have fun doing solid work with us."

Jim and his family discussed the possibility. His wife was at a point in her work where she could move. Indeed, the possibilities for her vocation were fuller in the new city. Their two oldest, both boys, thought that if the family were going to move, now would be the time, with the older son entering seventh grade and the next entering fifth grade. Waiting to move in a few years would be more difficult, when the kids would be in high school and the last part of junior high. Their daughter, three years old, seemed to be happy wherever they were. They made the move and were amazed at how graciously and generously they were welcomed.

They discovered a congregation delivering nine of the twelve central characteristics with extraordinary strength and excellence. The congregation shares three compelling missions in the community: with the poor, with families that have elementary children, and with youths and their families. There are multiple, stirring services of worship, with separate choirs for each of the six services. The spirit of the congregation has about it a dynamic of creativity and flexibility.

Jim knew he would be the senior pastor of a staff of fifty-some persons, each competent in his or her own field. He found them well organized into five team clusters: mission, outreach, and evangelism; worship and music; congregational and community care; groups and programs; and giving development, administration, and finance. Their continuity as an extremely competent staff, matched with equally competent key leaders, made Jim's coming even easier and more fun.

He discovered a streamlined dynamic of action and momentum. It did not take three months to make a thirty-dollar decision. The congregation and the staff spent more time in sharing action and mission, and very little time in committee meetings. There were many one-time, seasonal, and short-term projects, programs, and teams. The congregation had sufficient space and facilities for the mission. They were not burdened with overwhelming debt.

When Jim and I were together, he had been with his mega-congregation for three years. He shared with me how much he had grown in both his preaching and his leadership. I said to him, "You have learned a leadership of presence, not a leadership of always being present. You are loving, listening, learning, and leading with your congregation. You are trusting your leaders and your staff. You are not allowing yourself to be caught up in details. The results are that both your preaching and your leading benefit." We talked at some length about these two areas. Jim looks forward to serving for many years in his healthy mega-congregation.

Jim and his congregation are but one example of an increasing number of mega-congregations. Were we to look at a graph today showing the number of mega-congregations, we might make the measurement of the bar graph one inch high. When we gather again thirty years from this time, the bar graph for mega-congregations will measure closer to fifteen inches high.

There is an extraordinary explosion of mega-congregations happening, and not all of them are on television. Many of them are happening in medium-sized cities and smaller towns, not just in metropolitan areas. It is clear, as we look to the twenty-first century, that one of the strong futures for the Christian movement is continuing development of mega-congregations.

I have had the fun of helping many mega-congregations come into being. At the same time, I want to honor with you that this is only one future for local congregations. You will find a discussion of each of these four futures in my book *Building for Effective Mission*. I take a moment in this book to talk about all four, so you know that all four futures are emerging. I mention mega-congregations because of the array of literature that has come out—and will come out increasingly—which, regrettably, heralds the mega-congregation as the future of the church.

It is tough to do a mega-congregation in some parts of, say, South Dakota, Indiana, New England, South Carolina, or deep Southwest Texas. It is tough to do a mega-congregation in some parts of South America, China, Asia, Australia, India, Africa, and Europe. Moreover, even in large metropolitan areas, the mega-congregation is not the only viable future for congregations. In the twenty-first century, we will see a marked increase of small, strong congregations in metropolitan areas.

Small, Strong and Large, Regional

For the purpose of our current discussion, I want to confirm that there are four futures for congregations, and that for most congregations two of the four are likely the simplest futures to consider. One helpful future is small, strong. The other helpful future is large, regional.

I affectionately refer these two as the two "easiest" futures for congregations. It is tough to do small, strong. It is tough to do large, regional. The four futures mentioned previously are all tough, but of the four, these two are the "easiest tough futures" that God gives most congregations.

Some denominations used to know how to do small, strong congregations but have virtually forgotten how. They have not yet learned how to do large, regional. They have bet the farm on the middle. It is not accidental that some denominations are successfully declining or dying.

Small, strong is tough. Large, regional is tough. Both of them are an easier tough than the middle. The toughest future for a congregation is the middle. The middle is tough-tough. The middle gets beaten both ways. It is too large to deliver the intimacy of small, strong. It is not large enough to deliver the resources, programming, and staffing of large, regional. It is tougher than simply being a church caught on a plateau; it is the church caught in the middle. Moreover, it usually has fewer staff, more buildings, and a larger debt than is helpful to do the middle successfully.

It is not true that small equals declining. Many small colleges are doing very well. Many large, regional universities are doing very well. The ones in the middle are virtually gone. Think of all the small, strong colleges you know that have found a focus on their specific mission. They deliver it with excellence. They are thriving. Many students are drawn to the strengths and advantages that small, strong colleges offer.

Some small colleges are weak. Some are dying. Usually, these colleges have two problems. First, they do not deliver, with excellence, the behavior pattern—the way of thinking, planning, acting, and living—of a small, strong college. Second, they make the mistake of trying to think, plan, and act like large, regional universities. Thus, they do not share and develop the strengths of a small, strong college.

Certainly, there are some large, regional universities in trouble. There are, however, many large, regional universities that have a specific, focused array of key priorities. They deliver them with excellence and confidence, and therefore are healthy and thriving. Many students are drawn to the diversity and range of possibilities that large, regional universities offer. The point is that, in higher education, the middle is in trouble, is weak and dying, or has gone out of business.

Similarly, many large, regional shopping centers do well. To be sure, some are in difficulty, but many thrive. Some small specialty shops do well. Mostly, any store that tries to do the middle is in trouble, if not already out of business.

Regrettably, some denominations have staked their future on the middle.

Both small, strong and large, regional congregations that deliver nine of the twelve central characteristics of effective congregations are doing well. They have a spirit of creativity and flexibility. They honor excellent mistakes. They are being developed by a team of competent, compassionate leaders.

Small, strong congregations and large, regional congregations do what they do well—with extraordinary competency. They do not deliver mediocre, halfway behavior patterns. They focus on delivering the qualities that are distinctive to small, strong and large, regional churches, and they deliver them in so strong a fashion that both are healthy, constructive congregations.

The tendency of weak congregations is to try to do something that does not match their strengths and, along with that, to try to do too much. The art is learning to focus on only the few, key, essential strengths and priorities that deliver the future.

I think of the health of congregations in three ways: as strong, weak, or dying. There are, then, three types of small congregations: small and strong, small and weak, and small and dying. The same can be said for large, regional congregations. Some are large, strong; some are large, weak; some are large, dying.

Weak or dying is not the result of being a certain size. It is the result of a way of thinking, planning, and acting.

Regrettably, some congregations develop patterns of thinking, planning, and acting that contribute to their becoming weak or dying congregations. Some are small; some are middle; some are large, regional; and some are mega-congregations.

We have made the mistake of being preoccupied with the patterns of behavior in small congregations that contribute to their being weak or dying. We have been much engrossed with the sources of illness and weakness in small congregations. Then, we assume that these patterns happen only in small congregations. As a matter of fact, I find that these patterns happen in all four futures of being a church.

Here is a chart that illustrates a constructive way of thinking about the four futures God gives those of us in the Christian movement. It helps us to see that strong, weak, or dying can apply to any one of these four futures.

	Strong	Weak	Dying
Small congregations			
Middle congregations			
Large, regional congregations			
Mega-congregations			

The purpose of this book is to help you grow forward the distinctive future of being a small, strong congregation. Your congregation touches the lives and destinies of many people across the years as you share God's mission.

Emerging Possibilities

Small is strong.

The twenty-first century is the century of small, strong congregations. More people will be drawn to small, strong congregations than any other kind of congregation. Yes, there are many mega-congregations; their number is increasing greatly. Nevertheless, around the planet, the vast majority of congregations will be small and strong, and the vast majority of people will be in these congregations.

It is not the case, as some have suggested, that although mega-congregations represent a small fraction of the total number of congregations, their total combined membership is greater than the total combined membership of other churches. One might draw such a conclusion for the current pattern in this country. But as we look around the earth, we see that the vast majority of Christians are part of small, strong congregations. This worldwide pattern continues to grow across the planet, as well as in this country.

Years ago I developed a definition for large, regional (and mega) congregations: "A large congregation is a collection of small congregations that have just enough in common to share the same leadership team and the same general sense of direction."

If we do a closer analysis of a large congregation, we discover that a considerable number of small groupings provide the dynamic and energy of the larger congregation. The definition does not mean that several small congregations, which previously were separate and in their own locations, decide to cluster together as a large congregation. Occasionally this does happen. Rather, the definition points to the fact that, when we diagram the dynamics of a large congregation, we do not draw one large circle. We draw a number of overlapping circles that, although touching one another, each have their own differentiated identity and specificity.

Notice in the definition that I say, "have just enough in common." Frequently, these small groupings, or congregations, within a large congregation do not have a whole lot in common, but what they do share is just enough that they can hold together in one large congregation.

Notice also that I say a "general sense of direction." It is not as though these small congregations, gathered in this large congregation, agree on everything. Frequently, they do not agree on much. There is a considerable plurality of priorities, opinions, and ideas. Nevertheless, they have in common just enough of a sense of direction that they can, most of the time, function as one large congregation.

A large church is really a collection of small congregations. One might suggest that the genius of both large, regional and mega-congregations is their gathering of many small congregations. It is clear that these composite congregations develop their particularized goals and values, customs, habits, traditions, and leadership patterns. These distinctive groupings give people many options to find help, hope, and home within that large, regional or megachurch.

To some people, the words "the twenty-first century is the century of small, strong congregations" might suggest that I am building on my earlier definition of large, regional congregations. True, it is an accurate assessment of both large, regional and mega-congregations. However, this is not what I have in mind. I want simply to confirm that, as we look ahead, there is now—around the whole of the planet—an emerging trend causing the twenty-first century to be the century of small, strong congregations *in their own right.*

Small is strong. I invite you to memorize this conviction. Share it widely. Small is strong. Small can sometimes also be weak, and sometimes dying. Regrettably, however, we have virtually forgotten that small can be *very* strong.

We have made the near-fatal mistake of assuming that only big equals strong. I work with many very large congregations. I assure you that big congregations can be weak and dying just as often as can small congregations. We have romanticized big. We have fallen into a trap by thinking that bigger is better. As a counter to that, some people have romanticized smallness. They thank God that their group is small and getting smaller.

As the culture became preoccupied with bigness, the church became preoccupied with bigness. We determined to match the culture bigness for bigness. The bigger some institutions in the culture became, the more we sought to create bigger and bigger churches.

Regrettably, the myth, years ago, developed that bigger is better. Therefore, some concluded that bigger government is better government. Therefore, some concluded that bigger churches are better churches. It is worth noting that megachurches do not do or have everything. Small, strong congregations do not need to feel bad that they do not do or have everything. Some may say that megachurches may not have everything but they sure have a lot more. Do they? It depends on what one is looking for. Not everyone looks for big.

The truth is that bigger is bigger, not necessarily better. The truth is that small is smaller, not necessarily better. God invites you and your congregation to share a mission that matches both the mission field God gives you and the strengths with which God blesses you.

Small does small very well. Small does not try to do "mini-mega." Small, strong congregations are where we are headed in the twenty-first century.

Immensity and Immediacy

The more immense we discover the universe to be, the more immense we discover God's love is with us. The universe is a sacramental sign of the immensity of God's love in our lives. God creates the universe to be as immense as it is so that we know the immensity of God's love with us.

In very recent years, we have been discovering the extra-ordinary immensity of the universe. With the help of astro-physics, the Hubbell telescope, and radio astronomy, we have discovered the universe is vast, wide-ranging, rapidly expanding, and virtually unending. It is more immense than we would ever have imagined (which was always difficult enough in its own right).

There was a time in the history of humankind when we thought the earth was the center of the universe. Then, we thought the center of the universe was our sun. Then, we thought, if not our sun, surely the center was our solar system. With begrudging reluctance, we gave up those ideas and came to the notion that surely the center of the universe was our Milky Way. Now, we discover that our Milky Way is but a tiny speck in the vastness of the universe, not even in one of the larger clusters of stars.

There is an astonishing, remarkable immensity to the universe. It is as though there is a Milky Way for each grain of sand on the beaches of the earth. It is as if a distinct star system exists for each drop of water in all the rivers, lakes, and oceans across our planet. There is much yet to discover. We are amazed at how immense the universe is.

Thus, God comes to us in the manger so we know the immediacy of God's love with us. This extraordinary immensity could drive us to a sense of being alone in all that space. We are not lost in space. We are not left to ourselves. We are not some tiny speck in the galaxies, cast adrift in an ocean of stars. God comes and dwells among us so we can have the confidence and assurance of God's immediate presence in our lives, so that we know the nearness of God's love with us.

Immensity and immediacy are mutual longings in our lives. They are helpful dynamics that contribute to our sense of well-being. The immensity of the universe stirs our longing for immediacy, for nearness. We have a longing for immensity; we have a longing for immediacy. Both are important in our lives.

We go on vacation trips to admire the immensity of the Grand Canyon; the vast open spaces of the West; the tall mountains of our planet; and the height, breadth, and length of our monumental buildings. We fly, now here, now there, to discover the vastness of the planet. We take driving trips to see the expansiveness of the land in which we live.

Likewise, we are drawn to the immediacy of warm, intimate family meals. We look forward to rich, full conversations over tea or coffee with a few close friends. We share the closeness of a campfire with our family, and we experience looking at a full moon with a few of the persons we love deeply. We are grateful for the vastness and nearness of God's love in our lives. Both immensity and immediacy are important to us.

The current experience of immensity contributes directly to the desire for immediacy. The more we experience immensity, the more we are drawn to immediacy, intimacy, and nearness. This hunger for immediacy is one way of understanding all of the small, strong groupings that are cropping up in our communities.

These groupings range from religious to recreational. They focus on life stages, human hurts and hopes, community interests and concerns. They gather around business, boating, civic interests, and quilting. Hobbies and interests, vocational similarities, and worthwhile mission projects gather people in a vast, diverse array of groupings. Amidst the immensity of the universe, people have developed deep-seated longings for community that helps them discover roots, place, and belonging intimately and immediately. The immensity of the universe strengthens our attraction to the small.

The increasing immensity we feel in our time drives us to want immediacy in things as fundamental as the design of our houses. New trends show the development of smaller, intimate floor plans that help people have a sense of immediacy, warmth, friendliness, and family.

Earlier, somewhat less recently, the trend seemed to be toward bigger is better. Popular floor plans contained 1,500 square feet, then 2,500 and 3,500, and then 5,000 square feet and more of space. Frankly, a family can only live in so much space. Given the immensity of the universe in which we now find our home, there is a sense in which many people long for a house that is warmer, simpler, more immediate, more intimate. Even within larger houses, there is renewed emphasis on intimate gathering spaces. The focus is on an immediate, intimate space such as a family kitchen, a family room, or a recreation room.

Amidst the immensity of the universe, in which we now find ourselves living, we are learning anew how to do small, strong. This is happening in our cities, our towns, and our rural areas. It is happening in our vast metropolitan areas, precisely because they have become so big and enormous.

I was at an airport, waiting on the plane. I struck up a conversation with a man sitting nearby. I learned that he works as part of a large American corporation. He was sharing with me how big the corporation has become in recent years. He went on to describe his cabin on a lake, where he and his family can share close, immediate relationships. He told me how, when he takes his wife out to dinner, they go to a small, intimate restaurant. It is their favorite place. The larger the corporation has become, the more important the cabin and the restaurant have become for him—to have a sense of balance.

Spirit

Amidst the immensity and immediacy of our times, a new spirit is dawning. There are many signs of promise. We are discovering, even more fully, now here, now there, possibilities to help pastors and leaders bring solid leadership to small, strong congregations. We are developing ways to advance the morale of members and ministers in small, strong congregations. We are helping small, strong congregations learn how to deploy their resources to serve people richly and fully. We are discovering how to use modern methods of communication and transportation to serve small, strong congregations scattered across metropolitan and rural areas.

We are learning how to value our resources as a gift of God. We are coming to appreciate the leaders and ministers with which God blesses us. We are discovering ways to share our generosity to advance the financial resources of small, strong congregations. We are becoming more encouraging, open, welcoming, and invitational with people. We are finding new possibilities to help people deepen their spiritual lives and discover the mission field with which God blesses them.

We are learning how to take advantage of the competencies and compassion of older adults; equally important, we are discovering how to help children and youths be actively part of small, strong congregations. We are learning how not to separate children, young people, adults, and senior adults into departments. We are discovering how to be a whole congregation together. We are learning how to develop a strong, healthy future.

One year, I was watching the Final Four in college basketball. A team with a fast break and full-court press got more than twenty points ahead by halftime. During the third quarter, they came out, began to lose their lead, and fell disastrously behind.

The coach/announcer was asked, "What's happened to this team?"

He replied: "I've always taught my teams that we play to win. During the first half, with their fast break and their full-court press, that's what this team did. They played to win. After halftime, they came out and began to play to avoid losing. That's where they got off their game, and that's why they're behind."

I've worked with some congregations where the banner out front is "We play to win." This is their spirit. They see themselves as the Christmas people, the people of the Cross, the Easter people, the people of Pentecost. They live the Christian life with confidence and assurance, knowing that God surrounds them with grace, Christ shares with them compassion, and the Holy Spirit leads them with hope to the future.

I've worked with some congregations where the banner out front is "We play to avoid losing." With a retrenching, retreating spirit, they hope simply to avoid losing any more than they have already lost in recent years.

I've even worked with congregations where the banner out front is "We play to lose." Some people develop an identity of failure. They look down on themselves, think more poorly of themselves than they have a right to do, and suffer from low self-esteem. Sometimes, they make good headway; things are going well. Then, just at the point of success, they marshal their considerable competencies to ensure that they fail yet again. Why? Because to succeed would disrupt the identity of failure and the comfort with that failure that they have grown in themselves. Some congregations do the same.

I've worked with some congregations where the banner out front is "We do not plan to leave the locker room; it is safer here." But the game is won on the field and on the court, not in the locker room. The church is the locker room; the world is the field and court.

Small, strong congregations have the spirit of "We play to win; we plan to help people with their lives and destinies, with the grace of God." Small, strong congregations focus on the strengths God gives them, not the ones they wish they had. The art is to grow a stronger congregation, not necessarily a larger congregation. The focus is on spirit and strengths more than size.

The people of God do reverse supposed trends. We do create new trends. We do create a new future for the culture and the church. God does invite us to advance and develop the future to which God leads us. We invest our time and our lives somewhere. We can retrench and retreat or roll over and play dead, and in so doing we can let the inevitability of stable, then declining, and then dying happen. Or we can choose to invest our lives, time, gifts, strengths, and competencies in moving toward the strong, healthy future to which God invites us.

More and more congregations, leaders, and pastors are *choosing* to head toward the future to which God invites them. Small, strong congregations are a significant part of the future to which God is inviting us. Small, strong congregations are flourishing across the planet. We will see more of them in the years to come.

Strengths

Small, strong congregations are strong because of their spirit and their strengths. There have been too many conversations about size. Size is a by-product of spirit and strengths. You create a strong congregation by focusing on a spirit of developing the future to which God invites you. You create a healthy congregation by focusing on building on the strengths of the congregation with which God is blessing you.

Those leaders and pastors who worry about size create congregations that worry about size. Congregations that worry about size do not concern themselves with people. They are too interested in either getting bigger or else protecting (by retreating and retrenching) the size they now have. Focusing on size for its own sake is unhealthy. Focusing on spirit and strengths advances the future of your congregation.

The art is to look at the twelve central characteristics of strong, healthy congregations:

1. Specific, concrete missional objectives
2. Pastoral and lay visitation
3. Corporate, dynamic worship
4. Significant relational groupings
5. Strong leadership resources
6. Solid decision making
7. Several programs and activities
8. Open accessibility
9. High visibility
10. Adequate land and parking
11. Adequate space and facilities
12. Solid financial resources

Strong, healthy congregations deliver nine of these strengths. My book *Twelve Keys to an Effective Church* gives you a fuller understanding of each of these.

For our purposes now, I simply want to confirm that *Small, Strong Congregations* and *Twelve Keys to an Effective Church* are complementary resources. They are good friends. You will benefit from this book and you will benefit from the wisdom and insights you find in *Twelve Keys*.

Small, strong congregations deliver nine or more of the twelve central characteristics. Small, weak congregations deliver perhaps five to eight of the twelve. Small, dying congregations deliver one to four of the twelve. The same ratio applies to middle; large, regional; and mega-congregations. From one congregation to the next, it is a distinctive nine. Each congregation delivers the nine that match their specific strengths and their particular mission field. What small, strong congregations have in common is that they deliver a dynamic of nine characteristics that focus on spirit and strengths, not size and bigness.

One of the mistakes people make—particularly in small congregations—when they look at the twelve central characteristics is to ask, "Do we have all twelve?" Here is that old friend, the compulsion toward perfectionism, again showing up in our lives. We do not need all twelve! Indeed, congregations that try to deliver all twelve end up delivering none of the twelve.

What takes wisdom in small, strong congregations is to grow forward one or two strengths now. You cannot steer a ship unless it is moving. A ship sitting dead in the water— whether a sailboat or a motor boat—cannot be steered. The nautical term is that the ship "is in irons." The art is to get your ship moving. Then you can make course corrections, tack here or there, as you head toward a solid future.

Look for the strengths you have, not the ones you wish you had. This is an important principle for individuals as well as for congregations. If we look for the strengths we wish we had, we miss the strengths God gives us.

Regrettably, some small congregations look for the strengths of being a busy, bustling suburban church with lots of programs and activities. The notion of a suburban church is an invention of the church culture of the 1940s and 1950s. In that time in the United States, as well as many other places on the planet, the emerging pattern was to build new suburbs.

Following World War II, those suburbs held the promise of being better places to live. They provided us a decent home and a good school. Following our nearness to the abyss in the war years, we were rebuilding civilization. In addition, each new suburb needed one or more new churches. These churches had lots of programs and activities. They did good work and were appropriate for their time and place.

However, God's mission moved forward on this planet for nineteen hundred plus years without ever knowing what a suburban church looked like. We have inner-city churches; county-seat town churches; open rural country churches; and all sorts of small, strong congregations in rural and metropolitan areas. Regrettably, many of them still imagine that being an effective, successful church is to look like the busy, bustling suburban church of the 1940s and 1950s. Remember the Babylonian captivity. I call this preoccupation the "suburban captivity" of the church. We have lived too long in this captivity.

Know that the suburban churches of the 1940s and 1950s did good work. Their strengths matched those times. Having just fought the largest war to date among humankind, people longed for something more enduring and lasting. With the wartime disruption of family clans, with sons and daughters spread across the planet, some never to come home again, the search for some sense of community was desperately strong.

There was a sense that we could start over: "We can rebuild. We can begin again to build a sense of hope and future. We can discover a new and promised land." All these longings contributed to the growth of new suburban communities. Remember, also, that in the aftermath of the war, social conformity was strongly pressing people to be in church. And it worked. It was the thing to do to go to church. After the abyss of the war, it made sense to be active in a church. By and large, suburban churches played an important part in making these new communities work.

Even though those days are long gone, the lingering image, the haunting picture that some congregations still have is that the best kind of church to be is a busy, bustling suburban church like those of the 1940s and 1950s. Fortunately, this lingering picture is passing.

Regrettably, some have replaced this picture of the busy, bustling suburban church with the busy, bustling mega-church. I want you to know that people are not looking for busy and bustling churches, whether suburban or mega.

Given the immensity of the universe, given the scattering across the globe of extended family clans, people in our time bring with them to congregations the search for help, hope, and home. They are already busy and bustling enough in their everyday, ordinary lives. *They neither need nor want the mixed blessing of a church that now invites them to be even more busy and bustling than they already are.*

They bring with them a search for community, not committee. They bring with them a search for hope amidst the difficulties, the despair, the depressions, and the defeats that abound in this life.

Steadfast Love

In small, strong congregations, people discover the steadfast love of God. In our time, people are looking for a congregation that delivers steadfast love, a congregation where they can discover and share steadfast love in their lives. People discover the steadfast love of God in a variety of places and groups. The small, strong congregation is one of the most significant groups. People want to participate in a steadfast love—both giving and receiving. They do not want just to receive. They are not just consumers. They look toward giving of themselves with love, sharing, and caring.

The God we know is steadfast in love with and for us. In an ancient time, some thought the gods were whimsical, that they were not steadfast. The thought was that the gods played with humankind, that they were fickle and capricious, that they did not love humankind. People were the victims of the pranks and capers of the gods. Some people, regrettably, continue to think that way today.

Love lasts. The love of God is steadfast. We therefore live with confidence and assurance. This sense of confidence is not, finally, in us. It is not in our own doings, accomplishments, and achievements. Our sense of assurance is in the love of God. We know God loves us. Our feeble strivings and anxious fears wither. We are at peace.

People are looking for a congregation that helps them live whole, healthy lives. In a small, strong congregation, they discover a group that, with confidence and assurance, focuses on its strengths. This helps people focus on their own strengths. They look for a congregation that focuses on a spirit of progress—that expands one existing strength and adds one new strength. This helps them expand one strength and add one new strength in their own lives.

People are not looking for a congregation that is trying to do too much too soon. They intuitively know that such a congregation only contributes to their trying to do too much too soon in their own lives. They look for a healthier future than that. People are not looking for a congregation that is going to be something for everyone. Most of us have tried to be something for everyone and have discovered that it does not work. People have the wisdom to know that it does not work for congregations either.

I helped a congregation in Florida one year. Ten years earlier, they had looked around and seen this sea of gray hair across the congregation. They said, "The future of our church is at stake. We need to reach the youth of our community, or we will grow old together." They built a gym, but it sat virtually empty most of the week for the next ten years.

Ten years having come and gone, they invited me to come and help. After I had been there a while and had a chance to study the community, I said, "Think about the community God gives you with which to be in mission." In that community, there is a high density of persons over sixty-five years of age. There are very few children and even fewer adolescents and teens. We had a helpful discussion.

I work with many congregations in Arizona, New Mexico, and Florida where there is nobody in the church under sixty-five, because there is nobody in the community under sixty-five. In these congregations, the "children's division" is for people sixty-five to seventy-five, the "youth" program is for people seventy-five to eighty-five, and the "adult" division is for people eighty-five and above!

I suggested to them that the focus of their mission be with new retirees in their community. In a very real sense, these are the new children and the new youth who will see to the future of that congregation for years to come. It is not true that a congregation needs to reach from cradle to grave to be an effective, healthy congregation. Their mission could certainly include the new retirees who are projected to move to that part of Florida from Indiana, Ohio, and Pennsylvania during the coming twenty-five to fifty years.

The art is to grow the real strengths God gives you in ways that match with the community God gives you. That takes wisdom.

Fortunately, God has given me the privilege of sharing with countless small congregations, across the years and around the planet. Some have been dying. Some have been weak. Some have been strong. I am grateful to have the opportunity of working with so many small congregations, and for their contributions to my own thinking and wisdom.

We have learned much together. We have shared excellent mistakes and we have made new discoveries. We have pooled our mutual wisdom and experience. We have learned how to expand one current strength and to add one new strength. We have learned to do well what small, strong congregations do well.

Small, strong congregations do not try to do everything. Many small, strong congregations do not deliver numerous competent programs and activities. They may or may not have open accessibility or high visibility. They may lack adequate land and parking. They may not have adequate space and facilities.

Over the years, with the help of many leaders and pastors, I have learned that small, strong congregations focus distinctively on certain qualities of being a congregation together. You can grow and develop some of these qualities as you help your congregation. These qualities are present in many small, strong congregations across the planet:

- Mission and service
- Compassion and shepherding
- Community and belonging
- Self-reliance and self-sufficiency
- Worship and hope
- Leaders and team
- Just enough space and facilities
- Giving and generosity

Wherever some of these are present, with excellence and strength, you are likely to find a small, strong congregation. Hence, the focus of this book.

The psalmist describes the strength and steadfast love of God. Our strength is not in bigness, buildings, and budgets. We do not match the culture bigness for bigness. Our strength is in God. Our strength is not of our own doing. Our strength is the gift of God. Our steadfast love with people is the gift of God. We are steadfast in our love because God is steadfast in God's love with us. We are not fleeting and fickle. We do not waver and wander. Our love is steadfast.

People who discover our congregation discover the strength of God and the steadfast love of God. They live strong, healthy lives, rich and full with the love of God. They live with trust in the grace of God, the compassion of Christ, and the hope of the Holy Spirit.

Small, strong congregations live with this confidence and assurance: they know *small is strong.*

2

Mission
and Service

Go and preach the Gospel.
Use words if necessary.

—FRANCIS OF ASSISI

Alice is tall and thin with graying hair and a purposeful
stride. If you look closely, you can see that she favors her
left ankle slightly. She once fell and broke that ankle while
climbing a mountain. Her ankle teaches her when the
weather is changing. Alice is now in her seventies. She lives
alone; her three children live in other parts of the country.
Her husband died ten years ago, and she still misses him
greatly. Her comfort is in her church.

Alice asked to visit with me during one of the seminar
breaks. The whole group from her congregation came with
her for our visit. In her slow, gentle, easygoing way, Alice said
to me, "Dr. Callahan, we want to share with you what has
happened in our congregation during the past year."

I had led a seminar with a number of congregations in the
area the year before, and she and many of the members of
her church had participated. Now, I was back a year later,
leading a follow-up seminar to continue being helpful.

31

Alice said to me, "Last year, Dr. Callahan, you invited us to a theology of service, not a theology of survival. You invited us to a theology of mission, not a theology of maintenance. We remember your exact words.

"On the way home from the seminar, we talked with one another about what you had said. You see, our church has been down to fourteen people. We have been dying off slowly over the years. Those of us who are left are in our seventies and eighties.

"We decided we wanted to do something worthwhile in mission before our church was dead, done, and gone. Shortly after the seminar last year, we approached the principal of the nearby elementary school and said to him, 'Our church is down to fourteen people. We have been dying off for years. It will not be that many years before we are gone. Before that happens, we'd like to do something to be helpful with the children and the faculty in this elementary school.'

"The principal said, 'Oh, you're such-and-such church?'

'Yes,' we answered.

"'Oh, I thought your church had died years ago.'

"In a way we had," Alice continued. "Our mission statement had become: 'We are down to fourteen people, and it won't be that many years before we're dead, done, and gone.'

"We made an agreement with the principal that we would be helpful in whatever ways we could with the children and the teachers in that elementary school.

"It has been a remarkable year, Dr. Callahan. We've made, as you would say, some excellent mistakes along the way, and at the same time, our church is alive in ways we never could have imagined.

"As we look back, we know now that our church was really already dead when we adopted a theology of survival. We have new life with a theology of mission. We're still not a big church, but we have about ninety people coming for worship on Sunday morning now.

"We no longer worry about being bigger. We worry whether we will be helpful with the children with whom we are working. And we see people from the community who come to help us with our mission in the elementary school.

"We want to thank you for helping us see that our lives can count in ways we would never have dreamed possible. Now, we are precisely what you have described: we are a small, strong congregation."

Discoveries About Mission

Over the years, working with a wide range of small, strong congregations, certain discoveries have come to me about mission. I am grateful to the vast numbers of congregations who have helped me to think through these discoveries about how congregations discern and share their mission:

- Small, strong congregations share one excellent mission.
- The congregation shares its mission as its gift with the whole community. The participants of the congregation live a theology of service, not survival.
- The mission begins, frequently, with some precipitating event, some planning event, or some other decisive event that stirs people's discovery of their longings and strengths.
- The mission begins with three to five people. They share their mission with the spirit of a team. They deliver concrete, effective help.
- The mission is mutual. The consequence is that new helpers for the mission come from among the persons helped. The congregation is a legend for the mission and service of a few people in the congregation.

God calls each congregation to its mission in a distinctive way that each congregation can hear. There is no universal, repeatable checklist of steps whereby all congregations discover their mission. The events and processes whereby congregations come to their mission vary greatly. Congregations travel many paths to find the mission to which God invites them. There is no one ubiquitous method. Your congregation will discover its mission in a way that is distinctive for you. Here are some observations that give you clues to help your congregation discover its specific mission.

One Excellent Mission

Alice and her congregation share one excellent mission. Their focus is families with elementary children. They do this singular mission well. Because of their direct helpfulness, their congregation is known as the congregation that loves children.

In another congregation, Betty, Sally, and Jim share an excellent mission with shut-ins across their community. Both the shut-ins and their families greatly appreciate the thoughtfulness and kindness with which they help. For their mission and service, their congregation is known as the congregation that loves shut-ins.

The one congregation has as its focus elementary children and their families. The other focuses on shut-ins and their families. Neither congregation tries to major in both missions. Each has good wisdom.

Small, strong congregations share one excellent mission. You will notice that I emphasize *one excellent mission.* As healthy congregations, they share one compelling mission with considerable competence, compassion, and continuity. Their mission is more than mere interest. They do not trifle, whimsically, in now this and now that fashionable mission. They are not blown hither and yon by one faddish mission after another. They are not dilettantes about mission, dabbling in this or that popular vogue: recreation one year, vaccination programs the next, literacy the year after that. For healthy congregations, mission is more than one flavor of the year after another. They do not do mission hopping. They focus on one excellent mission.

It is not that they focus on one excellent mission because, as a small congregation, they have limited resources. Rather, it is simply that *one mission*, compellingly well done, is sufficient to have this quality of small, strong congregations well in place.

Having one excellent mission is somewhat like college. People who have one major tend to graduate with a degree. To be sure, they may have one or two minors, a number of requirements, and many electives. However, the person who has four majors tends not to graduate. This person spreads his or her resources too thin. The person loses a sense of focus and direction. Moreover, he or she does not need four majors to achieve a degree. With one major, people graduate.

You do not need two, three, or four mission priorities to have this quality of mission of the small, strong congregation in place. Some, who have an enthusiasm for mission, think that the more missions we do, the better we have this quality in place. More is not better. More is not necessary. Yes, in your congregation there are a range of minor missions and many electives. The art is to discover one excellent major for your congregation.

I was helping one congregation. The people said to me, "Dr. Callahan, we have decided on two primary mission priorities. One: we want to be a congregation that is in mission with couples who have small children. And two: we plan to become known as the church in the community that sings only classical music in our services of worship."

I said to them, "You have two excellent mission priorities. One of them heads you this way, and the other heads you the opposite way.

"You could have taught me that you plan to be in mission with couples with young children and that you plan to have the best preschool and after-school programs in the community. You would have taught me a linkage between two program objectives that head toward one primary mission priority. You would be heading in the same direction.

"Or, you could have taught me you plan to be the church that is known and distinguished for singing only classical music in your service of worship. You could have said that you plan to have the best preaching in the county. Then, you would have taught me that you have complementary, linking priorities that head toward one excellent mission."

As a footnote, I said to them, "If you plan to sing only classical music in your service of worship, you will want to have the best preaching in the county. You will dearly need it, and it will help greatly."

Julie and I spend quite a bit of our time listening to a rich, full range of classical music. I am not against classical music. However, I happened to know the radio marketing surveys in that particular community. In that community, young couples listen primarily to two kinds of music: soft FM and country western.

I did not propose to them that they focus the music in their worship service in that direction. What I did suggest to them was that they find one excellent mission that matches their gifts and their community, and then live that mission out in a legendary way that serves the people of their community.

I suggested, given the strengths they have, that their one excellent mission could focus on preschool children and their families. I mentioned the possibility of their sharing that mission by having the best preschool program in the community.

As time passes, they might also see their way to adding an excellent after-school program. They could help their service of worship to be "children and family friendly." They would be building and developing one consistent, excellent mission with families with young children.

My dad opened the first A&P supermarket on the planet. Supermarkets focus on one primary mission. Their core mission is foodstuffs. They do this mission very well. Supermarkets do not manufacture parachutes. They do not produce cars. They do not do service-industry work. They do not construct houses, office buildings, or factories.

Supermarkets do carry a range of minor and elective products. You will find some simple hardware goods, some electric supplies, and some seasonal items for Halloween, Christmas, and Easter. The corner grocery stores of an earlier time did the same. But for all of the vast array of products on their shelves, the primary mission of supermarkets is foodstuffs. Moreover, in the largest of supermarkets, we find a focused, distinctive array of foodstuffs on the shelves. A store belonging to the same chain, eight to ten miles down the road, has *its own* distinctive array of foodstuffs on the shelves. It is not the same, and neither store has everything.

Supermarkets are intentional about whom they serve, what they do, and what they do not do. They are selective about what gets on their shelves and how many inches of shelf space each product has. As vast as the number of items in a supermarket is, more food items do *not* make the shelves than do find space. Excellent supermarkets tailor what is on the shelves to the area and the people they serve. The important point is this: they cannot have on their shelves everything on earth, so they have only those things that specifically help the people in their area of service.

Small, strong congregations follow a similar principle. Yes, there may be fewer products and fewer shelves, but the principle is the same. The church that tries to do a multiplicity of missions scatters the resources with which God is blessing it. It ends up creating a mediocre middle across the board. A small, strong congregation is intentional in the one excellent mission it shares with the community.

A Gift

Small, strong congregations share one excellent mission as their gift with the whole community. They live a theology of service, not a theology of survival. The mission they share is a gift. There are no strings attached. There are no conditions put forward. The gift is freely given. There is no hint of anything like, "We will do the mission, if you will become members." We do the mission for the sake of the mission.

Andy said, "I've had enough. We keep talking about how we want to grow our congregation. We are too preoccupied with getting bigger. There's more to life than just getting larger." The silence that followed Andy's statement was a healthy silence. No one spoke for some time.

Andy was responsible for much of the growth the congregation was experiencing. He was chair of the evangelism team. He gathered a competent team of people. They did excellent work in reaching first-time worshippers, occasional worshippers, constituent families, and newcomers to the community. Before Andy, the congregation had been slowly declining. However, in the past four years, with Andy's leadership, and with the team he drew together, the congregation experienced solid growth.

Andy went on to say, "We started out to reach and help people with their lives, but somehow, somewhere along the way, we got caught up in our own success. We have forgotten about helping people. We have become too preoccupied with our own growth. We are too concerned about church growth. We need to rediscover what we set out to do."

After the silence, there was much animated discussion. Although the people of the congregation enjoyed their new-found growth, they all agreed that they had become too caught up in the chase. The group spent time in prayer. They found it hard to give up their interest in church growth, precisely because they were being successful at it.

The clue came when they remembered, perhaps more fully than before, God's way of relating to them. They experienced the love of God in their own lives. Andy shared with the group: "God's love is freely given. God shares God's love with us as a gift. There are no conditions. There are no stipulations. God's love is freely given. We can do the same."

The result of Andy's comments was rediscovery of what they had set out to do. They became less concerned with whether they were growing bigger. They returned to their focus on helping people with their lives. They focused on their one excellent mission as a genuine gift with the community. Now, more richly than before, they relate to the community the same way that God relates to them.

All congregations—of whatever behavior pattern—benefit from giving one excellent mission as a gift. They benefit from focusing on mission growth more than church growth. A congregation that shares a specific mission as a gift is, in fact, a congregation. A congregation without a mission is a club, not a congregation. The benefit of having a mission is especially helpful with small congregations.

Small congregations, more than large, regional or mega-congregations, have a tendency to become preoccupied with survival. Perhaps small congregations have a right to become so preoccupied. In comparison to large, regional and mega-congregations, they have considerably fewer resources. Sometimes, small congregations do seem to live on the brink, compared to the resources of large, regional and mega-congregations.

Further, we live in a culture that prizes bigness. Although this is changing as we enter the twenty-first century, the current preoccupation with bigness can most certainly be intimidating to a small congregation. People might, therefore, be forgiven for their temptation to be preoccupied with their survival.

Thus, it is urgent that a small congregation have some mission, given as a gift. The mission helps the people of a small congregation focus on someone beyond themselves. In so doing, they overcome any tendency to be preoccupied with their own survival. Their focus is on others, not themselves.

The Pharisee and the Levite were favored by the culture. They had standing. They had prerogatives, prestige, perqs, and power. Perhaps they were impressed with their status. Perhaps they saw themselves as headed to do bigger, more worthwhile things than helping a man in a ditch. I sometimes think the Pharisee was on his way to a church growth conference. I sometimes think the Levite was busy with a study of rules and regulations, data and demographics. For whatever reasons, preoccupied with themselves, their own journey, their own worries, their own larger agendas, and their own destinations, they moved to the other side of the road, ignored the wounded man, and hurried on.

The Samaritan had little standing in the culture. Of the three, he might have been forgiven for passing by on the other side of the road. It might be anticipated, even expected, that the other two would stop. Yet, it is the Samaritan who stops, binds up the wounds of the injured man, and sees him safely to an inn. The unexpected one stops.

The Samaritan's theology of mission kept him from being preoccupied with himself. He illustrates a theology of service, not a theology of survival. Some large, regional and mega-congregations, like the Pharisee and the Levite, are so caught up in themselves and their own journey that they do not stop to help. The same can be said for some small congregations.

Small, strong congregations are "good Samaritan" congregations. Precisely because they have so little in comparison with large, regional and mega-congregations, they share richly what they have. They are disproportionately generous with their mission and their service. They live for their mission and service with others rather than for themselves. Their interest, their passion, is mission growth, not church growth. Their compassion leads them to their mission.

The text in Matthew 16:25 (RSV) suggests, "For whosoever would save his life will lose it, and whoever loses his life for my sake will find it." The text applies to groups, as well as individuals: "Whatsoever congregation would save its life will lose it, and whatsoever congregation loses its life for my sake will find it."

Small, strong congregations are gift-driven, not getting-driven. They are strength-driven, not weakness-driven. They are spirit-driven, not size-driven. Small, strong congregations are high-compassion congregations. They are mission-driven congregations. They do not ask, "What's in it for us?" They are not interested in church growth. They are interested in people growth.

The mission is a gift precisely because the focus is on helping people with their lives. There is no ulterior motive. The focus is not on growing the membership of the congregation. At the same time, there may be some expenditure involved in the mission. I do not want to imply that the nature of the gift suggests that the mission is always free. Sometimes, the mission is free. Sometimes, the participants help with the expense of the mission.

For example, the mission may be an after-school program for the elementary children in the community. The after-school program has the best director, the best faculty, the best volunteers, and the best program in the community. There are solid salaries for the director and the faculty. There is appropriate tuition for the program, and—precisely because the preschool has the best director, faculty, volunteers, and program—the preschool is in the best position to raise excellent scholarships in the community. Thus, all children who want to can be a part of the preschool. The gift nature of the program is that the preschool is the gift of the congregation to the community. It is not an implicit effort to recruit more members for the congregation.

In one seminar, I lifted up the possibility of small, strong congregations being gift-driven and mission-driven. A young woman asked, "Dr. Callahan, is there a difference between a mission-driven church and a purpose-driven church?"

I responded, "A purpose-driven church with one excellent mission is, in fact, a mission-driven church." Regrettably, some purpose-driven churches have as their primary purpose growing the size of their churches. Their purpose is to get bigger. Such a purpose is self-seeking and self-centered. It is an institutional, organizational effort. It has nothing to do with sharing one excellent mission in the community as a gift.

Some churches say, "We are a purpose-driven church. We have this purpose: blank, blank, blank, and blank." However, what they want to talk about is not how they help people with their lives and destinies, but how they are going to help their church. Their focus is inward, on themselves.

There are churches that call themselves purpose-driven churches. They have said, "Our mission is with children and their families in this community in the name of Christ." They are delivering one excellent mission as their gift to the community. I think of them as gift-driven, mission-driven, high-compassion congregations. If they are using the terminology of *purpose-driven*, that is fine.

A healthy congregation, at its best, sees its mission as sharing a gift of grace. The mission "We love families and their children in Christ" is central to everything they do. They lose themselves in service to the mission to which God is inviting them. Their mission with children and their families drives everything they do. It is not that the congregation goes about a busy list of programs and activities, and on top of that lays on a mission that is also important. The gift of mission leads, informs, strengthens, and shapes everything the congregation does.

Decisive Events

The mission begins, frequently, with some precipitating event, some planning event, or in an informal conversation or gathering, that stirs people's discovery of their longings and strengths.

The driver of the tractor trailer said that he tried to stop. The anguish and weeping with which he shared those words, the wrenching and wracking of his body, the grief with which he shook were evidence that he had tried, desperately, to stop. The deep skid marks on the pavement were further testimony to his valiant efforts to halt his truck.

He knew, when he felt the slight, almost imperceptible bump, that it was not in time. He was going a few miles per hour less than the speed limit. He had been through the area before, and he was aware of the children in the neighborhood. He was coming up the grade of the hill. Just at the top, almost before he could see her, the young girl dashed out between two cars immediately in front of the truck. He tried his best to stop, but as he climbed down from his truck to her side, he knew she was dead.

No one faulted him. He had done the best he could. She had not looked either way. Two neighbors, with horror, had watched her, with her enthusiasm for life, dash, too quickly, into the street.

This precipitating event stirred the longings and strengths of three women. In honor and memory of that young girl, they launched what became the best after-school program in that community. The young girl was in third grade. The tragedy had happened in the late afternoon. Both of her parents worked. The young girl was a latchkey child.

She would come home from school and do the best she could, until her parents got home from work. It was not as though she was left to her own devices. Several children in the neighborhood did the same. They frequently played with one another. Some thought she was headed across the street to a friend's house.

Her death made it clear something more should be available to the elementary children of the community. Harriet, Gladys, and Sandra talked it over with one another and discussed it with their small congregation. They decided they would launch an after-school program as a gift to the community from their congregation. They talk of how much they feel their lives are counting. The elementary children are thriving. The community is deeply grateful for the gift.

Stewart, Jane, Dan, and Ida were leading the planning event. It was the first one for their congregation in years. For so many years, there had seemed to be no hope for their future. Across the years, several denominational leaders, well intentioned and admittedly preoccupied with big churches, told them that their congregation would grow old together and eventually die. They almost came to believe that.

Then a new pastor, Richard, came. He was new to them, but in fact he was a seasoned pro. He had retired—with distinction. He had rattled around his house for two years, grew increasingly restless, and asked to serve a small congregation. The denomination thought he could be chaplain to the congregation until they died off.

He liked the people. They liked him. After he had been there six months, for lunch one day he gathered Stewart, Jane, Dan, and Ida. He proposed they be the steering team for a congregational planning event. They were not, at first, certain the idea would work. He suggested that they make it a good-fun, good-times event. They warmed to that idea. He described how the event would benefit the congregation and the community. They agreed to develop the event.

Everyone was surprised at the strong turnout. Virtually everyone came, although Miss Merrill had to go out of town to care for her mother, who had fallen and broken her wrist, and Mac Conners was delivering a shipment of goods to another part of the state. Everyone else was there. There was good food and good fun. Richard shared with them some of the data and demographics he had discovered. There were an increasing number of retired, older persons in the community. Most of the other congregations in the community, as best he could discern, were focused on young couples with small children.

He observed to everyone at the planning event that their strengths were in dealing with retirement and growing older. He noted the phrase that someone once said: "Growing older is not for amateurs." He suggested that one of their strengths was that they were pros at the business of growing older. They had considerable wisdom and experience, insights and possibilities to help persons learn, as best one can, the art of growing older.

They shared much conversation during the planning event. They observed that they had spent too much time in trying to become a "younger congregation." What they knew how to do, where their strengths were, was in helping people with the process of growing older.

They look back on that planning event as decisive. Partly, the new data helped them to discover the emerging older population around them. Mostly, it was the discovery of the strengths they have for helping people with their lives. They were looking for the strengths they wished they had, and they were missing the strengths they really have.

The mission begins, frequently, with some precipitating event or planning event. In addition, it may begin more informally, in a conversation or gathering that stirs people's discovery of their longings and strengths. Looking back, people in the congregation view the conversation or gathering as decisive for the congregation's mission.

The mission may focus on any of these possibilities:

- Life stage
- Human hurt and hope
- Sociology
- Vocation
- Geography
- Community and civic interests
- Recreation
- Music and arts
- Health
- Religion

Life Stage. At Brady Lake, it became clear to Orville and Mary, Harold and Wilma, and Julie and me that our mission was with the youth of the community. We were sitting on Harold and Wilma's screened-in porch one evening, visiting, looking out over the lake as the sun set, talking about this and that. Somehow, we came to the sense that our mission would be with the youth of the community of Brady Lake.

Human Hurt and Hope. Tom, Glenn, Merrill, Olive, and Lester would sometimes talk of how they "stumbled" into a mission with people who wrestle with alcoholism and their families. The mission began with Tom's longing to help; as the rest of them became part of the team, the mission stirred their own longings to help. As best they could remember, it was a first telephone call for help that stirred the mission.

Sociology. I have the privilege of working with a congregation that shares an amazing mission with the poor. Their primary focus is with this specific sociological grouping. Their mission grew out of an informal gathering one Friday evening at Jill and Bob's house, when they gathered to talk about ways to improve their Sunday school. Somehow, no one quite remembers how, the conversation "drifted" to a discussion of the children of poor families in the community. They found their way to a mission with the poor. Their compelling compassion for the poor of the community is a legend. They look back on that Friday night as decisive for their own lives and for their congregation.

Vocation. People frequently live in what I call "a vocational village." The coal mine is one. The office skyscraper is another. (In many communities, the skyscraper is the coal mine, simply rising to the sky rather than going deep into the earth.) Many people spend much of their lives with their vocational family.

In one mill town, a congregation discovered its mission to help the persons who work in the mill. The conditions of the mill were abysmal. The mill owners did little to improve them. In their customary informal gathering after church on Sunday, out under the oak tree, the conversation "gravitated" to the plight of the mill workers. The group sensed that they needed to do something to improve the mill and help better the lives of the people who worked there. A mission was born.

Geography. On a prayer retreat, the leaders of a church in a metropolitan inner city discovered their mission with the people who live in the immediate area of the church. They were on a prayer retreat, primarily to advance their own prayer lives and to improve their individual spiritual growth. Somehow, in the midst of the retreat, they felt an "invitation" to serve the people God had planted all around them. Their individualistic interest was transformed into a community mission.

Community and Civic Interests. Marge, Judy, and Doris gathered for a good-fun lunch. They were sharing about their grandchildren. The conversation "moved" to a discussion about the educational concerns in their community. Marge is a retired teacher. Judy has an active business in finance. Doris is a leading civic and community leader in many worthwhile groupings in the city. All of their grandchildren are in the school system. The number of children per class is too high. The teachers are in need of fuller support. The three of them shared their concerns with the rest of the congregation. Time has passed. They have accomplished much to advance the educational resources of their community.

Recreation. A primary value in some communities is basketball. In other communities, it is tennis. In others, it is football, or hockey. Many congregations have discovered their mission in relation to a primary community value centered on recreation. The vast number of boys and girls clubs is an extraordinary testimony to a mission through recreation.

Years ago, I was walking across a piece of land on which a new church building was being developed. The pastor and I were talking as we walked. He mentioned that one of the central interests in the community was tennis. I knew of his interest and competence in tennis. I suggested he build the mission of his congregation on the tennis courts of the community, that he become, in effect, the shepherding pastor of the people who "lived" on the tennis courts. He is a legend for his love and shepherding in the community, and it began on the tennis courts.

Music and Arts. Howard teaches music in college. He is the choir director in his local congregation. The congregation has a long tradition of music. It is one of their great loves. During a rehearsal one Wednesday night, at the break, the conversation turned to doing a given work of music as their gift to the community. The idea emerged that some of the students at the college could be part of the choir for that specific work. They decided, in addition, to invite people in the community to be part of the choir for that work. The choir, with students and community persons, had a grand time together preparing the work. New friendships formed. New relationships developed. The mission continues.

Quilting is an art. Julie is active in quilting. She is a gifted quilter. She is a member of the local quilt group and the state quilting association. She participates in the fall and spring quilting retreats. Seminar leaders from across the country come in and teach specific arts and techniques of quilting. Much happens on the retreats in the way of sharing and caring, fellowship and belonging.

Years ago, I was helping one congregation. I mentioned Julie's interest in quilting. Several women in the congregation shared their love for quilting. I offered a brief word about the fall and spring retreats. They decided to conduct a similar retreat as their gift to the community. In the years come and gone, many people have found the retreat helpful in their lives.

Health. The newspaper made the urgent announcement of an emerging, compelling concern to deliver vaccinations to the children of the community. The possibility of an epidemic was slight. Nevertheless, the wisdom of the community leaders was to be safe rather than sorry. One small, strong congregation decided to offer its help. Rowena, the daughter of one of the leaders, had been a nurse in Asia. She had gone there as a missionary to help vaccinate the children of the countries in which she worked. She had been there many years and done good work. Just before she was to come home for a sabbatical, she contracted a rare disease, fell desperately ill, and swiftly died.

In honor and memory of her life, the congregation decided to help with the vaccination effort. They turned out their friends and work associates, their neighbors and their acquaintances. They became the primary volunteer group of the city's effort. They continue to be so today, in similar emergencies.

Religion. Sonny, Ralph, and Dee found their longings to help people discover the richness of the Bible. On a Saturday morning, they offered a one-time Bible study. They did solid advance work in inviting friends, family, work associates, acquaintances, and neighborhoods. They described it as a good-fun, good-times gathering. They focused on several passages in Luke. The turnout was good. People found the Bible study helpful in their lives.

People have lost track of the number of "one-time" Bible studies that Sonny, Ralph, and Dee have offered in the years come and gone. These too are good-fun, good-times gatherings. They focus on a specific range of passages. They are immediately helpful in peoples lives. A rich sense of community has grown up among the people who come. They bring their friends and acquaintances with them. Congregations are helpful in a mission that touches the religious longings that people have. However, this does not mean that the only mission for a congregation is a religious mission. I have intentionally put this one last on the list. I have done so in the spirit with which Jesus answers the disciples of John the Baptist, who ask, on behalf of John, Are you the One to come, or should we look for another? Jesus responds by sharing that the lame walk, the blind see, and the Gospel is being shared with the poor. The religious mission is shared last.

I rather like the focus of the Salvation Army, on soup, soap, and salvation. We are in mission with the whole person. Sometimes, I say it this way: God invites us to share the whole Gospel with the whole person the whole of the time. Ultimately, the rich variety of ways of sharing mission lead to helping people live whole, healthy lives with the grace of God, the compassion of Christ, and the hope of the Holy Spirit.

Yes, there are a vast array of possibilities with which congregations share their mission:

- Life stage
- Human hurt and hope
- Sociology
- Vocation
- Geography
- Community and civic interests
- Recreation
- Arts, music, hobbies, interests
- Health
- Religion

I encourage you to be open to the variety of ways with which God is inviting you to discover your one excellent mission.

Three to Five People

The mission begins with three to five people. They discover their common longings, their matching competencies, and one another. They share their mission with the spirit of a team. They deliver concrete, effective help.

Don, Sam, and Greg were having fun visiting one Saturday. They were cooling down. They had just finished running their usual three miles together. From one Saturday to the next, they varied the route they ran. Frequently, their course took them by the local neighborhood park.

The same group of high school kids seemed to hang out there. Usually, they were shooting baskets, or playing three-on-three basketball. Sometimes, they would be playing softball or wrestling. On occasion, their activities, especially the wrestling, would lead to fighting with one another until someone in the neighborhood called the police. Then, shouting and bedlam would ensue, as the various participants in the fighting would blame one another and try to convince the police that the fight was someone else's fault.

Don, Sam, and Greg felt some stirring to help. It seemed such a waste for these high school kids to be bickering, fighting, and beating one another up. Surely, life could be more constructive than that. Their first attempts to reach the kids failed. The kids wanted nothing to do with them. They were too old, too straight, and too nice. After several Saturdays of less-than-positive response, the three challenged the kids to a game of three-on-three basketball. The kids could play their best three players. They could substitute players, in and out, as they wanted to.

Don, Sam, and Greg lost the first game by a disastrous score. They lost the second by a few points. They won the next six games by solid scores. The youths were duly impressed. They wanted Don, Sam, and Greg to help them advance their skills. A neighborhood tournament was on the horizon. There would be a city tournament after that. They began a coaching relationship together. Over time, this expanded into a constructive mission with the young people in the neighborhood.

Don, Sam, and Greg simply began the mission. There were no lengthy studies. There were no long committee meetings. There were no drawn-out discussions as to whether this would be the mission of their congregation. They did not labor over the exact wording of a mission statement. They did not have a complete plan as to where their mission might head. They were open to the leading of God. They simply discovered a possibility for mission, and they began.

They did not feel the need to enlist lots of volunteers in the mission. They had two reasons for this decision. First, to do so would have been unnecessarily intimidating and over-powering with the youths with whom they were working. The kids already had their share of authority issues. Too many people would have exacerbated those issues. The presence of the three of them was sufficient, and it worked, in large measure, because the originating relationship was built around a common, shared interest, namely, three-on-three basketball.

Second, they understood the biblical principle of a diversity of gifts. God blesses people with a diversity of gifts. Not everyone in a congregation has gifts to work with high school kids. Their gifts are in other areas of mission. Regrettably, some congregations discover a specific mission and then almost insist that everyone in the congregation participate in that mission, whether it matches their gifts or not. Indeed, the insinuation is sometimes made that if you were really committed, you would volunteer. Fortunately, people have a reasonable sensibility as to whether a given mission matches their gifts and strengths.

For Don, Sam, and Greg, the mission was a match. They functioned together with the spirit of a team. Depending on the situation, each of them took the lead in the mission. Had they created an authoritarian system as to which of the three of them was boss of the team, they would have scared off the very youths with whom they hoped to work. These particular kids had been burned enough by a variety of authority systems. They did not plan to relate to another one. Don, Sam, and Greg shared their teamwork together so well that the young people learned the behavior pattern of relating with one another as a team.

Don, Sam, and Greg delivered concrete, effective help. They did not share glowing generalities or syrupy sentimentalities. They did not share vague intentions or banner slogans. Fortunately, the youths were wise enough to see through all that stuff, and even more fortunately, Don, Sam, and Greg were down-to-earth, commonsense people. They knew that pious platitudes and vague aphorisms do not help. They directly helped youths with their lives, practically, day to day, one day at a time.

Over time, as the mission expanded, the three persons became five persons, then, eight, ten, twelve. The eight, ten, twelve became fifteen, eighteen, twenty-plus. Both adults and youths became leaders on the mission team. The mission continues to grow in its helpfulness in peoples lives. Many youth and their families are being helped. It began with Don, Sam, and Greg. Sometimes, an excellent mission develops with the leadership of a committee, a council, or a board. Frequently, the one excellent mission of a small, strong congregation begins with three to five people who discover their longings and competencies and one another, and they begin.

Another congregation has a mission with young people and their families. It began with three people as a remarkable leadership team. Two doors down from the church location is a junior high school with twelve hundred kids. The principal of that school had been there for a long time—thirteen years. One day, three members of the congregation went to visit the principal. They felt led to do so. They said to the principal, "Our congregation would like to help in whatever way we can."

The principal responded, "I've been waiting thirteen years for some congregation in this community to come and say that to me."

"How can we help?"

The principal said, "I find myself having to suspend students for three days when they commit any major infraction of our policy. It is simply the rule set by the school board. But I do not want to penalize them for missing homework; I want them to stay caught up with their lessons.

"What your congregation can do is to tutor and mentor these students during their three-day suspension. I will see that the school bus drops them at the church. Your gift will be to provide the tutors and the mentors that will help these students."

This mission now leads, informs, strengthens, and shapes everything the congregation does. Sometimes, God plants a mission virtually on our doorstep.

Mutual

The mission is mutual. The consequence is that new helpers for the mission come from among the persons helped. The congregation is a legend for the mission and service of a few people in the congregation.

In an excellent mission, the mission is mutual. It is never quite clear who is helping whom. In the parable of the Samaritan, the question is asked, "Who is the good neighbor?" One way of understanding the parable is that the Good Neighbor is the man in the ditch, beaten and robbed. The good neighbor is the one who draws forth the best in the other. It is the man in the ditch who drew forth the best in the Samaritan, who, in the centuries come and gone, has become known as the Good Samaritan. Sometimes, the person we are helping is helping us live our life at its best.

When the mission is mutual, no dependency-codependency patterns are created. When the mission is shared in a top-down fashion, where we imagine that "we" are helping "them," codependency becomes the fatal pattern. Unhealthy relationships are created. We deliver too much help, and the help becomes harmful and intensifies the dependent-codependent pattern.

Mutuality is central to mission. It is the mutual encouragement people share as they help one another, as they discover a mutual relationship with one another. The person being helped discovers mutuality, encouragement, new life, and hope. The person helping discovers mutuality, encouragement, joy, and peace. Together, they discover a mutual relationship of helpfulness and encouragement as they discover one another in the grace of God.

When the mission is mutual, some of the new helpers for the mission come from among those who have been helped in mission. One congregation has a mission with people wrestling with alcoholism, and their families. Every alcoholic the mission team helps brings five more to be helped. Two or three out of five who are helped become part of the helping team. The mission team grows not from within the congregation but because the people who have been helped become part of the team.

When the mission is mutual, members of the community help. These are people who come to have a sense of mutual respect, trust, confidence, and credibility in the mission of the congregation. They are grateful the congregation is sharing this specific mission as a gift with the community. They want to help with this worthwhile project, because of its helpfulness in the community.

The Salvation Army—among the most remarkable movements with which I have the privilege of working and sharing—discovers that many of the volunteers who help them with their mission are community persons. They have not been served in mission. They do not "belong" to the army. They simply want to share in the mission with the poor.

When the mission is mutual, friends of the congregation who live elsewhere help with your mission. They may have grown up in your church. They may have been part of the church for two or three years when they lived in your community. During that time, the church became family and home to them. These friends may not even be directly related to your congregation, but someone in their family was, and thus for them your congregation has a special place in their heart. For whatever reasons, they look to your congregation as home and think well of your mission.

Although they live somewhere else, if you let them know they send money to help with your mission. Moreover, if, once a year or on some special occasion, you plan a work project to help with the mission, they return from wherever they now live and are glad to help with the mission project.

Many people travel elsewhere to give time and help to Habitat for Humanity, or to a project in Appalachia, or in South America, or somewhere on the planet. For a worthwhile project, they come back "home" to help with your mission. You may invite them to be part of a one-time or seasonal event that helps in some special way with your mission. Invite them to be part of an event that is directly related to your one excellent mission. They are glad to help. They gain a source of satisfaction from helping. If you thank them well, they look forward to helping again.

When the mission is mutual, constituents help with the mission. Your constituents are those who participate in some program or activity in your congregation. They are not persons served in mission or community people. They are not friends of your church who live elsewhere. They are not members.

They may come to worship from time to time—Easter, Christmas, or Christmas Eve. They may participate in some grouping in your congregation. It may be vacation Bible school. They may be part of your after-school groups. They may sing in one of your music groups, or play on one of your recreational teams. They may come to a Bible study. They may participate in some of your major congregational events.

They are glad to help—particularly with one-time projects, seasonal projects, and short-term projects that directly relate to the mission you are sharing in the community. They help not because they are members. They help because of the integrity of the mission and the excellence with which it is shared as a gift to the community.

When the mission is mutual, members of your congregation help. We are a small, strong congregation. We do not have lots of members. Some help. Fortunately, the two largest groupings that are glad to help you with your one excellent mission are those served in mission and community people. These two are the numerically greater groups and, likely, have the deepest range of competencies to share. Precisely because your mission has integrity, is worthwhile, and is done with profound competency and compassion, they are gratified to help. The stronger the mission, the more the number of people who help.

Life is both inductive and deductive. Sometimes we find our mission deductively, from leaders to congregation. Frequently, we discover the mission with a grassroots, inductive spirit. This is especially so in small, strong congregations. The mission grows up among the grass roots of the congregation.

In the process, we discover our longings and our strengths. We find our spirit of encouragement. Laughter becomes our good friend. Deep sources of satisfaction fill our lives. We discover mutual relations with people. We find wonder and joy, new life and hope. We discover prayer. Our mission leads us to prayer. Prayer leads us to mission. Our mission draws us to our knees in prayer.

We do the mission for the integrity of the mission—for the sake of the mission. The by-product is that—sometimes—some of the people helped in the mission become part of our mission, become part of our worship, and become part of our family. Our focus is mission growth, not membership growth.

We think of mission objectives. In the long-ago past, we set membership objectives. Now, we think of those we look forward to serving in mission during the coming three years, not of the number of new members we plan to get. Sometimes, in that earlier time, we were too preoccupied with membership objectives. Now, we focus on our mission objectives. We are thereby living in the world God now gives us, not the world that existed in the 1940s and 1950s.

A mission culture thinks about "missionship." A church culture thinks about membership. A mission culture thinks about the number of persons served in mission in the community. A church culture focuses primarily on the members of the congregation. A mission culture focuses on the "whole family" of the congregation, including persons served in mission, community people, friends of the church who live elsewhere, constituents, and members. Together, these five groupings are the "family" of a small, strong congregation.

Welcome to the first century. Welcome to the twenty-first century. Welcome to Southern China, Eastern India, and Northern Africa. Welcome to the Pacific Rim, to Central and South America. On any of these mission fields, we would be thinking primarily about mission, not membership. We would be focusing on people's human hurts and hopes. We would know that we were serving at the front lines. With wonder and joy, new life and hope, we would see the mission God gives us.

Welcome to North America, to your hometown—one of the richest mission fields on the planet. If we were to do in your hometown what we wisely do in any other mission field across the planet, we would do well in your hometown. God would bless the mission.

People under forty-five teach me that they long for and yearn to participate in a mission group, not a maintenance group. Many of those over forty-five teach me that, although they would sit loyally through endless committee meetings in the past, now they long for and yearn to participate in a mission team. In the old, old days of the church culture in the 1940s and 1950s, the notion was to put someone on a committee; he or she would then feel ownership for the church. Times have changed. In this time, people do not want another committee meeting. People want to be part of a mission team. They want to feel rich, full ownership of their congregation's mission.

People are loyal. Now, people are drawn to mission loyalty more than to organizational loyalty. They look for a theology of service, not a theology of survival. They are drawn to mission-driven, gift-driven congregations, not program-driven, money-driven, bigger-driven, or maintenance-driven congregations. People want to serve, not simply survive.

Mission is grassroots. Mission grows from among the grass roots of the congregation. Three to five people discover their longings to help with a specific human hurt and hope. They discover their competencies to deliver concrete, effective help. They find one another. They become a mission team. They do solid work. They share one excellent mission. They discover new helpers for the mission from among the people being helped. The mission flourishes. For the work of these persons, the congregation becomes a legend on the community grapevine for its one excellent mission. It lives out a theology of service, not survival. It is a small, *strong* congregation.

3

Compassion and Shepherding

Maiream croi eadrom I bhfad.
(A light heart lives long.)

—IRISH SAYING

Mason likes building things. From the time he was little, he has enjoyed seeing new things come into being. Early on, it was with wooden building blocks. As he grew a bit older, he moved to models of planes and boats. In high school, he had a part-time job at the local lumberyard. When he finished college, he went to work for a building firm to learn the building trade. He worked in the field; he worked in the office. He learned quickly.

Some four years ago, he started his own contracting and construction company. He had married his high school sweetheart. They had two young children. But, if he was ever going to have his own firm, now was the time.

The hours are long. The pace is hectic. He loves what he is doing. His company is thriving. He has construction projects scheduled for two years out. He feels blessed. His spirit of generosity flows forth.

He wanted to give something back to the community. Older persons would benefit. He wanted to share his sense of compassion and shepherding in ways that would help his community. Beyond his own construction company's work, he put together a team of volunteers, from his congregation and from the community. This volunteer team is especially helpful with older people who need assistance with modest projects around their homes. In the midst of the house projects, the team shares its compassion and shepherding with the people helped.

Kailey, early on, fell in love with music. Her mother talks of watching her in her crib. When the music came on, Kailey's eyes and head would turn toward the music, and she would listen with intensity. In preschool, her favorite times were the music sessions. From elementary school through high school, she learned and played a variety of instruments, and she has always loved to sing.

Now older, with three children, she sings in her church choir. She plays in a local group that gets together to play for fun. From time to time during the year, Kailey has ten to fifteen music students. Most are piano students; several study flute with her; two are learning the hammered dulcimer under her teaching. All of her students have great fun being with her. She has about her a quiet spirit of joy and enthusiasm for life.

She is glad to help anyone learn the gift of music. A team of volunteers works with her, especially to help junior high kids discover the gift of music for their lives. In the midst of the music lessons, Kailey and the volunteers share their compassion and shepherding with whoever they help. On behalf of their congregation, this is their gift to the community.

Tom had it hard in his early years. There were many trips to the doctor and several surgeries. His leg works well now; he runs faster than the wind. He has become the local champion in marathons and sprints. He loves the sprints the best. When people watch him run, they say they can almost see the braces falling off his legs as he heads swiftly toward the finish line.

Tom works for the local public works department. He has been with them now for a number of years and has developed considerable seniority. He is known around town as someone who is glad to help you in whatever way you might need help. Several of his friends in his congregation are glad to assist him. Together, Tom's team has helped many people in the community.

Rachel works in a local restaurant. Sometimes, she works as the hostess. Sometimes, she works as one of the servers. She helps with the cooking in the kitchen. She clears tables and washes dishes. Most of the people who go there know that Rachel owns the restaurant. She started in the restaurant as a server, became hostess, and worked her way up to manager. When the owners moved to Florida, she bought the business from them.

Under Rachel's leadership, the restaurant thrives even more than it did before. The food is good and hot. The helpings are generous. The deserts are remarkable. The prices are reasonable. When people come to the restaurant, they find a staff with friendly spirit and a warm welcome. Rachel is active with her congregation. Mostly, Rachel is known for helping many families in the town.

Mason, Kailey, Tom, and Rachel live full, happy lives. Each of them participates in a small, strong congregation in his or her own local community. Because of who they are, with their spirits of generosity and graciousness, of helpfulness and caring, their sense of compassion and shepherding, it is because of each of them that their local congregations—albeit small—are legends in the communities for their compassion and shepherding.

Importantly, it is not for what each of them does inside the church. It is because of how they share their shepherding in their daily lives. Small, strong congregations are strong not because of the compassion and shepherding, which they live out with one another in the church. They are strong because of the generosity with which they share their compassion in the whole community. Mason, Kailey, Tom, and Rachel live lives of compassion wherever they are. As they work and share in everyday life, they naturally help and serve the people in their community. The compassion of their congregation is shared, richly, fully, generously, through each of them.

Compassion-Driven

In the words that open Chapter Two, St. Francis of Assisi said it well: "Go and preach the Gospel. Use words, if necessary." Mason, Kailey, Tom, and Rachel—and thousands more who participate in small, strong congregations—live out the words of St. Francis in their local communities. They preach the Gospel by how they live and how they share, more than by the words they speak.

Mrs. Pershing was, for more years than anyone could remember, the history teacher of the local high school. She and her husband married when they were both in their early thirties. They came from another state to begin their home together. He worked in the hardware store. She taught school. Both were active in the life of the community.

The fall from the ladder was not far. It was not that high a ladder inside the store. He was reaching for something for a customer. Somehow, when he fell he hit his head. There was a gasp, a shudder, and he was dead.

Years passed. Mrs. Pershing did not remarry. There were offers. She threw herself into her teaching. Her family became the kids to whom she taught history. She loved them. They loved her. She was voted Teacher of the Year more times than she could remember. The state teacher's association recognized her achievements.

Classes came and went. She watched "her kids" move on with one graduation after another. She always thought she would, one day, marry again. She never did. She came quickly to retirement; the years had moved by so swiftly. She was honored greatly by the whole community. It was a going-away celebration as well.

Her cousin, Mabel, convinced her to move back home, where they both had grown up. Mrs. Pershing had not been there in years. She could hardly remember what it looked like then. She certainly could not picture what it looked like now. Mabel had not been there in years either. She had worked for a shipping company in another state but always hoped to move back home. The year Mabel retired, their one living relative back home, an aunt, left Mabel her house in her will.

Mrs. Pershing had second thoughts as she watched the movers pack her belongings. She was amazed at how few she had, after all the years. She kept hoping someone would ask her to stay. But they were so happy for her in her leaving. They thought that was what she wanted. After all, it did make sense. She and Mabel would share the small home together. They would be company for one another and look after each other. They would have fun together in their remaining years.

They did. They had fun. They enjoyed being together. For four years. One day, Mabel did not wake up. She died in her sleep. Fortunately, in her will, Mabel left the house to Mrs. Pershing, or else she would have had no place to go. Mabel had distant relations who thought the house now belonged to them. The court judged the will to be sound, and Mrs. Pershing had someplace to live.

With the loss of Mabel, the local congregation surrounded Mrs. Pershing with their love. They had not known Mabel or

Mrs. Pershing for long. Just the four years they had lived there. Some of the old, old-timers could remember (way back) kin in their family. But Mrs. Pershing, without Mabel, was essentially alone. Or so she thought.

In the years following Mabel's death, the congregation continued to share their compassion with Mrs. Pershing. Not out of a prolonged sympathy. They liked her spirit. They appreciated her wisdom. She was fun. She did the best she could to respond with a like spirit. She made friends. They treated her like family. She was amazed to discover how they included her in their lives. She had come as a stranger. They welcomed her as family.

There came the day went she could no longer fend for herself. She dreaded moving to the nursing home, but there was no alternative. Even the small house had become too much to care for. She had fallen three times, hard. Nothing was broken, but each fall was a scare. One moment, she would be walking across the room. The next moment, she would find herself on the floor. Her hands and feet simply did not move the way they used to. Dressing herself was difficult. Fixing meals was a challenge. Simple household chores were virtually impossible. Her hands, feet, and eyes could not cooperate with one another the way they used to.

Mrs. Pershing lived in the nursing home the last ten years of her life, until she was ninety-eight. Her congregation did not forget her. They treated her as one of their own. They visited with her. They took her out on short trips. They helped her with her shopping. They celebrated her birthdays with her. They picked her up for church. They saw that she got to her doctor. They were like family with her. In her closing years, bedfast for her last three years, they were especially helpful. Their shepherding, across the years, was gracious and generous.

In one visit, near the end, she remarked to her friends visiting with her, "How blessed I am. I have had five wonderful families. The family I grew up in was a blessing. My husband and I had a good family together. I lost my husband. I found a new family with my students. I taught class after class of high school kids. I loved them. They loved me. We were family. Many of them still stay in touch with me. There are cards and letters. I came back home to discover home was not what it used to be. Mabel and I had each other. I lost Mabel. Yet, I have found a dearer home with all of you than I could ever imagine. Thank you for your shepherding. Thank you for being family with me. I am home."

Small, strong congregations share a remarkable spirit of shepherding and compassion:

- A small, strong congregation is compassion-driven.
- The congregation shares the sacrament of compassion.
- The congregation lives a theology of forgiveness.
- The congregation is a legend for its spirit of a loving heart.

Small, strong congregations are compassion-driven. They are not vision-driven. They are not challenge-driven. Small, strong congregations have a compelling compassion with people. They have a spirit of sharing and caring. They share a sense of loving and serving. To paraphrase the text in Matthew 18:20 (RSV), "For where two or three are gathered in my name *with compassion,* there I am in the midst of them." Indeed, to be gathered "in my name" is to be gathered with compassion.

The small, strong congregation is a high-compassion community, not a high-commitment church. It has the sense of the living, moving spirit of God. The congregation shares generous compassion and shepherding—precisely because of their gratefulness and gratitude that God is generous with compassion with them. They shepherd in the community in the same way God shares compassion with the world. They love because they know they are loved. Their love is not of their own doing; it is the gift of God.

Small, strong congregations have a security about their own relationships with one another because they are secure in God's relationship of grace, love, and encouragement with them. They are therefore able to share with new people the same grace, love, and encouragement with which God is blessing them. They are grateful God has sought them out with his compassion, and they are glad to do the same with people in their community.

The vision of a small, strong congregation—if it ever thinks in terms of vision—is that of the Good Samaritan and the Good Shepherd. Small, strong congregations are not interested in vision-driven statements, challenge-driven goals, or commitment-driven objectives that advance the organizational growth of the congregation or institutional welfare of the denomination. What stirs people in a small, strong congregation is their spirit of compassion.

In recent times, much has been said about helping congregations develop a vision, develop a challenge. Vision-driven, high-challenge, achieving, and accomplishment-minded persons primarily lead these well-intentioned efforts. Naturally enough, these appeals resound well with those who are vision-driven people and high-challenge types. However, such appeals do not resonate with all people.

Many people in this life's pilgrimage are compassion-driven. What stirs their strengths and actions is a spirit of compassion. They live out their sense of compassion with persons in the community. They share their compassion with people they serve directly through their work. They welcome newcomers to the community in a spirit of love. People in hospitals and shut-ins feel the touch of their compassion.

They live their compassion in the community groups in which they participate. Their spirit of compassion is evident in the congregation's one excellent mission. With their deep, abiding compassion, they include in the family those served in mission, community people, friends of the church who live elsewhere, constituents, and members.

Small, strong congregations live a life of compassion and shepherding more than a life of challenge, achievement, and attainment. Many people in congregations I have gone to help across the years have said, "Dr. Callahan, help us find a pastor who will come and love us and whom we can come to love." Underneath that statement is an understanding that a foundational purpose for congregations is to share compassion and shepherding in people's lives and destinies.

We learn as much from what the text does not say as by what it does say. The text does not say, "for God was so challenged by the world." God may very well be challenged by the mess we are making of God's world. But what the promise of the Gospel is, what the text affirms, is this: "for God so *loved* the world" (John 3:16 RSV). We do not say that Christ died on the cross because he was committed to us. We affirm that Christ died on the cross because he loves us. We have the confidence and assurance that God surrounds us with the richness of grace and compassion.

We are the movement of grace more than law, love more than legalism, compassion more than commitment. The text does not say "now abideth vision, challenge, and commitment, but the greatest of these is commitment." What the text does affirm is the priority of charity, of compassion. The text says, "now abideth faith, hope and compassion, these three, but the greatest of these is compassion" (I Corinthians 13:13 KJV).

It has become popular in our time to encourage congregations to develop a vision statement, a challenge statement, or
a purpose statement. If you were going to develop a statement of any kind, I would encourage you to develop a compassion statement. Briefly and simply, share whom you are
loving and serving in mission. Mostly, small, strong congregations live out a compassion statement with one another and
the community in which they dwell.

I was helping two new congregations. One of them, regrettably, printed its first brochure and passed it out into the
whole community before I had the opportunity to be with
them. On the front of the brochure were the bright, bold
words, "Come, join in the challenge of starting this new
denominational church." Inside the brochure was their vision
statement, describing all the things they planned to do with
programs and activities in their early years and how they
planned to grow bigger.

Fortunately, I was able to help the other new congregation before the members printed their brochure. The only
words on the front of the brochure were "Your Friend, Next
Door." Inside the brochure, what one saw were people: pictures of people sharing compassion and shepherding, fellowship and family with one another. The spirit of the brochure
is "We love children in Christ." The focus of the brochure was
on helping people to live whole, healthy lives in the grace of
God. Guess which new congregation was strong and healthy,
helping people with their lives; guess which congregation
reprinted its brochure.

The people who are primarily drawn to developing vision
statements and challenge statements are people for whom
these ways of looking at life work. There are books written on
vision-driven, challenge-driven, high-commitment churches.
Many good people write these excellent books. They are
vision-driven, challenge-driven, high-commitment persons.

Frequently, they fail, however, to include the chapter that describes the grassroots compassion of the people in the congregation. They do not mention how the people of the congregation quietly go about sharing compassion and shepherding with one another. In fact, the reason a vision-driven church works, when it does, is not ultimately because it is vision-driven but because, behind the scenes, it is compassion-driven.

To be sure, compassion, vision, challenge, and commitment are good friends. However, what people long for and look for is someone who will share with them the gift of compassion. They already belong to enough groups trying to convince them to adopt a given vision or a challenge.

We long to both receive and share compassion. We do not simply want to receive it. We know we live, richly and fully, as we give, as we share, compassion with those around us. We want to be part of a group where compassion is central. We know that what strengthens our lives, like rain in a scorching desert, is a spirit of compassion.

Sacrament

They were holding hands. It seemed natural. No one had suggested they do so. After the doctor left, they simply joined hands. The waiting room was old. It had not had a coat of paint since the new Wal-Mart opened, and that was at least ten years ago. The waiting room was cluttered with hand-me-down chairs and sofas people had donated to the hospital rather than carry them to the landfill.

The room was crowded. Everyone who could had come. Esther had been part of the congregation for more years than anyone could remember. As they waited, they began to recall the acts of compassion and shepherding Esther had shared with the whole community across the years. Someone would remember an act of generosity. The silence would return.

Someone would recall another act of compassion. The silence would return. Slowly, and then more swiftly, with a gathering sense of appreciation, they recalled the many people with whom she had been helpful and generous.

The tightness in her chest, her gasping for breath, the pain in her head had come on that morning. Someone, hesitantly and hopefully, said, "If it had to happen, it was good that it happened here rather than in Europe."

Esther and Douglas had planned a trip to Europe. Their passports came. They were to leave in three days. The packing was completed. The post office was notified to hold the mail. The UPS man knew what to do with any packages that came. The kennel was looking forward to a visit by Whiskers, their wonderful, happy cairn terrier. Everything was in readiness. They were going to celebrate their fortieth wedding anniversary. The congregation gave them a going-away party two nights before their departure date.

But they were not going.

Douglas called their doctor the minute Esther fell down. She was rushed to the hospital. Jodi, their doctor's receptionist, alerted the congregation. She placed six phone calls, and each of those people called five households. Within minutes, the whole of the "family" received the word. Someone in the clan was in trouble. As many as could do so headed for the hospital. Esther and Douglas were well loved. The family planned to be present to lend their support.

The doctor said that they would know something just as soon as the lab tests came back. He was not gloomy. He was not hopeful. He simply recited the fact that nothing could be determined, for the moment. Perhaps the uncertainty of the moment led them to join hands. Someone prayed. Perhaps their love for Esther and Douglas stirred their longings to hold hands. Someone else prayed. Silence followed. Someone coughed. Someone sighed. Someone cried, softly, with gentle embarrassment.

They waited what seemed a long, long time. Somewhere in the waiting, Douglas gathered himself together and thanked them for their presence. The doctor came with the news. Esther was likely to remain in the hospital for three days. The tests suggested she would be all right. It was a case of exhaustion and fatigue. She had been doing too much to get ready for the trip. She had not been eating well. With the excitement of the trip, she had not been sleeping well.

The doctor said that her family could go in and see her. Everyone in the waiting room got up to go. The doctor said that only her family could see her now. They all continued toward the door. One person said to the doctor, "We are her family. We are her congregation. It's the same thing." They assured him that only a few would go in at a time. They would stay just a minute. They wanted Esther to know of their love and prayers for her. Together, all of those gathered with Esther and Douglas shared in a sacramental event of compassion and shepherding.

Later, the doctor told his receptionist, Jodi, that the best medicine Esther received was the love of her family, her congregation. Jodi made certain the congregation knew of the doctor's words.

Small, strong congregations share the sacrament of compassion, the sacrament of shepherding. A sacrament is a sign of grace, compassion, community, and hope. The sacrament of shepherding is an outward and visible sign of the inner and invisible grace of God, compassion of Christ, and healing hope of the Holy Spirit. When you care with another person, you share one of the richest sacraments in the Christian movement.

The sacrament of compassion is grounded in God's sacramental way of relating with us. We love, because God first loved us. An act of compassion has sacramental value precisely because it is shared in the same spirit with which God shares acts of compassion with us. It is not simply that we love one another because it is a good thing to do, or because that way we get along better. It is not simply that we favor motherhood, apple pie, and good intentions (and we do). Our compassion, our shepherding grows out of God's sacramental compassion with us.

We are not always lovable. Hasty words leap from our mouths. Hurtful acts of harm come from us. We are difficult to live with. We are preoccupied with our own problems. We vent our anxiety and anger. Our fear overtakes us. Rage escapes from us. We are sullen and silent. We are overbearing and obnoxious. We are not our best selves.

We are not always loving. We do not always love. We remember slights. We allow grudges and resentments to block our compassion. Old shadows and past griefs hinder us. Doubts and difficulties cloud our minds. Despair and depression freeze our hearts. We want to forgive former hurts but cannot quite bring ourselves to do so. Worries and frustrations get the better of us. Sometimes, we find it difficult to share our compassion.

Amidst the frailties and foibles of living, a small, strong congregation discovers how to share the sacrament of compassion, of shepherding in everyday, ordinary life. Acts of kindness, thoughtfulness, courtesy, and gentleness are shared with those around us. We live simply, one day at a time, a life of compassion with the people with whom we are in contact. Sometimes, anxiety, fear, anger, and rage come upon us. We have moments of doubt, despair, and depression. We have times when we are so busy we hardly look at one another. Old grudges and resentments sometimes overtake us.

When we are at our best, we share acts of compassion during the course of the day. We share them with our work associates and our customers. We share them with our friends and our family. We "see" one another. We take time with one another. We do so whether the day is dull and boring, new and exciting, or simply an ordinary day. We are generous with acts of compassion because God is generous with acts of compassion toward us. We live a sacramental life of compassion, not because of our own doing; it is God's gift to us.

Small, strong congregations share the sacrament of compassion, of shepherding as they share events of *good fun and good times*. It may be a picnic or a party. It may be an early morning walk. It may be a family gathering around a special meal. It may be a happy, good-fun evening, enjoying a gentle breeze on the porch and one another's company. It may be a late night, sitting out back, looking at the stars and the vastness of the night sky. Whatever the good fun event, the spirit of compassion is shared.

Small, strong congregations share in the sacrament of compassion in times of *remarkable celebration*. Anniversaries, births, birthdays, graduations, major promotions, significant community events, and retirements are events we experience with a sacramental spirit. We sense our closeness with one another. We sense our nearness to the grace of God. These special events become sacramental in our lives.

We sang "Amazing Grace." We were gathering for the last time. The closing gathering was a time of remarkable celebration. Our voices filled the room. We had come from across the planet. We had been together for two extraordinary weeks. We were in London, England. The general of the Salvation Army had gathered officers and leaders from across the planet. We were invited to develop a sense of future possibilities for where the Salvation Army can head in the twenty-first century, particularly in the area of faith education.

We prayed with one another. These would be our last prayers together. From diverse backgrounds, and with a multitude of distinctions, we lifted our prayers unto God. We were gathered from all of the continents and from many cultures. We shared work sessions, fellowship times, breakfast, morning tea, lunch, afternoon tea, tea, and supper together. We worked well. We lived well. We loved well.

It was a remarkable two weeks. Papers were read and shared during the first week, and during that week, I made it a point to come to know each person at the gathering. I would suggest, with one, that we share breakfast together. With another, we would visit over morning tea, or lunch, and so on. During the second week, I led the planning process. We all sensed the stirring, moving, living presence of God's grace with us.

We held hands as we shared together the closing blessing. For everyone, those two weeks were among the most remarkable celebrations in our lives. The sacrament of compassion, of shepherding was richly and fully present. As I look back, I see our closing time of singing, praying, and blessing gathering all of us together in that one remarkable, sacramental event. We celebrated all we had done. Even more, we celebrated who we were. It was not simply what we had done. It was who we had become. The sacrament of compassion drew us together in the grace of God.

Small, strong congregations share the sacrament of compassion in *tough, tragic times.* Esther and Douglas are living testimony to the spirit with which small, strong congregations share the sacrament of shepherding together.

Clara and Marie were sorority sisters. Many, many years ago, Clara was Marie's big sister in the sorority of which they were a part. Clara has amazed the doctors who treat her cancer. They projected, nine years ago, that she had six months to live. With her spirit and good treatment, she has lived nine good years.

Clara is weak and frail now. She gets around only in a wheelchair. She cannot do much for herself. Both she and her doctors know the end is near. Marie remembers Clara's help and caring with her as her big sister all those years ago. She knows Clara will benefit from special help in her last weeks and months.

Marie has taken a leave of absence from her job. She left the state where she lives and moved halfway across the country. Marie has decided that she wants to come and spend these last weeks and months with Clara. Marie shares the sacrament of compassion as her final gift to her beloved friend. Clara shares the sacrament of compassion with Marie as well. The sacrament is mutual.

Clara and Marie share a special relationship with one another. It began in their sorority. It has continued throughout their lives. What the two of them share is typical of the nature of shepherding in small, strong congregations. To be sure, both of them are part of Clara's congregation in these last weeks. Both of them feel surrounded by the shepherding of the congregation. They know they are loved. They know they love one another. They know God loves them. Because of the nearness of Clara's impending death, each moment has the quality of a sacrament for them.

Jane was suffering from Lou Gehrig's disease. D'Wayne, her sister, decided it was important for them to share the remaining months of Jane's life together. D'Wayne moved to Jane's community. Each day they shared with one another the sacrament of compassion. Together, they worked on this book during Jane's closing months of life. D'Wayne did the typing of the original manuscript, and together they made helpful editorial suggestions. It was a project they could share in common.

As best as one can be, both Jane and D'Wayne were at peace in the closing days. They sent their suggestions to me.

Jane died while I was completing the final editing of the book. D'Wayne called to let Julie and me know. As I look back on preparing this book, I see how much we have shared in one of the richest sacraments of the Christian movement. We experienced, with one another, the grace of God, the compassion of Christ, and the hope of the Holy Spirit. Both of them have contributed their wonderful, remarkable spirit to the book.

What happens in small, strong congregations are remarkable acts of compassion. Everyday people, with solid gifts and competencies, share these generous acts of caring. They do so in everyday, ordinary life; in events of good fun and good times; in events of remarkable celebration; and in tough, tragic times. As a result, they live this life, richly and fully, helpfully and hopefully. It is precisely for this reason that some small congregations are strong.

Small, strong congregations have good wisdom. They know, intuitively and consciously, the importance of sharing acts of compassion in everyday, ordinary life, in events of good fun and good times, and in events of remarkable celebration. By doing so, the sacrament of compassion in tough, tragic times takes on a deeper significance. Small, strong congregations do not simply show up in tough times. We live the whole of life together, not just the tragic times.

Moreover, we are wise enough to know that showing up only in the tough, tragic times burns us out fast. It takes the balance of sharing both the good times and the tough times for us to have the sense that life is more than death. People who share shepherding in good times and tragic times have two advantages. First, they develop a richness and depth of relationships during good times to be fully helpful in tough times. They are not strangers; they are family. Second, by sharing good times and tough times, they benefit from the balance. They do not wear out. They renew themselves by sharing in all of life together.

Forgiveness

Art and Tim could not even remember what they were arguing about. Their falling out had happened three years earlier. As good friends, they had been close, growing up together. They shared similar interests. During high school, they enjoyed good times hiking, camping, and canoeing with one another. They went to different colleges, largely because of the dissimilar majors they decided to pursue.

But the colleges were nearby, and they continued sharing good times together. They enjoyed double dating. They had fun camping and canoeing during the summers. One summer, they worked together on the same construction crew. They were at one another's graduation. They served as best man at each other's weddings. They were present in the hospital when each of their children was born. Their families were active in the same congregation. They enjoyed their newfound interest in golf together.

What started out as a simple conversation became a raging feud. They remembered the heat and fire, the shouting and shoving. They did not finally come to blows, but almost. It was close. The argument raged for too long. Huffing and puffing, they left, vowing never to speak again.

Time passed. They did not speak.

Three years came and went. At the congregation's covered-dish suppers, each of them made it a point to approach, separately, the table where all of the dishes were spread; otherwise they might have to speak to one another. They sat on opposite sides of the sanctuary. They made it a point to be on different project teams in the congregation. They played at different golf courses. They adopted differing travel patterns. They made every effort to be sure they would never speak again. They did it well.

Over the three years, people made various efforts to get them back together again. Their wives gave it a go. To no avail. Friends tried blind-date strategies. Golf matches were set up, but, invariably, Art or Tim caught on and did not show. People in their congregation sought some form of reconciliation. Art and Tim were not interested.

Words were said. Clamor and bedlam filled the air. Accusations were made. Harmful, hurtful statements spewed forth. Neither of them could remember what was said, nor could they recall what the argument was about. But individually, they concluded it must have been a massive quarrel to break up a lifelong friendship.

Now, life is not as simple as saying that they finally remembered what the quarrel was about, and that they laughed about how silly and insignificant their argument was, and that they went on to make up. Nor is life as simple as their discovering the quarrel was about something significant, and they continued to have nothing to do with one another. The reality is that they have not remembered, to this day, what the argument was about.

Art's oldest son, Lyle, was injured in a soccer game. A head injury. The ambulance rushed him to the hospital. Art was assistant coach of the team. He encouraged his son to play soccer, but the youngster was less than interested. Lyle loved music. But to please his father, and also because he had two friends on the team, he went along with the idea of playing. It was the next-to-last game of the season when he was injured.

Art's wife called Tim's wife. Tim's wife put Tim and their children in the car and headed to the hospital. Art's wife also called several members of the congregation: "Please pray."

They did more than that. They got into their cars and headed to the hospital. This is what family does when someone in the clan is in trouble. Through phone, cell phone, and e-mail, the word went out: "Art's son is in trouble. Come." And they did.

Compassion is tough. Compassion, community, challenge, reasonability, and commitment—these are powerful motivations for the Christian life. All of them are tough, especially compassion. Sometimes, when I am leading a seminar on motivations, someone will say, "Dr. Callahan, we appreciate your emphasis on compassion, and we agree, but when are we going to get around to the really tough one, namely, commitment?" Compassion is as tough as commitment.

I invite them to think of a person who has injured them and harmed them, someone who has grievously damaged them—someone with whom they have a grudge and resentment. They can almost taste the bitterness they feel. That person has wronged them. Badly. Woefully. They experience a sense of anger, hostility, and revulsion toward that person.

I invite them, with the grace of God, sometime during the coming week, to forgive that person. Compassion is tough because it is the motivation that includes forgiveness. It is tough to forgive. We do not do so easily. We can conjure all sorts of reasons why we should not forgive. We justify our bitterness. We make the case that we are in the right. Frequently, we are. It is really tough to forgive when we are right. It is not easy to forgive and be forgiven when we are wrong.

Small, strong congregations share the quality of compassion precisely because they have developed their capacity for forgiving. They do compassion well because they do forgiveness well. High-compassion congregations are high-forgiving congregations. They have learned that compassion without forgiveness is so much sentiment and soap. They have discovered that genuine compassion involves the capacity to forgive.

The best of families are the best of families because of the presence of compassion, forgiveness, reconciliation, and moving on. It is not true that the best of families are the best of families because conflict is absent. The only people I know who do not have conflict are those buried at the nearest cemetery—and sometimes, when I walk by late at night, I am not so sure about them. I hear the mutterings and the murmurings.

Art and Tim forgave one another that day. It was not easy. Both are headstrong. Both had deep resentments, built up over three years. Later, they regretted it had taken the accident with Art's son to bring them together. There was a concussion. Several weeks went by before Lyle was back up to speed. Everyone in the congregation was glad for Lyle's healing—and for the healing between Art and Tim.

The congregation prayed well. They surrounded Art and his family with the sacrament of compassion. Likewise, they surrounded Tim and his family with their compassion and shepherding. The congregation sensed a turning point. Through the experience, the whole congregation deepened its understanding of compassion. They value compassion even more as one of the central qualities of their life together.

A Loving Heart

The qualities, values, and objectives of small, strong congregations have more to do with compassion and shepherding than with growing bigger and bigger. In these congregations, the sacrament of compassion is central. Compassion and shepherding are what they do best. In our time, people increasingly long for and look for (1) a grouping that helps them with compassion and shepherding and (2) a grouping in which they can share their compassion and their shepherding.

People want, are drawn to, and thrive on opportunities to share their own caring. It is not the case that new people are simply looking for a small, strong congregation to love and care for them. They want their lives to count. They know, albeit sometimes intuitively, that compassion is mutual. They look forward to giving, to sharing, to offering their compassion as much as they want to receive compassion.

At the end of their days, people want to have the sense that they have lived a life of compassion and a life of shepherding. People are less interested in their lives counting because of an array of achievements and accomplishments. They have the sense that, in the end, these accomplishments can be lonely and dreary. Rather, people want God to say "Well done" for the compassion they have shared with those around them.

Small, strong congregations have this remarkable spirit of compassion. This spirit is central to who they are and whose they are. Their shepherding in the community is legendary. People love and are loved. People are helped and help. Mason, Kailey, Tom, Rachel, and thousands more who participate in small, strong congregations live out this spirit of compassion and shepherding in their lives each day.

God invites us to live life with a light heart—to live a life that is happy, cheerful, and spirited. We can encourage a light heart, or we can encourage a heavy heart. God invites us to a buoyant, lively sense that we are the people of wonder and joy. To be sure, despair, depression, and despondency visit us. Sickness, tragedy, and disaster find us. We walk in the valley of the shadow of death. We weep. We feel lost and forlorn. We lose track of who we are and whose we are.

In the midst of the heavy stuff of life, we discover God loves us. Our life is full of wonder and joy. God's love with us is sure and certain, not fickle and vague. We are amazed. God loves *us*—with a steadfast love. We are bubbling over with gladness. It is like the delight two people have in discovering their love for one another. Or it is like the wonderment of a new child being born, and, happily, enthusiastically, we share the good news with everyone we meet—strangers and friends.

Our heart is light. We are filled with joy and wonder. We have a light heart because we know God loves us. It is in the Irish saying that opens this chapter: a light heart lives long.

I add these words of my own: a loving heart lives well. We can encourage a loving heart, or we can encourage a selfish heart. God invites us to have a loving heart that lives out the love with which God blesses us. A loving heart is warm and forgiving, tender and caring, thoughtful and kindly. A loving heart does not think too much of itself. It is not puffed up. It does not fuss and bicker over minor matters. It is not caught in selfishness, egotism, and greed. It is not preoccupied with its own advantage, prestige, and power. It has left those things behind.

A loving heart longs to share and serve. It does not get caught up in the perpetuation of organizations and institutions, or the retrenchment and retreat of authoritarian establishments and confused bureaucracies. A loving heart is not drawn to an imprudent, foolish, frivolous frenzy of accomplishments and achievements, challenges and activities, however busy and frantic.

With a loving heart, we live well with those God gives us. Anxiety, fear, anger, and rage do not rule us. We love deeply. We discover grace and peace, simplicity and encouragement. We are creatures of grace, not law. We do not live by law. We have already had enough law. We can encourage compassion, or we can encourage law. God invites us to choose compassion.

Two things are true. A light heart lives long. A loving heart lives well. Small, strong congregations live with a light heart. They live with wonder and joy. They live with a loving heart. They live with compassion and shepherding. People discover both truths in small, strong congregations. People live with light, loving hearts. They live whole, healthy lives in the grace of God.

4

Community and Belonging

We may not have it all together, but together we have it all.

—AUTHOR UNKNOWN

Barb's parents wanted nothing to do with her. She had embarrassed them; she had shamed them. It was not so much that she was sixteen. It was more that she was pregnant, unmarried, and had carried on an affair with a boy whom her parents considered unacceptable and undesirable. He was from the wrong family and the wrong side of town.

Moreover, he did not want to marry her and make her "an honest woman." The complexities of her predicament almost overcame her.

The parents refused to allow her to continue living with them. For a time, Barb stayed with the family of a close girlfriend. That became awkward. Then she stayed for a time with her aunt. The aunt had never married, had devoted her life to a business career, and was active in civic and community projects. Her aunt took pity on her and took her in, but the pity finally got to be too much for Barb. She wanted to get on with her life. She did not want to wallow in pity.

Soon, she found a job working in a store that paid her a modest weekly salary. With just a few more hours, she could be self-supporting, but the store did not want to use her full-time. That would oblige them to pay for her medical insurance, and the store did not intend to do so. She found a second part-time job to make ends meet.

She rented a room in the house of a widow who had taught in the elementary school for many years and known her parents. Her landlady did not know her parents well, but she knew them well enough. She knew that it would have been very difficult for Barb to live at home, even if her parents allowed her to do so.

Her landlady let her be. She did not pester. She did not pity. She shared her home, much like the innkeeper in the story of the Samaritan. She provided just enough of a home that Barb could get on with her life, with her journey.

Weekends were tough. The store and her second part-time job afforded structured opportunities and relationships Monday through Friday, but the church in which she had grown up made it clear that they wanted nothing to do with her. They were the large, respectable church in town—the church mostly for "good people."

She thought about going back to her former church anyway. She thought she might just show up one Sunday and see what they would do. She mentioned the idea to one of her friends, and the word came back that the church would not welcome her, nor would her parents, who continued to attend the church.

Time passed.

She was getting on into her pregnancy, past six months now. One day in the store, a customer said to her, "I'd like to invite you to come to our congregation. We aren't big, and we don't have a lot of programs and activities to offer, but why don't you come some Sunday? We would really welcome you."

Barb was sharing the story of her pilgrimage over lunch one day during a seminar I was leading in that state. She said, "You know, Dr. Callahan, I went that first Sunday, and I knew I had found home. They really did welcome me. They could see that I was young, pregnant, and alone.

"They knew from the community grapevine I'd been kicked out of my own house. My parents shunned me, would have nothing to do with me. My former boyfriend justified his behavior by saying I had enticed him. I really hadn't enticed him, but I'm glad he's not part of my life any longer.

"I'm looking forward to the birth of my child; we'll do the best we can together. And now we have a family here. They'll help us and support us, and we can help and support them as well."

Barb went on to say: "Frankly, I was surprised they welcomed me. This congregation is known in the community for its strict ways of living, for its sense of discipline and discipleship. In a way, I think it's their love of children that helped me to be accepted.

"They have the best vacation Bible school in our community. They do wonderful work with their preschool program. The church isn't big; they don't have lots of space." Then she corrected herself: "*We* don't have lots of space. But we do love our children, and we do well with them. We aren't a big church, but we do have a big heart.

"You know, Dr. Callahan, I never thought I'd find such a warm, caring family in my whole life. I'm so glad I have found home."

As she spoke, I was reminded of the text in Ephesians that says, "Now therefore ye are no more strangers and foreigners, but fellow citizens with the saints, and of the household of God" (Ephesians 2:19 KJV). With the grace of God, we are in a new fellowship with God and live as God's own family in this time.

Open and Inclusive

One of the significant qualities of small, strong congregations is that people discover a deep sense of community. Countless millions of persons around the planet, with all sorts of human hurts and hopes, from all paths of life, discover a sense of home, community, and belonging in a small, strong congregation. This spirit of belonging strengthens and enriches their lives. Small, strong congregations share a remarkable spirit of community and belonging:

- A small, strong congregation is open and inclusive.
- The congregation helps people discover family.
- The congregation serves multiple neighborhoods.
- The congregation lives a healthy life as one, or three, or more groupings.

Small, strong congregations are open and inclusive, warm and welcoming. These qualities are a matter of spirit, not size. To be sure, some small congregations are closed, exclusive, isolated, and cliquish. However, these qualities are not marks of only small congregations.

I have worked with middle; large, regional; and mega-congregations that have about them the spirit of being closed, exclusive, isolated, and cliquish. They are preoccupied with themselves and their own petty plans. They are almost glad when newcomers join; they need Sunday school teachers, ushers, nursery workers, choir participants, and youth counselors. There are vacant slots that they need to fill. There is money that they need people to give.

However, in these closed churches, the old-timers hold the newcomers at bay. Their help is appreciated, but they really are not included in the family—until, perhaps, they have been there for many years. They are still newcomers after thirty-plus years. They are not included in the key decisions that shape the life and mission of the congregation. They are not included in the power. The relationship is cordial and distant, polite and formal. Some small congregations do portray this closedness, but such an exclusive spirit is not limited to small churches.

By the same token, fortunately, some large, regional congregations are open, inclusive, warm, and welcoming. They include newcomers in the life and mission, the decisions and power of the congregation. They are welcome as full participants in the family. Some are less so. Some small congregations, too, are open, inclusive, warm, and welcoming. Some of them are less so. Small, *strong* congregations are open and inclusive, warm and welcoming.

In our time, people search for community, not committee.

A small, strong congregation is marked by the dynamic of community, not the multiplicity of committees. The church-culture notion of committees, with its labyrinth of reporting, is not the mark of a small, strong congregation. The culture of committees may have worked in an earlier time. In this time, small, strong congregations have a healthy spirit of community, very few committees, and even fewer committee meetings.

The busy, bustling churches of earlier times had lots of committees. The model was a committee-laden, complex organizational structure. It was built on an institutional understanding of how middle-sized, suburban congregations operated. In that earlier era, both the church and the culture valued institutional, organizational, bureaucratic ways of involving people, making decisions, sharing power, and accomplishing objectives. Fortunately, most of the time the culture-of-committees approach did work in those congregations. However, those labyrinths of committees and organizational structures do not work in small, strong congregations, especially in our time.

Small, strong congregations invest their resources in helping people discover community; find roots, place, belonging; discover family and friends. They are wise enough not to invest their few resources of time and leadership in a multiplicity of committee meetings. The earlier, ancient organizational structure invited congregations to spend much of their volunteer time in committees. Small, strong congregations are wise enough to know that people come looking for community, not committee.

In small, strong congregations, there are just enough committees to be helpful, but not so many that the committees become harmful, slow down the mission, and detract from the depth of community people discover in their congregation. Indeed, most decisions in small, strong congregations are made informally and then are ratified and confirmed by whatever simple, formal process exists. The focus is on being open and inclusive, warm and welcoming. The spirit is more like being part of a family than being part of a church.

One small congregation I have had the privilege of helping has a preschool program. During the spring each year, people in the congregation and the community enroll their children—and by extension also themselves—into the preschool program that commences the following September.

This congregation is wise enough and welcoming enough to visit each family within two weeks of when they enroll their child. So in February, March, and April, families are visited. Most of the registrations for the following September happen in these three months.

During the visit with the family, the person from the congregation says, "Welcome. We're glad you're part of the Good Shepherd family." From the viewpoint of the congregation, they are part of the family from the time they register their child. The person from the congregation is seeking to include them now. He or she is not preoccupied with "Now, how can we get them to a new-member orientation class?"

Many people do not understand our neat, tidy distinctions between members and nonmembers. What they do understand is that they have entrusted their child to this preschool program. What they understand is that by this step they have entrusted their whole family to us through some of the most decisive, formative years in their life together.

From their point of view, when they enroll their child and themselves in the preschool program, they think they are becoming part of our family. Unless we teach them otherwise, they think of themselves as part of this congregational family. Regrettably, some churches, operating from a church-culture mentality, teach them that they are not yet really part of the family. Those churches put them in a second-class, one-down status as nonmembers.

In Good Shepherd congregation, and many congregations I know, the families of the children enrolled in preschool are included in the congregational family from the first contact made. When they share in any church gathering, they are welcomed as part of the family. To be sure, some families later go on to formal joining and formal membership. Nevertheless, the art in small, strong congregations is that we think in *informal, family* terms, not formal, membership terms. We think in *mission* terms, not membership terms. We think in encouraging, open and inclusive, warm and welcoming ways, not restrictive, closed, cliquish, isolated, exclusive ways.

Gatherings of small, strong congregations have the spirit of a healthy family reunion. We may not know every person gathered, but we know just enough people to feel part of the family. Frequently, we do know most everybody. Further, because we are all part of this congregational family, we have the sense that those that we do not know we could easily come to know. We discover the sense of roots, place, and belonging with one another.

Of course, we know some families are not like this. At the family gatherings, three sisters do not speak to each other. They have not spoken for years. They try to arrive at any gathering at different times, so they will not even have to say a one-word hello to each other. They don't really remember what happened so many years ago. However, they hang on to the memory that it happened, and they have allowed the gap to remain and widen over the years.

In one family, the father died. The mother had passed on years before. One son was at the funeral home, making the necessary arrangements for his father's funeral. The other son was at the old homestead, taking those "few mementos" he *just knew* his dad wanted him to have—the stove, the refrigerator, the furniture, etc. In the course of one swift day, he moved out of the house practically everything that was in it.

Understandably, the man who made the funeral arrangements felt his brother had robbed his father's house. He felt his brother had not honored their father's wishes in the will, which were that the household furnishings be divided equally. The two brothers have seldom spoken since. Some families and some congregations do exhibit dysfunctional behavior.

Small, strong congregations illustrate healthy, constructive behavior. Certainly, small, strong congregations have their difficulties and their problems. What they also have, however, is a capacity for forgiveness, reconciliation, and moving on. Small, strong congregations have the spirit of "Whatever these difficulties are, we will get through them together. Our relationship will be deeper, richer, fuller, and stronger than before."

What we know as part of a small, strong congregation is that God is open, inclusive, warm, and welcoming with us. Thus, with God's grace, our sense of community and belonging binds us together; draws us to one another; and helps us be open, inclusive, warm, and welcoming with new people. Members of a small, strong congregation have a healthy network of relationships *with one another,* and this promotes their ability to be open, inclusive, warm, and welcoming.

Some congregations are closed, exclusive, isolated, and cliquish. This is a matter of spirit, not size. This exclusive attitude can be found in small, large, middle, and mega-congregations. Regrettably, some congregations are so preoccupied with their own internal affairs that they freeze other people out. Usually, it is because they are insecure about the flimsy nature of their own relationships with one another, so they huddle up.

Wherever you find a congregation that behaves like a clique, you find two factors at work. First, you discover a congregation whose network of relations with one another is weak, fragile, insecure, and easily disrupted. They exhibit anxiety and apprehension over their own sense of belonging. They are not certain of the depth and quality of their own relationships.

Second, you find a congregation that is not secure in its relationship with God. The members are not allowing God's open, inclusive, warm, and welcoming grace to enrich their lives and their sense of being God's family together. Thus, they "cannot handle" the advent of new persons. They have enough trouble keeping their own relationships in almost reasonably good shape. They do not have the energy to include another person.

People in a healthy family congregation have solid relationships with one another. They are sufficiently secure about these relations, and with their relationship with God, that they are able to open their arms, welcome new people, and embrace them as they grow and develop as new persons. Life is a search and a pilgrimage. We grow and develop, advance

and mature as persons. We are not the same people today as
we were some years ago. Small, strong congregations include
us even as we grow and develop; advance; and build a new,
healthy life for ourselves. Small, strong congregations discover anew each day how God is open with them and includes them with love and grace. Thus, they are open and
inclusive with new people as well as with one another.

Family

Howard now knew he would make it in college. He was
beginning the spring quarter of his senior year. All of his
required courses and major courses were behind him. He had
only a few electives to complete this last quarter. He was at
his best with these courses. His scholarship was safe. Because
of his strong grades at the end of his first year, he was granted
a dean's scholarship as a sophomore. Now, he knew he would
finish. He would graduate at the end of this quarter. He had
never imagined he would get this far.

The guidance counselor had taken his parents aside during one of the high school open houses. With an air of subtle
arrogance and dammed pity, he informed them that their son
would never make it in college. There was no reason for them
even to try to help him to go. There was no chance for him. He
assured them that their son would flunk out in his first year.

For Howard's family, his completing college was important. When I write *family* here, you can read *congregation*.
Howard's genealogical family was part of his congregational
family. Neither he, nor his parents, could separate the two.
Indeed, no one could. They all thought of themselves as part
of the same family even though the participants in the congregation came from separate genealogical families. They
were one family in Christ.

Not many in the family (genealogical and congregational) had the possibility of going to college. Howard was the first to have the chance. They wanted him to succeed. The whole family-congregation got behind him. They encouraged him. His parents said nothing about what the guidance counselor had said. With the whole congregation, they supported his interest in going.

During the winter quarter of his sophomore year, he nearly stumbled. The courses in biology and physics were tough. He had not had the preparation from his high school for either course. He found himself having to learn things he should have learned in high school just to understand what he now needed to be learning in college. Notes and letters, phone calls and visits encouraged him. It was as if the whole family-congregation were with him in his struggle. He made it through. From then on, his whole family knew he would make it.

The family came to his graduation. His genealogical family came: his mother and father, his younger brother and sister, his grandparents, and his aunts and uncles. His whole family came. The congregation came, not because they were a church but because they were family. It was as if a grand family reunion gathered to celebrate Howard's graduation. To some, it seems out of the ordinary that the congregation came. For all of them, it was the natural thing to do. This is what family does.

Small, strong congregations are a family, not an institution. They are a relational, person-centered, and people-centered group. They are not functional, institutional, and organization-centered. Their best times are like a family reunion. One of the primary strengths of small, strong congregations is that they help people discover a deep spirit of family.

Small, strong congregations think, plan, and act like a healthy, extended family. The goals and values are those of a family. The customs, habits, and traditions confirm that we are family together. Compassion and shepherding are primary values. Most of the decisions are made informally. Much of what happens is spontaneous, on the spur of the moment. There is a wonderful family spirit, fully open to new people.

Hundreds of times over the years, in interviews with members of small, strong congregations, I have asked the question, "Why did you decide to join this congregation?" Again and again, people have said to me, "The first Sunday we came, Mary so warmly welcomed us that we knew we had found home."

In answer to that question they do not say, "Well, the first Sunday we came everybody rushed over and welcomed us." That would have been overpowering and intimidating. They do not say, "Well, on the tenth straight Sunday that we came to worship, Mary came over and warmly welcomed us." What they do say is, "On the first Sunday we came here, Mary so warmly welcomed us, we just knew we had found home."

The names change. It may be Mason or Mallory, Kailey or Tom, Rachel or Sue, Lynne or John (or whoever). What happens is this. On a Sunday morning, someone, stirred by God's leading in life, makes his or her way to this congregation. The person is graciously, warmly welcomed. He or she is invited into the new family.

You can never make a first impression a second time. The first impression small, strong congregations make with new people is that "we are a family; you are welcome." In warm, winsome, welcoming ways, they include new people into the family. Small, strong congregations have an informal understanding that people who are connected in some way are part of the family.

The small, strong congregation includes in the family *persons served in mission:* those whom the congregation has helped or is helping directly in some specific way. The phone call came from the funeral home. The undertaker said, "One of your members has died. The family needs you as their pastor." The minister could not remember the name. He quickly looked through his membership file. The name was not there. He said, "I'm sorry. They're not members of my church. You must have the wrong church."

Ten minutes later, the funeral director phoned back. He had talked further with the family. He said, "This is one of the families whom your congregation has helped with food and clothing in recent years. They think of your congregation as their congregation." The minister did the funeral. He helped the family of the deceased. The family helped him. From that day on, he included in the congregational family every person served in mission.

The congregation includes *constituents:* people who participate in some way in the life and activities of the congregation. People who participate in your congregation on Easter and Christmas are teaching you that they think of themselves as part of the your congregation. It is not accidental that they are there. They could be anywhere else.

In this culture, it is no longer the thing to do to go to church. People could instead be on an outing. They could stay at home. They could be involved in some recreational activity. They could be worshiping with some other congregation. By their presence, they are teaching you that, if they have a congregational family, it is with you.

Those who participate in any grouping or activity in the congregation are constituents—are part of the family. They may be part of vacation Bible school, a mission project, a youth event, a Bible study group, a shepherding project, a fellowship event, or a worship gathering. Formally, they may not be members of the institutional denomination, but they think of themselves informally as part of the whole family, and so does their small, strong congregation.

The congregation includes *friends of the church who now live elsewhere*. They may have grown up in the congregation, or they may have come to the community, found a sense of family with the congregation, and been active participants for several years. Now, because of schooling or because of job transfers, they are living somewhere else. They continue to feel part of the congregation. For them, this congregation is family.

They continue to "participate" in the same ways distant family members continue to share with one another. There are phone calls, e-mail, and visits back home. They help with their prayers, their giving, and their participation in one-time projects that the congregation is doing. In some congregations, they go on the mission service project with congregation members. In some, they come home to help with one-time events such as vacation Bible school, the congregational homecoming, the Christmas Eve service, the Easter service, or the congregational retreat. They participate, as best they can, because they have found family with this congregation.

The congregation includes *community people:* those who live in the community, think well of the mission of your congregation, and are glad to be as helpful as they can. They are not people whom your congregation has helped directly. They are not constituents; they do not participate in the life and activities of the congregation. They do not live elsewhere. They are not formal members.

One congregation has a legendary mission with children and their families. The members live a theology of service with the children in the community. They do what they do with excellence. They share one-time, seasonal, and short-term events with children as their gift to the community. They do them well. Precisely because these events are so well done, three teachers in a nearby elementary school are glad to share their wisdom, strengths, and experience with the congregation. As a result, they see themselves as part of the family. The congregation includes them in the family.

The congregation includes *formal members*. These are people who have formally joined the membership of the denomination. In small, strong congregations, the sense of an organizational, institutional joining of a denomination is not a preoccupation. Regrettably, institutional congregations think in terms of members, nonmembers, prospective members, and inactive members. They even organize their "membership" rolls that way.

The spirit of small, strong congregations is informal, not formal. The understanding of communityship, of familyship is informal. People become part of the family with an informal sense of community and belonging. The whole family includes persons served in mission, constituents, friends of the congregation who live elsewhere, community people, and formal members. Their "family rolls" include all of these people. Together, we are a whole family.

In the first century, the family vows, becoming part of the household of God, were something like this:

> Will you love the Lord, your God, with all your heart and soul and mind and strength?
>
> Will you love Jesus Christ as your Lord and Savior?
>
> Will you love your neighbor as generously as you love yourself?
>
> Will you be part of this family of grace, compassion, community, and hope?

By contrast, institutional membership vows sound something like this: "Will you be loyal to such-and-such denomination and uphold it by your prayers, your presence, your gifts, and your service?" In the early years of the Christian movement, people did not think institutionally and organizationally. There were no denominations to join. There was the family, the household, of God.

In our time, people join a family, not an organization. People join a congregation, not a denomination. People join a movement, not an institution. In our time, people are drawn to a community, not a committee. They are draw to the spirit of a movement more than the structure of an institution. In a small, strong congregation, people become part of a healthy family and live rich, full lives as a part of the family.

There is a time for family. There is a time for organizations. There is a time for congregations. There is a time for denominations. There is a time for movements. There is a time for institutions. All of these do solid work.

This is a time for family, congregation, and movement. This is not a time for organization, denomination, or institution. At a later time, seventy to ninety years from now, it may once again be a time of organization, denomination, and institution. It is certainly the case that in the 1940s and 1950s, the church as organization, denomination, and institution did remarkable work all over the planet.

That earlier time was a churched culture. It was the thing to do to go to church. Social conformity delivered people to the church. Extended family clans delivered the sense of community, roots, place, belonging, friends, and family. The culture was more institutional in its orientation. Then, in that time, local churches could get away with being slightly more organizational, denominational, and institutional.

I do affirm that much of that earlier time had a focus on community and belonging. The church scrapbooks are filled with pictures of Sunday school class picnics and parties. Yes, there are institutional pictures of the annual congregational meeting, of the visit of the denominational leader, and of the national denominational gathering. But most of the pictures are about people and groups in the congregation. Even then, the longing for family was strong. Now, the longing is even stronger. We are drawn to a grouping of people who live whole, healthy lives; who are spontaneous with one another; who are relational more than functional, who are family.

The search for family is more desperate now because many of the extended family clans that used to deliver this sense of family have been scattered asunder across the landscape. Certainly, it is the case, whether I am working with rural, county-seat town, suburban, or inner-city congregations, that mostly what I find are congregations seeking to be family together. They do not object to being part of some institution, some organization, some denomination, but their compelling focus is on their life together as community and family, not as organization or institution.

A congregation is a matter of being. An organization is a matter of doing. A congregation lives together as a family. A church functions as an organization. Families do not function like institutions. Some of the denominations have organizational structures that they think each local congregation should replicate. For small, strong congregations, there are three difficulties.

First, the denomination recommends an organizational structure that is designed for middle congregations, and in some instances for large congregations. It is a fairly elaborate structure, built on the notion of some committees reporting to other committees. Even in denominations that permit a truncated, abbreviated form of structure, it is still extensive.

Small, strong congregations do not have enough leaders to serve on all of the prescribed committees. What happens is that the same group of leaders meet, essentially wearing different hats. Now we are the finance committee. Now we are the council. Now we are the trustees. Now we are the worship committee. Now we are the education, or the evangelism, committee. This "let's pretend, wearing different hats" is almost laughable to some leaders. Some small, strong congregations seek to combine the committees. The typical response of the denomination is reluctant consent, along with the admonition that all of the recommended functions must be retained.

The second difficulty follows from the first. As a congregational family, small, strong congregations make most of their decisions together, and they make most of their decisions informally. They have a sense of the whole, not the parts. The denominational organizational structure is built on the premise of parts, not the whole. In a formal manner, this "part" of the organization makes these several decisions. In a formal fashion, another part makes those several decisions. Reports are brought to a formal, central group that coordinates the work of the parts. Regrettably, the formal, central group functions "representatively." In small, strong congregations, there is no representative group. With an open, inclusive spirit, everyone in the family is invited to participate in the decisions of the group.

The third difficulty follows from the first two. The recommended denominational organizational structure is built on the premise that a congregation is a matter of certain functions that it must be doing. However, small, strong congregations understand themselves as having certain qualities of *being* a family together. For them, life is being, not doing. They see themselves as being a congregation, not doing church. They do not see themselves as functioning like an organization. It is not that they are against that way of thinking. Rather, it is simply that they have discovered a way of living together—of being God's family.

For them, gatherings of the congregation—whether for mission, shepherding, fellowship, worship, study, or planning—are like the gatherings of a family reunion. There is a spirit of informality and generosity, of spontaneity and compassion.

Not everyone may know everyone else at a family reunion. But they know a number of people well enough to feel that they belong, that they are at home, with family. Birthdays and anniversaries are celebrated. New births are celebrated. Significant accomplishments and achievements, graduations and promotions are celebrated. They gather close with one another in times of sickness and tragedy, disaster and death.

In our time, what people long for and look for is not busy, bustling programs and activities that take them out of life and put them inside a church. What they look for—especially in a small, strong congregation—is a grouping of people whose spirit of family helps them live life, richly and fully, in the day-to-day world God gives us.

Neighborhoods

Small, strong congregations serve multiple neighborhoods. In our time, we live in a multiplicity of neighborhoods. Precisely because small, strong congregations help us live life well in the world, they help us live well in the multiple neighborhoods in which we live.

On the other hand, small, weak and small, dying congregations, preoccupied with their own survival, focus on their members' living life inside the congregation. They image that the more people they can get to focus inside, the more likely they are to survive. The difficulty is that we benefit from learning how to live in the world with which God blesses us. We are not helped to do so if the congregation, in a closed and separatist fashion, focuses its attention and ours on a life primarily within the congregation.

An open, healthy congregation helps us live well in the world. Such a congregation helps us live whole, healthy lives in the multiplicity of neighborhoods in which we find ourselves. Constructively and effectively, the congregation helps us embrace these varied neighborhoods. The congregation, in helping us embrace creatively these varied neighborhoods, comes to an understanding of these neighborhoods. In doing so, the congregation becomes, in a certain sense, a multiplicity of neighborhoods.

We live in a *relational* neighborhood of acquaintances, friends, and family. This neighborhood is the primary one in which most of us find a sense of community and belonging. Usually, this is an informal network of relationships. This is our day-to-day, significant relational grouping. We construct, both intuitively and intentionally, this relational neighborhood network. Thereby, we can participate in a grouping of sharing and caring, community and belonging. We enrich our lives through the primary relationships we discover.

We live in a *vocational* neighborhood. This neighborhood includes those with whom we work. We share much of our energy, creativity, and sense of direction with this grouping of people. This neighborhood also includes those with whom we come into contact during the course of our work. These may be regular customers, vendors, suppliers, or subcontractors. Many of us spend much of our lives at work. This vocational village is primary, especially when we discover rich sources of community and belonging in our lives.

We live in a *sociological* neighborhood. In some parts of the planet, these sociological neighborhoods are rigidly structured. There are clear lines of demarcation between one neighborhood and the next. There are distinctive goals and values. These groupings are particular because of quite differentiated customs, habits, and traditions. To be born into a given sociological grouping is to remain in that grouping for the rest of one's life. In many places now, these sociological neighborhoods are becoming less structured, more open and flexible, and more overlapping than was true in earlier times.

We live in a *geographical* neighborhood. The geography of a neighborhood is measured in minutes more than miles. We develop an average trip time in terms of going to work, major shopping, and major social and recreational activities. We create for ourselves a trip-time horizon. We are perfectly willing to drive up to that trip-time horizon insofar as the activities to which we are driving interest us and serve our sense of belonging. Our geographical neighborhood is more than the two or three blocks around where we live. With the advent of modern transportation, our geographical neighborhoods have become considerably expanded.

We live in a *genealogical* neighborhood. We are born into a given set of genealogical relationships. As we marry, we become part of additional genealogical relationships. There are first cousins, second and third cousins, aunts, uncles, nephews, and nieces, in addition to parents, siblings, grandparents, and great-grandparents. The genealogical relationships go on and on. With people living longer, and marrying more than once during the course of their lifetime, these relationships can be both expansive and complex.

There is *overlap* between the five neighborhoods in which we live. Frequently, our relational neighborhood overlaps with our vocational neighborhood. Sometimes, our genealogical neighborhood overlaps our relational neighborhood. Our sociological and geographical neighborhoods often overlap with the others. We participate in a kind of dynamic overlap in terms of these distinctive neighborhoods in which we live.

There is the process of *interchange*. We interchange one neighborhood and another with considerable flexibility. We attend one gathering that is primarily in our relational neighborhood. We go on to an event that is primarily a gathering of our vocational neighborhood. We go on to another gathering that is primarily in our genealogical neighborhood. We feel reasonably at home in all of our neighborhoods. Most people have learned to accomplish these interchanges constructively and happily.

There is *multiple belonging* in these neighborhoods. Perhaps a better term is *multiple community.* We find some sources of community and belonging in each of the five neighborhoods God gives us. We appreciate the value and worth of each. We experience a sense of community and belonging with our participation. We live whole, healthy lives because of the constructive influence of these neighborhoods.

To be sure, sometimes, one of these neighborhoods may be destructive and harmful to us. We may discover that the vocational neighborhood in which we find ourselves is blocking the development of our strengths and competencies. We may find that our genealogical neighborhood has unhealthy patterns of behavior, whether of fear, anger, abuse, or neglect. Most often, we are drawn to the neighborhoods that contribute a healthy influence in our lives. Sometimes, we may behave self-destructively and allow ourselves to become mired in an unhealthy set of relationships. Fortunately, we tend to learn from these excellent mistakes. We grow and develop, and move on to healthier relationships.

These five neighborhoods of everyday, ordinary life come together in a small, strong congregation. Our neighborhoods are part of who we are. We bring all of our neighborhoods with us to our congregation. Our congregation is open and healthy. Thus, what we frequently find in a small, strong congregation is convergence of relational, vocational, sociological, geographical, and genealogical neighborhoods. A small, strong congregation offers the richness of these overlapping relationships with amazing subtlety and abundance.

Years ago, the people who gathered at Piney Grove Church were the people who lived up and down Flowery

Springs Road. They were essentially all a part of the same relational, vocational, sociological, geographical, and genealogical neighborhoods. The convergence was amazing. Most of the people who came to that church were all part of the Lott family clan.

Were you and I to go to Piney Grove Church today, we would find that some of the Lott family clan still live where they have lived for years. Others now live some distance away, toward the east. Others of the Lott family live in another direction, even farther away, toward the west side of the county. These families have moved to other vocational and geographical neighborhoods, but they continue to come back to Piney Grove. They bring with them the sense of the new neighborhoods in which they live.

There are new people in the area. These new people, living up and down Flowery Springs Road, are now part of the congregational family. They bring with them a rich array of relational, vocational, sociological, and genealogical neighborhoods. There is a rich multiplicity of neighborhoods now present in the Piney Grove congregation. The congregation is more diverse, and at the same time richer and closer, than was true years ago. These people—old and new, young and old, scattered, dispersed and living close by—have come together and found a sense of community and belonging in the Piney Grove congregation.

The small, strong congregation gathers a convergence of neighborhoods and reshapes them. The parts become a whole. The varied neighborhoods inform, and the constructive values of each neighborhood draw forth, the best of the other neighborhoods. They enrich one another. The result is that the sense of community and belonging people discover strengthens the whole of the neighborhoods in which they live. Fortunately, the small, strong congregation does not replace these multiple neighborhoods with an inside-the-church neighborhood.

Rather, the distinctive convergence of these multiple neighborhoods provides a fullness and richness that benefits those in the congregation. They live whole, healthy lives.

It is not so much that a small, strong congregation finds its niche. This is a marketing term, and small, strong congregations are more into mission than marketing, more into community than homogeneity. It is not that they are trying to find their church-growth marketing niche. Rather, the small, strong congregation reaches out to the convergence of multiple neighborhoods that network with it and, in that sense, serves these neighborhood networks. People find a sense of roots, place, and belonging in the neighborhood of God's family.

A small, weak or a small, dying congregation frequently serves one sociological, geographical, or genealogical neighborhood. There are also large, regional congregations that are weak and dying precisely because they serve one geographical or one sociological neighborhood. By focusing essentially on one of the five neighborhoods, they do not help people constructively deal with the multiple neighborhoods in which people live. Further, they do not extend the richness and depth of neighborhoods that a small, strong congregation does.

A small, strong congregation gathers the multiple neighborhoods in which we live and transforms them—with the grace of God—into God's family. What is happening in a small, strong congregation is that these five neighborhoods, these networks in which we participate, are no longer stratified in the way they may have been in an earlier time. They no longer function as separate compartments of relationships in our lives. They no longer divide us inside ourselves. Fragmentation and compartmentalization are gone. Strict differentiation gives way to a dynamic interchange between these distinctive neighborhood networks.

With the grace of God, the multiple neighborhoods in which we live, with their fragmentation and compartmentalization, discontinuity and disunity, are transformed into a whole. We still live in several neighborhoods, but now they make sense. There is a unifying whole, a purpose, a unity as to how we live.

Perhaps the best way to describe this phenomenon is that we now live in the neighborhood nearest our heart, not our house. We no longer live primarily in a geographical neighborhood, or a vocational neighborhood, etc. The saying is, "A house doesn't make a home; people do." In a small, strong congregation, the neighborhood is no longer a collection of houses placed side by side in the same area of town.

The neighborhood of a small, strong congregation is a collection of people who bring with them interconnecting relationships with the five neighborhoods in which they live. The participants of a small, strong congregation may live scattered across an area. They may have the same average trip time in common. More important, these people have found just enough in common in terms of their search for individuality, community, meaning, and hope to decide to gather and live as God's people, as God's family in this time.

One, or Three, or More Neighborhoods

Small, strong congregations live healthy lives as one, or three, or more groupings. With the grace of God, a small, strong congregation gathers the multiple neighborhoods in which people live and transforms them into God's family. At the same time, it is easier to gather one, or three, or more neighborhoods as God's family than it is two.

"The table has always been in the narthex."

"It's too big for the narthex. We can use it better in our social hall."

The members of the congregation had heard these two statements for longer than they wanted to. They were tired of the controversy and argumentation. With an air of insistent authority, Hector would declare the first statement. With a rush of relentless enthusiasm, Wilbur would immediately respond with the second. Hector and Wilbur would be off and running. It was as if they were a duet with their chantings and rantings. The congregation had virtually memorized the litany of bickering and squabbling that would unfold.

Hector had been part of the congregation for all of his life. His parents, grandparents, and great grandparents were active before him. He was the avowed leader of one grouping in the congregation. Some said that his great grandfather was among the founders of the congregation. Mostly, Hector said this. No records could be found to support the claim, since the fire in the mid-1900s destroyed all of the earlier church records. Hector was known for liking things the way they had always been.

Wilbur was a newcomer. That is, his parents were active in the congregation. He had grown up with the congregation as his primary family. He had been a part of the congregation for all fifty-some years of his life. He was looked to as the leader of the second major grouping in the congregation. Nevertheless, from Hector's point of view, Wilbur was a Johnny-come-lately. His views were to be taken lightly, or better yet ignored altogether.

Some months before, the congregation held a community-wide dinner in the social hall. It was open to everyone in the area. Wilbur's wife was the team leader for the event. It was the first time that someone in Wilbur's grouping was the leader for the event. They were going to have a larger turnout than ever before. They would run out of tables. She asked Wilbur to find some extra tables. Wilbur and his crew moved the table from the narthex to the social hall.

It was a plain, sturdy table, not fancy. No one ever used the table in the narthex. The ushers had their own table nearer the main door. This plain table was off in a corner. Mostly, it had been "stored" there for years. In the social hall, the table was put to good use. So much so that Wilbur and his crew decided to leave it there. It would be a helpful addition for future events. When Hector found out the following Sunday that the table had not been moved back to the narthex, the argument began.

Time passed.

The congregation asked me to come and help them think through how to reach the youths in their community. While I was there, I learned that they were having this argument over where the table should be. The bickering had gone on for some months. Several leaders said to me, "Dr. Callahan, we're glad for your wisdom in helping us reach the youth of our community. This is why we invited you to come. If, while you are here, you can give us any help or peace on 'the table matter,' we would appreciate it greatly."

They recited for me the continuing chants that Hector and Wilbur would spew forth in virtually every gathering. The feuding embarrassed people in the congregation. Wilbur made it a point to talk with me. He wanted me to know the table was being put to good use in the social hall. Hector sought me out with his side of the story. He wanted me to know the table had been moved from "where it had always been."

When I heard those words, and as I listened further, I knew I was helping an unhealthy two-cell congregation.

A *cell* is another term I use for a grouping. A cell is a grouping of people who have developed significant relationships of sharing and caring with one another. It may include people from a range of relational, vocational, sociological, geographical, and genealogical neighborhoods. The cell has bonded together in some manner. Frequently, the cell, as a significant grouping, exercises some form of leadership in the congregation.

In a healthy cell, the grouping helps people deal with and integrate the multiple neighborhoods in which they live in everyday life. The healthy cell grouping is open and inclusive, warm and welcoming. People discover a healthy sense of family in the grouping. Healthy congregations create healthy people. Healthy people create healthy congregations. The two are close friends. They go together. Each helps the other. In this healthy environment, the cell exercises whatever leadership it does with a constructive, creative, open spirit.

In an unhealthy cell, the bonding of the group is such that it does not help people with the multiple neighborhoods in which they live. The cell tends to suggest that it is the only neighborhood. The nature of the bonding of the cell tends to be closed, exclusive, isolated, and cliquish. The unhealthy cell tends to focus inside itself. It has difficulty in relating to other groupings. It tends to look at life primarily from its point of view. It exercises whatever leadership it does with a domineering, restrictive, dictatorial spirit.

In an earlier time, in rural America, the people living up and down a given road were frequently from the same genealogical family. They also shared a common vocational neighborhood, namely, farming. Moreover, they tended to share the same relational, sociological, and geographical neighborhoods. There was a sameness to the neighborhoods in which they lived.

This sameness was also true in many mill towns in that earlier time. Even in county-seat towns and cities, similar genealogical families tended, as they migrated to this country, to live in the same section of the town or city. Frequently, they developed congregations that lived out a sameness of neighborhoods. This pattern was common in small congregations.

In some instances, it was true of midsized and large, regional congregations as well. In some mill towns, county-seat towns, and cities, the interconnected genealogical neighborhoods were sufficiently large that middle-sized congregations and large, regional congregations emerged. A sameness of neighborhoods prevailed.

Even in the midst of a sameness of neighborhoods, many of these congregations learned to develop their capacity for relating to other, distinct neighborhoods around them. They developed healthy patterns of behavior that would stand them in good stead in the future. As the multiplicity of neighborhoods increased, they would have the capacity to relate to them.

During that same time, there were congregations that did not need to develop their capacity for dealing constructively with multiple neighborhoods. Indeed, even if they wanted to, there were not enough multiple neighborhoods around for them to learn how to do so. Thus, in that earlier time, what one found in many congregations were people who shared a mutual relational, vocational, sociological, geographical, and genealogical neighborhood. This is still evident today among those recently migrating from other countries, who, in the early stage of their pilgrimage in a new country, tend to bring with them, or create here, a congregation with a sameness of neighborhoods.

There is nothing inherently wrong with this. The difficulty arises as people encounter a multiplicity of neighborhoods in their everyday life. The healthy congregation helps people learn and develop their capacity for dealing constructively with the multiplicity of neighborhoods in which they find themselves. A congregation that has learned how to do this helps the people in the congregation learn how to do this.

A grouping that has not learned how to do this is less helpful to the people in the group. It is not helpful to retreat to a grouping that seeks to isolate itself from the multiple neighborhoods in which we now live. Such a grouping discourages an open, inclusive spirit of community and belonging. It deprives people of the richness and fullness of relationships that help them grow and develop whole, healthy lives. Such a grouping is an unhealthy cell.

As I listened to the discussion, I knew that there were two unhealthy cells in this congregation. We had the old-timers. They were one of the cells. They insisted on life being lived the way that they thought it should be. Hector's grouping consisted of an overlapping sameness in his relational, vocational, sociological, geographical, and genealogical neighborhoods. Moreover, his group had not learned the capacity to relate constructively with other neighborhoods. Some old-timers are not this way, but Hector's group was.

We had the newcomers. They were the second cell. The newcomers were not that new. They had come thirty and fifty years before, but from the standpoint of the old-timers, they were new. Wilbur's grouping consisted of an overlapping sameness in his relational, vocational, sociological, geographical, and genealogical neighborhoods. It was a differing neighborhood from Hector's, but as in Hector's grouping, Wilbur's group had not learned the capacity to relate constructively with other neighborhoods. Some newcomers are not this way, but Wilbur's group was.

Here we have two unhealthy cell groupings in direct opposition to one another. If we had two healthy cell groupings with differing perspectives, we would be in a stronger, healthier position.

I said to them, "I will be glad to help you with the table fight, and then work it out with Julie for me to come back in about six months and help you with your next fight." I went on to say, "Work it out with her for me to come back about every six months and help you with whatever fight you are having at that time."

They said, "What do you mean?"

I said, "You have taught me that you are an excellent two-cell congregation of old-timers and newcomers. The thing two-cell congregations do best is fight. Right now, you are fighting over where the table should sit. Then, there will be a period of truce and resting up for the next fight—which will take about six months. You will then find something else to fight about, take a period of truce and resting up, and then there will be another fight.

"Someone will write the history of this congregation about forty years from now. Those of us who can read between the lines will chuckle at all of the 'table' fights that have gone on in their various degrees of intensity and turmoil over the forty years."

They said, "That does not sound like a promising future. What can we do?"

I said, "We can grow a third cell and become a three-cell congregation. Three-cell congregations still fight, but they take turns. They fight *around*." As I said that, they smiled, and chuckled, and then began to laugh. They understood the value of what I was suggesting.

I went on to suggest that our mission with a third grouping would help us to grow forward our capacity to deal with multiple groupings. As we learn how to relate to the third grouping, we discover fuller ways to relate with one another. By reaching out to a third group, we have a considerable advantage in developing our ability to relate with multiple neighborhoods. With this group, no harsh words, no bickering scenes, no shoutings and rantings have happened. We learn how to relate to this new group. In doing so, we discover ways we can relate more fully with one another.

Some leaders and pastors think the way forward is to concentrate on bringing a two-cell congregation together—to help them learn how to get along with one another. They focus solely on the two cells. If the two cells were going to learn how to get along with one another, they would have done so at some point during the last thirty years. Two-cell congregations tend to have "difficulty" getting together. The solution is to grow a third grouping.

They said to me, "How do we do that?"

I said, "First, we will find a couple of old-old-timers. Old-old-timers are people who can remember the time when we did not do things the way we have always done things. They can remember the time when there was no table over which to have an argument!

"We will find a couple of old-old-timers, a couple of old-timers, a couple of newcomers, and one or two new-new-comers. We will invite this group of people to be a mission team for the coming three to five months. Their task is to create, sponsor, and deliver three one-time events. The purpose of these events is to reach a new grouping of people in the community whom we are not now reaching."

I pointed out to them that if we got together just old-timers and newcomers on a mission team, they would simply begin a new two-cell church fight on how to do the mission. The presence of a couple of old-old-timers and new-newcomers helps the mission team focus on the mission, not on a fight.

They began to think of the people who could be part of the mission team. There was, in fact, a kind of relief at moving beyond the fight over where the table should sit. Mission beyond ourselves draws us to our best true selves.

Time passed.

The mission team did solid work. They sponsored three one-time events to reach and serve a grouping of people in the community. Because of the nature of the community and the strengths in the congregation, the focus was on reaching families with elementary children, particularly in the third, fourth, and fifth grades. I pointed out to them that this focus would also help them develop their long-term mission with youth. The new youths are the current third, fourth, and fifth graders, the youth grouping of the near future.

Two of the three events went well. The people they were seeking to reach found each other. The older elementary children and their families began to develop a rich, deep, informal network of relationships with one another. They decided to sponsor the next four events themselves. As time passed, they became the new third grouping in the congregation.

If you visit with that congregation today, you will find that, on occasion, they still fight. Three-grouping congregations do fight. But they take turns; they fight around. The balance of power shifts. It is no longer simply a fight between the old-timers and the newcomers. Likewise, four groupings fight. They take turns. They learn how to live with one another.

Two-cell congregations tend to be dysfunctional. Granted, a two-cell congregation of healthy cells does well. I have had the opportunity to work with some of these. At the same time, there seems to be a tendency for two cells, particularly when one or both are unhealthy, to fight. We hear of such congregations. We hear of the bickerings, the feudings, the fussings, and the heated arguments. Much noise is made. Much damage is done.

Regrettably, it is precisely because of the heat, noise, and damage that some people have concluded there is no future for small congregations. I concur that there is no future for unhealthy, two-cell, small congregations. However, we have paid too much attention to the noise of two-cell church fights in small congregations. Many small, strong congregations go quietly about their life together as a healthy one-cell, or three-cell, or more-cell congregation.

Indeed, two-cell church fights are not limited to small congregations. I have worked with many middle-sized and large, regional congregations engaged in their own two-cell controversies. The heat, noise, and damage in these congregations are horrific to behold. To be sure, a midsize or large, regional congregation is a gathering of many groupings. As I shared earlier, a large congregation is a collection of small congregations.

What sometimes happens is that two of the groups rise to the top and become competing leadership groups. Frequently, they see themselves as old-timers and newcomers. They exhibit the same patterns of behavior that Hector and Wilbur did. They argue over this or that. They seek to have power over one another and over the other groups as well. They bicker, feud, and fuss.

We do a disservice to small congregations if we think that two-cell church fights occur primarily in them. It may be that some people's preference for middle-sized and large, regional congregations causes them to notice this phenomenon more in small congregations. Thus, they have an excuse to focus on midsize and large, regional congregations.

They point to the few small congregations in their area that are having two-cell church fights, and in effect they say, "See what happens in small churches?" They fail to mention the midsize and large, regional congregations in the same area that are having equally difficult (if not more difficult) two-cell fights.

In our time, a small, strong congregation gathers informally. People discover with one another a sense of roots, place, and belonging; community, friends, and family. It may be a small, strong congregation with one cell—one major grouping in which people find family, community, and belonging. In a whole, healthy fashion, this one significant relational grouping gathers the multiplicity of neighborhoods in which people live in everyday life. As a consequence, this one-cell congregation is open, inclusive, warm, and welcoming. The diversity of neighborhoods that come together in this small, strong congregation enable it to be open to the new neighborhoods with which people increasingly live.

A small, strong congregation may be a healthy three-or-more-cell congregation. It has three or more significant relational groupings. Each draws together a beneficial multiplicity of neighborhoods in a whole, healthy spirit. The outcome is that this three-or-more-cell congregation is open, inclusive, warm, and welcoming. This small, strong congregation has become a gathering of a rich variety of neighborhoods. This enables the people in the congregation to benefit from a richness, depth, and fullness of community and belonging.

A healthy small, strong congregation is the result of one open cell, or three or more open cells. Feel free to encourage one. Feel free to develop three. Feel free to encourage more. The thing not to do is to drift into being a two-cell congregation. Two-cell congregations are usually weak and declining, or dying. No one wants to join a fight. (Well, mostly, no one wants to join a fight.) Healthy people do not. The thing two-cell congregations do best is fight.

Certainly, in healthy congregations, we have our share of fusses and feuds, bickering and disagreements. Hostility and argument overtake us. We do not always taste our words before we speak. Contention and controversy find us. There are disputes and conflicts. Angry words are spoken. Bitter words escape our mouths. We do not always get along. Sometimes, it is not pretty.

Importantly, if we do fight, we now fight about the key mission projects that serve well the multiplicity of people we are now helping. We do not allow ourselves to get caught up in lesser matters. Oh, occasionally, it happens. Mostly, we share in mission, compassion, and community together.

In small, strong congregations, we share a common sense of community. Barb is welcome. We are family. John and Nancy are invited. We belong together. Herb and Doris are included. We become whole, healthy persons. Dan and Pat discover home. We are God's family.

Dave and Joan, Sue, Ned and Nancy, John, Dick and Joyce, and Valerie are part of the family. It is amazing. We share the richness of community, the fullness of belonging. Blake, Mason, Brice, Kailey, Tom, Rachel, Naomi, Leila, Renee, Christen, Mallory—they all find home in this small, strong congregation. We may not have it all together, but together—with the grace of God—we have it all.

5

Self-Reliance and Self-Sufficiency

What lies behind us and what lies before are
tiny matters, compared to what lies within us.

—RALPH WALDO EMERSON

We came of age in that meeting."
During the course of the small-group gatherings and the individual interviews of my consulting with Jim's congregation, I heard this message from one person or another many times. Actually, the coming-of-age meeting took place some years before. It was the last in a series of crisis meetings in the congregation. Jim and I talked about it. He said to me, "I don't know where the words came from—save God. I simply felt led to share those words that day."

The words which Jim had shared were these: "We have taken help from our denomination long enough. It's time that we help ourselves."

This particular congregation had developed a pattern of depending on the denomination to help them. There was the time the roof leaked. They appealed to the denomination, and the denomination gave them money. There was the time—for a number of years—they asked the denomination to supplement what they were able to pay their pastor, and the denomination did it—for a number of years. There was the time when the congregation needed help with the stained-glass windows. They appealed to the denomination, and the denomination sent money. There was the time at the end of one year when the congregation was short on money and could not pay all of its bills. The denomination sent money.

It became a pattern for the congregation to depend on the denomination to help them from one crisis event to the next. They developed the syndrome of denominational dependence.

Several people involved in my consulting with their congregation described the meeting to me, and their accounts were remarkably similar. The meeting had not gone well that night. There was another crisis, and any number of people there were saying, "Well, we'll appeal to the denomination for a grant."

There was some wrangling, feuding, and fussing over how much money to request from the denomination. They talked about this amount and that amount. They talked about asking for a little more than they really needed, so they could use it to help with some other things. Some people thought that was less than honest. Words were spoken back and forth, back and forth.

In the midst of the fussing and feuding, Jim stood. People say that he doesn't talk a lot in meetings, doesn't talk a lot any time! He listens well. People like to visit with him. His small store is a gathering place on the town square. Mostly, people come in and talk with one another, and the gift Jim gives them is that he listens. It was a bit unusual for Jim to stand.

He asked to say something. People did not immediately quiet down. There were still words back and forth. Jim is not that tall. They say he talks almost in a whisper.

When they finally did settle down, he quietly said to them in a spirit of assurance and self-reliance, "We have taken help from our denomination long enough. It's time that we help ourselves."

With a gentle spirit, he went on to say, "Our denomination has been good to us. It has wanted to help us, and has been glad to help us. It has been too good to us. Almost every time something comes up, we turn to our denomination for help. We have come to rely on the denomination rather than on ourselves. This time, let's rely on ourselves."

As Jim and I were talking about that earlier, decisive event, several people joined the conversation. Mostly, I listened. In their own words, each of them shared what they had learned. It was in that event that they discovered they could be self-reliant and self-sufficient. Since that event, the congregation has found resources within itself and in its community to move forward with the mission. On occasion, the denomination has asked them if they needed any help. The denomination was so used to helping them that, even after the congregation had broken its pattern of denominational dependency, the denomination was having difficulty breaking its own part of the codependent-dependent pattern of behavior.

Consistent

Small, strong congregations share a solid spirit of self-reliance and self-sufficiency. They claim well the strengths, gifts, and competencies with which God blesses them. With the grace of God, they move forward with the mission to which God invites them:

- A small, strong congregation has a consistent spirit of self-reliance.

- The congregation encourages creativity and improvisation.
- The congregation benefits from community resources.
- The congregation has reasonable pastoral resources.

Small, strong congregations have a solid spirit of self-reliance and self-sufficiency. Their spirit is consistent and steady, not wavering or occasional. It is not that they depend on themselves for this project, and then ask the denomination to help them with that project. It is not that they are on one occasion self-reliant, and on another occasion give way to being denominationally dependent.

Glenn was a recovering alcoholic, some of the time. One day, he would be working his Twelve Step program of recovery. With the wisdom, strength, and experience of his sponsor, he would be growing forward a whole, healthy life. Two days later, he would give way to a codependent-dependent pattern of behavior. He would be back in dependency, depending on his codependent spouse. She would want to be helpful to him. He would need her help. She would deliver whatever help he needed and wanted.

One day, Glenn's sponsor was kind enough to say to him, firmly and straightforwardly, "Your inconsistency is doing you in. You can be consistent. You can decide, one day at a time, to work your recovery program. Let me know when you decide to do so." Glenn was taken aback. Inwardly, he had hoped he could have it both ways. He finally figured out that he wanted to be well, whole, and healthy. He worked his program. This year, he is celebrating his fifteenth birthday in the program.

It is easier to be consistent. It is hard to be inconsistent. It is easier to count on oneself to work toward one's health and recovery. It is tougher to depend on someone else to do it for one. When someone else tries to do it for the alcoholic, it does not work. Even if it did work, the alcoholic would have no ownership of his recovery.

Jim's congregation discovered that it was easier to grow their mission forward, grow their sense of health and wholeness, if they did not allow themselves to be drawn into a pattern of denominational dependency. It is not that they are too proud to take help from others, particularly from their denomination. It is more that they learned that they could depend on themselves.

Small, strong congregations practice, one day at a time, a life of self-reliance and self-sufficiency. They learn that the money matches the mission. The stronger the mission, the more generous the money. The weaker the mission, the less generous the money. They learn that God provides resources sufficient unto the mission. With the steadfast grace of God, they are consistent in their self-reliance and self-sufficiency.

Three things are true in small, strong congregations:

1. There is a shortage of personnel and money.
2. There are inadequate supplies.
3. There is hardly enough of anything.

With the grace of God, and with the resources with which God is blessing them, small, strong congregations share competent, compassionate mission in the community.

Three things are also true of weak and dying congregations:

1. There is a shortage of personnel and money.
2. There are inadequate supplies.
3. There is hardly enough of anything.

Regretfully for them, members of weak and dying congregations become preoccupied with what little the congregation has. They do not claim the strengths God gives them. They allow themselves to suffer from low self-esteem. They look down on themselves. They think more poorly of themselves than they have a right to. Frequently, they develop a pattern of denominational dependence.

It is not that the small, strong congregation has more resources in personnel, money, and supplies. Small, strong; small, weak; and small, dying congregations all tend to have about the same range of resources. The difference is what they do with the resources they have.

Self-reliant leaders create self-reliant congregations. Self-sufficient pastors create self-sufficient congregations. Conversely, dependent leaders and pastors create dependent congregations. Pastors who depend on the denomination create congregations that depend on the denomination. Leaders who depend on the company, the government, etc., create congregations that depend on the denomination. Their pattern of dependency in life contributes to their growing a comparable pattern of dependency in their congregations. How they live life shapes how they live as a congregation.

In small, strong congregations, the spirit is "We do not put our future in the hands of someone else; we do for ourselves. We have no interest in codependency; we do well for ourselves." Such congregations are this way because they have leaders and pastors who live the whole of their lives with this consistent spirit.

Regrettably, some people work from the notion that resources, strengths, and power are external. They may not yet have developed their own internal sense of their strengths and power, or they may be in the beginning stage of doing so. In a misguided fashion, they may hope that someone external to the organization will do it for them. This difficulty occurs. The person has no ownership for the externally granted strengths, resources, and power.

A further difficulty is that only you can grow you. No one can do it for you. God gives you the internal capacity to advance and develop your strengths and competencies. God gives you the freedom to grow yourself at whatever pace works for you. God wants you to have the power to grow you.

It is inherent within a congregation to be self-sufficient and self-reliant, but unfortunately some congregations learn a pattern of codependency. Sometimes, a denomination, too eager to be helpful, teaches a pattern of codependency. The denomination delivers too much help.

Cooperation between a congregation and a denomination is helpful. Codependency between the congregation and the denomination is harmful. This works both ways. It is important that congregations not be codependent on the denomination. It is equally important that the denomination not be codependent on congregations. The art is for each to give almost enough help to be helpful, but not so much that the help is harmful and creates a pattern of codependency.

Congregations are tough and resilient. Congregations last a long, long time. I have been in congregations where, some twenty-five years before, an alleged expert said, "If you do not do such-and-such, you are going to die." They did not do what the person proposed, and when I go there a quarter of a century later, they are still there.

You might be surprised at how many times a statement much like this is made to someone who wrestles with alcoholism: "If you don't give up drinking, you are going to die." In my years of knowing and working with many people, I have never yet met someone who gave up drinking because of this threat. Often, they drink more.

Mostly, I have learned, across the years—and this is especially true with small, strong congregations:

- Under threat, people whither. With encouragement, people grow.

- People are not persuaded to do something because someone tries to frighten them.

- Congregations are tough and resilient and last a long, long time.

Small, strong congregations are consistent in their spirit of trusting and hope. They are not blind to the difficulties they face, but they do not wince and whine, lament and moan, grumble and complain. They trust God. They pray. They build on the strengths God gives them. They know that their present is not of their own doing; it is the gift of God. They know God leads them to the future that God is preparing and promising for them.

There is an ancient Irish prayer, whose author is unknown, that goes like this:

Take time to work; it is the price of success.

Take time to think; it is the source of power.

Take time to play; it is the secret of perpetual youth.

Take time to read; it is the fountain of wisdom.

Take time to be friendly; it is the road to happiness.

Take time to love and be loved; it is the privilege of the gods.

Take time to share; life is too short to be selfish.

Take time to laugh; laughter is the music of the soul.

The following words came to me one day, as I was thinking of small, strong congregations. I think of the following prayer as a prayer for you and me as persons. I also think of this as the prayer for small, strong congregations.

Take time to claim your strengths; they are gifts of God.

Take time to have fun; it is God's way of teaching you your strengths.

Take time to grow yourself; only you can grow you.

Take time to live well; this is the life God gives you.

Take time to trust yourself; God trusts you.

Take time to be self-reliant; it is better than being dependent.

Take time to share with others; they will bless you, and you will bless them.

Take time to have hope; you are the child of God.

Small, strong congregations live the spirit of these two prayers.

I encourage you to keep these two prayers before you: the ancient Irish prayer and the prayer that I have written. You can paste them on your mirror, put them on your computer as a screen saver, set them on your desk, or post them on your calendar. Let these prayers be a steadfast blessing in your life and your congregation.

I wrote the following words as well. You are welcome to read them. I do not encourage you to focus on them. Simply know them, for this moment, and move on. Concentrate on the two prayers above.

Take time to develop dependency; your own strengths will diminish.

Take time to fear; it is the source of anxiety and anger.

Take time to frown; it is the secret of growing old while you are yet young.

Take time to be bored; you will miss the creativity you have.

Take time to be exclusive; it is the road to loneliness.

Take time to carry grudges; it is the privilege of bitter people.

If we develop dependency; our own strengths diminish. If congregations develop a pattern of dependency, the strengths they have diminish. Strengths are like muscles. If they are used, they grow firmer and stronger. If they are not used, they weaken, atrophy, and decay.

It is not that small, strong congregations are too proud to accept help. Indeed, small, strong congregations have a remarkable humility. They are humbly grateful for the gifts with which God is blessing them. With deep humility, they are amazed at the richness of the resources with which God blesses them. They live with the confidence and assurance that God gives them strengths and resources unto the mission that they share.

They live with the spirit of self-reliance and self-sufficiency. They are consistent in this spirit. They rely on the grace of God. They rely on the strengths, gifts, and competencies that God supplies. They have no interest in developing a codependent-dependent relationship with some denominational entity. They want their future to be in God's hands and their own, not in the hands of someone else. They know the steadfast love of God. They are consistent in their reliance on God's grace and the strengths God gives them.

Creativity and Improvisation

The capacity for creativity and improvisation and the capacity for a consistent self-reliance and self-sufficiency go together. They are good friends. The more consistently self-reliant a congregation is, the more creative the congregation is. The more self-sufficient a congregation is, the more improvisational the congregation is.

By contrast, if a congregation allows itself to develop a pattern of dependency, it loses its creativity and improvisation. The more dependent a congregation becomes, the less creative it is. If it depends on some other entity to do for it, it loses its ability to grow its own creativity forward. It becomes dependent on the creativity of the entity with which it has decided to develop a dependency pattern.

One of the remarkable traits of small, strong congregations is their capacity to be creative with the resources they have. They have discovered how to make do. They improvise wonderfully. They have learned how to build on the resources they have. They are open to new possibilities, to new ways of being a healthy congregation. They encourage people in the congregation to live, in everyday life, a spirit of creativity and improvisation. They live with this confidence. The more creative people are in their lives, the more creative they are in their congregation. They live with this assurance. The more creative people are in their congregation, the more creative they are in their life.

The focus in small, strong congregations is on creativity and improvisation, *not* on complaining and whining. To be sure, some people have developed a gift for bemoaning and lamenting, whining and complaining. In Australia, it is called "whinging." I have worked with congregations where some people have developed their gifts for complaining in remarkable ways. In so doing, they deny their capacities for creativity and improvisation. They deny resurrection.

God creates us to be creative. God creates us to *claim*, not complain. God creates us to claim the creativity, the new life we discover with God's grace. God does not create us to complain about things not going our way. The gift of the resurrection is the gift of new life. God invites us to be creative with the new life God gives us. God invites us to be improvisational with the strengths with which God blesses us.

We learn a behavior pattern of complaining. It takes considerable effort to learn such a pattern because we are learning something that is foreign and alien to how God creates us to be. Once learned, it takes even more emotional energy and stamina to sustain such a pattern because we are swimming against the flow of the life God wants for us. We are swimming hard in the opposite direction. People who complain a lot are drained a lot.

It is easier to learn a constructive habit. It is tougher to learn a destructive habit. If we can learn a counterpattern of behavior, we can learn a creative way of behaving, thinking, and acting that flows with and matches how God intends us to be. Frankly, it takes more energy—emotional, spiritual, and physical—to complain than it does to claim. We can be creative. Or we can complain. Claiming our strengths, being creative and improvisational, takes less energy, because we are working with the way God created us to be. Complaining about our plight takes more energy, because we are working against the grain—against the way God created us to be.

Some people adopt an attitude of "poor little me." They carry their "cross" with self-pity, lamenting what life has done to them. They assume that their preponderance of bemoanings and complainings represents a theology of the cross. This is not true. Jesus carried the cross without complaining. The central message of the cross is love. We discover a spirit of mercy and sacrifice. Christ forgives those who are crucifying him. The theme of the cross is, "Father, forgive them, for they know not what they do."

The cross points to the resurrection and new life in Christ. Small, strong congregations live in this spirit of love and new life in Christ.

Once I was helping a congregation. I had been there several days, sharing in interviews and small-group discussions. I learned that a group of people in the congregation—small in number and small in spirit—had developed to an advanced level the art of complaining, bemoaning, whining, and lamenting. They knew how to do it really well!

They would complain that the pastor never visited. When the pastor went out to visit, they complained that they could never find the pastor in the office. On one Sunday, they would complain that the temperature inside the church was too hot. The next Sunday (or even later that same Sunday) they would complain that the temperature was too cold. They complained about the type in the bulletin—they couldn't read it. The type would be changed, and they complained that it was too big.

They complained that the front door swung out, which did not help them when they were coming into congregation, particularly on a rainy day. So, against the fire marshal's policy, the door was changed to swing in. Then they complained that the door swinging in made it difficult for them to get out after services.

They would complain about this or that, now one thing, and then another. They were never satisfied. Nothing and no one could please them, even as people in the congregation spent quite a bit of time preoccupied with what the small group was going to complain about next, and trying somehow to satisfy them.

I was there near the beginning of Lent. In the congregational gathering, I said, "My wisdom as a consultant teaches me that all of us—as part of our spiritual growth and development—give up something for Lent.

"This Lenten season, I propose that we in this congregation—just for this Lent—give up complaining. Let us, in the spirit of prayer, thoughtfulness, and hope, decide that during the course of these days approaching Easter, the thing we will give up is any complaint."

I had thought about this before the congregational meeting. I talked with four of the creative, respected leaders: Verne, Sue, Janet, and John. I asked Verne, Sue, and Janet if they would serve as sponsors for this Lenten project. All three agreed. So I said then to the congregation, "If any of you feels any temptation *at all* to begin complaining or whining, call one of these three sponsors—Verne, Sue, or Janet. They will talk you through it, so that you do not complain.

"If people with alcoholism can figure out how to give up drinking by using this method, then I believe we can figure out how to give up complaining—one day at a time—for this short period of a few weeks."

I went on to say: "Now, during this Lent, with the creativity with which God blesses you, you may—with the stirring of God—discover an excellent idea or good suggestion that will help your congregation. Share your creative idea with John. You can talk with him. Or you can feel free to write it out, sign it with your name, put down your telephone number, and turn it in or send it to John. John will see that your excellent idea and good suggestion gets to the proper team for action. During this Lenten season, however, we are giving up unsigned notes that are bitter and complaining, angry and bemoaning."

Then I said to them: "I invite you now to talk with the person next to you—the person on your right or left—whoever looks reasonably friendly—smiling and in good spirits. Visit with them for the coming five minutes. Share with this person one thing: your capacity to give up complaining for Lent. Teach your neighbor how you plan to go about this decision for this short period of time."

There was considerable animated discussion in the congregation during the five minutes. There emerged a growing consensus that this would be a healthy spiritual practice, a healthy practice for their lives during Lent.

Then I said to them: "Now, share with the person with whom you have been visiting the beginnings of one creative idea you know will help our congregation. You do not need to share a finished creative idea. During Lent, you will have time to advance and improve your idea. Some time between now and Easter, you can share your fuller creative suggestion directly with John. For now, simply share the early beginnings of your creative idea. Take the next five minutes."

There was even more animated discussion. They liked the possibility of giving up an old pattern of behavior and discovering a new way of living. A new sense of creativity began to emerge.

It was amazing. During the whole season of Lent, no one complained! Oh, some people came close to it, and they would call one of the three sponsors, who would talk them through it. The coaching-sponsor team did solid work.

Several people sought John out to share with him a creative idea that had come to them. He was an excellent listener. People trusted him. They knew he would respect the creativity of their idea. A number of signed notes with excellent ideas and good suggestions were given to John. Some people simply telephoned him and shared a new idea that had come to them. Now, he was not flooded to overwhelming with hundreds of ideas. Nevertheless, the ideas that he received were sound and solid, workable and achievable. Less preoccupied with complaining, people came up with creative ideas.

Mostly, when people now look back to that Lent, they remember what they discovered, not what they gave up. They found their own creativity. They discovered their capacity to improvise in fresh new ways to build a whole, healthy future. They were so preoccupied with the complaining and whining that they had lost, neglected, forgotten, and tended less well their gifts for creativity and improvisation.

In that congregation today, from time to time, some people complain and whine. Old ways die hard. Significantly, what has happened is that people discover their wisdom, judgment, vision, and common sense. They discover their creativity with one another on behalf of God's mission. They improvise well. They make do with the resources God gives them. God gives them more. They advance their capacity for creativity and improvisation.

All of us have X amount of energy. If we invest our energy in creativity and improvisation, we flourish. Excellent ideas and good suggestions emerge. We discover new possibilities we have not considered. However, if we invest much of the energy we have in negative complaining and whining, we use up the energy we have, and we miss out on growing and developing our creativity.

People who seek to be creative some of the time are creative much of the time. People who try to be creative all of the time end up being creative none of the time. They put too heavy a burden on themselves. They try too hard. They freeze. Nothing comes. They block. They try to be too creative with too many things.

Creative people and creative congregations focus on being creative with the 20 percenters. The Pareto Principle states that 20 percent of the things a group does delivers 80 percent of its results. Eighty percent of the things a group does delivers 20 percent of its results.

You do not need to be creative with any of the 80 percent of things. They only deliver 20 percent of the results. With thoughtfulness and integrity, you can simply do the 80 percent. The art is to focus some of your best creativity and energy on the 20 percent that advance 80 percent of your future.

For small, strong congregations, the 20 percenters are the qualities we are discovering in this book. For a large, regional congregation, it would be a different set of qualities. We plan to be a small, strong congregation. Our 20 percenters are mission, compassion, community, self-reliance, worship, teams, just enough facilities, and giving. An objective that helps to advance one of these is a 20 percenter.

I would add this improvement to the Pareto Principle: invest 20 percent of your time in the 20 percenters. This will deliver 80 percent of your creativity and results.

With creativity and improvisation, invest some of your time in the 20 percenters. You do not need to invest all your time in the 20 percenters. Discover how you can invest 20 percent of your time, your creativity, and your strengths into the few key priorities that deliver the present and the future.

You do not need to be creative and improvisational all the time. You do not need to be creative and improvisational with everything you do. Some people lay that weight on themselves. Simply, some of the time (about 20 percent) be creative and improvisational with the few 20 percenters that advance your life and your congregation.

Small, strong congregations have discovered their creative and improvisational skills. They have a bias for creativity. They have a bias for improvisation. As someone once said, "This is a spirit of 'Ready, fire, aim.'" There is a preference for almost disorganized creativity over fully organized complaining. There is a preference for almost improvisational action over orderly inaction. The spirit is to value creativity and improvisation.

Our God is the creating God of the universe. We are amazed at the creativity of God. Our creativity is a gift of God. It is not of our own doing. It is God's gift. We are creative because God is creative with us. We live with a spirit of self-reliance and self-sufficiency. We claim the gifts of creativity and improvisation with which God is blessing us. We move forward.

Community Resources

The telephone call came. The woman caller said, "I understand that during August the congregation is having vacation Bible school for the children in the community. I would like to help with the music." Now, in that congregation, not so many telephone calls of this nature ever came. They were delighted with her gift to volunteer, as well as somewhat puzzled as to how it came to be.

During the course of vacation Bible school, they learned that she had spent many years as a teacher of music in elementary schools. She led music workshops across the state. She gave private lessons to countless students across the years. She helped them learn the piano and various musical instruments. She had gifts of vocal and choral directing. They greatly appreciated her talents and her help with the music program for vacation Bible school.

The children resonated with her spirit. She loved the kids, and the kids loved her. The parents loved her. She got along amazingly well with the other volunteers. She was helpful and generous with her encouragement. She was a source of cheerfulness and goodwill. Quietly and creatively, she shared her gifts of music. It was among the best vacation Bible schools they ever had in the community.

Time passed.

One of the leaders of the congregation was shopping in the local grocery store. She ran into the woman who had volunteered. Her curiosity got the better of her and she said, "We *really* appreciated your help. Tell me why you did it."

The woman said, "Many years ago, your congregation helped my niece when she was having a very tough time. She now lives in another part of the country. She's healthy, happy, and raising a good family. I got to thinking about how loving your congregation was with my niece. She mentions the compassion and graciousness of your congregation—of how much you helped her to turn around her life. I thought, 'You know, one good turn deserves another.'

"I certainly will never be able to repay your congregation for all you meant to my niece, but I decided the least I could do was help with the gift God gives me—music—in your vacation Bible school. I'm most grateful to you for allowing me to help."

There are countless comparable stories. It is amazing the ways in which the grace of God works. God invites us to have a solid spirit of self-reliance and self-sufficiency, to depend upon the resources God gives us. God encourages us to do so with creativity and improvisation. We discover that the more we depend upon ourselves and on God, and the more we give away in God's mission, the more community resources come to us to help with the mission.

Small, strong congregations live in this grace.

It is interesting how life works out. Small, strong congregations discover one excellent mission in the community. Through it, they share concrete, effective help. They deliver shepherding and compassion in deeply felt, extraordinary ways. They help people share a sense of community and belonging. They help people discover in the congregation, and also in their own lives, a spirit of self-reliance and self-sufficiency. Many people discover help with their lives and destinies. They experience the grace of God. The congregation, for its self-giving mission, becomes a legend on the community grapevine.

Such congregations are now given the gift of community resources. The congregation does not start out to draw on the resources of the community. What happens is that people in the community come forward to help this small, strong congregation with its mission. They honor the mission. They appreciate the sense of compassion, the spirit of belonging, and the self-reliance with which this congregation seeks to live. The more a small, strong congregation depends on itself, the more likely it is that people in the community will help the congregation with its mission.

The check came for $500. It was a gift to help the congregation send some of its young people to camp that summer. The treasurer of the congregation dimly recalled the signer's name but was not sure she could put the name and face together. She talked with one of her friends, and together they remembered that, some few years before, this man's mother had been ill with an incurable disease. She struggled and lingered long. Neither he, nor his mother, nor any of their family was active in any congregation. Nonetheless, some people in this congregation had visited, thoughtfully and helpfully, during his mother's illness.

There was the time of death, grieving, and mourning. There was the funeral celebrating the gift of her life. Lots of friends and family came from out of town, because she was the well-loved matriarch of the family. As a gift, some people in the congregation took food to the home as the far-flung family gathered after her funeral.

The man had never forgotten those simple acts of kindness. He knew of the congregation's mission with youth in the community. He heard somehow that there were more youths hoping to go to camp this summer than ever before. He wanted to help, and so he sent the check for $500.

Small, strong congregations may never have a youth director, part-time or full-time, on their staff. What often happens, however, is that a legendary teacher at a nearby school comes forward. She or he volunteers, usually for one-time events, to help in the congregation's mission with youth in the community. Frankly, we would be hard-pressed to find a person with the range of competencies and compassion possessed by this community volunteer. Out of respect for how this congregation lives, thinks, and serves, he or she is glad to help.

Small, strong congregations may never have a music director, part-time or full-time. What often happens is that community people with musical competence come forward. Sometimes, it is a music teacher, or an entire choir at a nearby school, a community ensemble, or a soloist or an instrumentalist from the community. Frequently, they are glad to help with one-time events. It may be the Christmas Eve service, the Easter service, a special Sunday, or a musical for the children and their families in the community. Most small congregations, whether in small towns or large, metropolitan areas, are grateful for the competencies in music that amazingly come forward from community resources.

Small, strong congregations may never have enough volunteers, teachers, and leaders to hold vacation Bible school. But if vacation Bible school is held, not only for the children inside the congregation but also as a gift for all the children in the community, people come forward, volunteer, and are glad to help. They look forward to being part of this significant event in the life of the community each year.

Small, strong congregations live in the community, not inside the congregation. The community delivers resources to the congregation because the congregation is sharing one excellent, helpful, compelling mission in the community. Community people help the congregation precisely because the congregation is sharing its gifts and competencies, compassion and strengths by helping people in the community.

In the Wesleyan movement, John Wesley never said, "The church is my parish." What he did say was, "The world is my parish." Weak and declining congregations and dying congregations think, plan, behave, and act with the mind-set of inside the church. They think, "How can we get people to our church so we will not die?" Their frame of reference is on how other people can save them. This is not a spirit of self-reliance and self-sufficiency.

Small, strong congregations think, plan, behave, and act with the mind-set of how they can serve in the world. They combine a rich spirit of service with a deep sense of self-reliance and self-sufficiency. In our time, countless small, strong congregations are sharing the resources with which God is blessing them in service with their wider community. If the congregation gives to itself, the community does not help that congregation. If the congregation gives to the community, the community gives to the congregation.

Reasonable Pastoral Resources

Small, strong congregations have reasonable pastoral resources. The art is to have almost enough in the way of pastoral resources to be helpful, but not so abundant an array of pastoral resources so as to be harmful. Some congregations learn the syndrome of denominational dependency. Some congregations learn the syndrome of pastoral dependency. Healthy congregations want just enough of a pastor to be helpful, but not so helpful a pastor that the pastor delivers too much help and the help becomes harmful and creates a pattern of dependency-codependency.

Roberta has been pastor with her congregation for six years. They have been good years for her and for her congregation. Her focus has been on being a good shepherd; a helpful preacher; a wise, caring leader; and a community pastor.

Sometime in the several months before she went to be pastor with her congregation, she and I talked. She described to me the fifteen years of pastors that had preceded her. The pattern in the congregations was one of ups-and-downs, turbulence and static, feuding and bickering, apathy and anger, declining and dying. She was uncertain as to whether she was looking forward to going to the congregation, once she learned more about it.

I asked her to describe, as best she could, how the four previous pastors had related to that congregation. There were four pastors coming and going during those fifteen years. Each of the previous pastors was sincere and willing, dedicated and committed. They invested considerable time, energy, and effort in trying to "save" the congregation. In their own way, each of them gave valiantly of his or her gifts, strengths, and competencies. Each worked long, long hours. A few people said of each of them, "If it weren't for so and so, our congregation would have died long ago."

When I heard those words, I began to have a sense of the problem. Each of Roberta's predecessors gave too much help. Each was like the mother or father who would keep doing so much for their kids and never let them grow up. It is a difficult predicament. On the one hand, the kids "enjoy" all the help. On the other hand, they resent not being allowed to do for themselves.

Some pastors do too much for their congregations.

Now, I am aware of the lazy, indifferent pastors who come into a congregation and virtually flop down on a couch and say to the congregation, "I'm here. Now take care of me." They infer, or sometimes state openly and publicly, that since this is a church, the people's task is to care for their pastor. They learned a pattern of dependency-codependency somewhere in their life and then they expect the congregation to take care of them.

Yes, I am aware of pastors who are angry and abusive, and of those who are dictatorial and autocratic. There are pastors who shout and pout. There are pastors with their own pet peeves, hobby horses, peculiarities, idiosyncratic quirks, troubles, and difficulties. Yes, there are as many distinct kinds of pastor as there are kinds of people in everyday life.

In our conversation, I suggested to Roberta that she share her particular strengths with her new congregation in a thoughtful, generous, and limited manner. Generously sharing one's distinctive strengths encourages the congregation to discover the generosity of its strengths. Sharing those strengths with some boundaries, some limits, helps a congregation discover limits for what it can and will do, and for what it cannot and will not do.

The pastor who does too much for a congregation creates a congregation that does too much for the people it seeks to serve. Consequently, the congregation experiences the same turbulent relationship with the people they seek to help. On the one hand, the people being helped enjoy all the help. On the other hand, they develop a resentment that they are not being allowed to learn how to do for themselves.

This is not really a discussion about whether a small, strong congregation has a volunteer, part-time, half-time, three-quarter-time, or full-time pastor. Rather, this is a discussion of how a pastor, whether part-time or full-time, relates with his or her congregation. Some part-time pastors try to do too much for their congregation. Some full-time pastors do the same.

If the pastor shares a reasonable amount of resourcing, with an encouraging spirit, the congregation learns how to be self-reliant as a congregation. Roberta had done that. Over the six years, she developed a balance of sharing her strengths appropriately. She did not give too much help. She did not give too little help. The balance was amazing, and her six years were remarkable. Roberta has shared her own strengths and helped people in the congregation discover and claim their own strengths. People have genuinely appreciated discovering their strengths and their capacity for self-reliance. They look forward to many years to come with Roberta as their pastor.

By contrast, in another congregation, the pastor did too much for the congregation. He would not let them fail. He would step in to be sure they would succeed. He would not let them succeed. They never failed. They never succeeded.

Some congregations never learn how to do for themselves because well-meaning pastors do too much for them. A congregation or a group in the congregation gather themselves to do some project. It could be vacation Bible school. It could be some one-time mission project, some one-time event for children, youths, or senior adults.

The group does just enough planning so that it can head into action. It can head for the mission. Somewhere in the planning or beginning stage of the action, there is the possibility that what the group is about to do may succeed or fail. Worried and anxious that the group might fail, the well-meaning, sincere, dedicated pastor steps in to ensure that the group does not fail. The result is that the group does not fail.

This simply reinforces in the pastor that stepping in to be sure the group does not fail is what pastors are supposed to do. Further, it reinforces in the group that they do not need finally to depend on their own resources to succeed, or to learn from their failure. The result of this pattern is that the group never fails. But it never succeeds, either. It never learns from its own excellent mistakes. It never learns from its own excellent successes. It never learns to develop its own capacity for self-sufficiency and self-reliance.

In one seminar, I was sharing these suggestions. I said: "Coaching helps people discover what they can do. Correcting tells people what they cannot do. Coaching helps people discover their own strengths. Correcting focuses people on their weaknesses. Coaching helps them discover their own self-sufficiency. Correcting focuses on making the specific corrections that the corrector wants the correctee to make."

At the seminar break, Albert came up to me, with a gentle excitement in his manner. He said to me that the suggestions I had just shared "named" for him one of the decisive events of his life. He went on to tell me what happened:

In one of the games heading us to the state championship, I started as pitcher. We were playing one of the better teams. We needed to win this one.

For some reason, I got off to a shaky start. The other team began to clobber my pitching. We were still in the first inning. We were nine runs behind. The bases were loaded. There were no outs.

Our coach had played pro baseball. He was known for his down-to-earth frankness. He did not put up with any foolishness. He planned to win games. He planned to take us to the state championship playoffs. As they scored each of their nine runs, he would almost wince.

Finally, he called a time out and steamed out to the pitcher's mound. I was not looking forward to the cussing out he was likely to give me. Nevertheless, I knew I could put up with it, because at least he was going to pull me from the game. Right then, I wanted off that mound in the most desperate kind of way.

When he got to the mound, he paused. Said nothing. Stood there. Looked at me, as if he was trying to make up his mind about something. Then, in a low, determined voice that gathered all his resolve and determination, he said: "Albert, I don't know what the hell you think you're doing out here, but you'd better figure it out pretty soon, because I am not pulling you from this game. You're going to finish this game, come hell or high water. There will be no one from the bullpen coming in to relieve. You are it."

The coach turned, walked off the field, sat down in the dugout, crossed one leg over the other, took off his cap, picked up a cup of water, and nodded to me to continue.

Albert went on to describe how he pitched his way out of that inning, and how, with the help of the team's hitting, scoring, and fielding, they went on to win the game. He told me: "My coach gave me a great gift that day. He knew I had it in me more than I knew it. He let me succeed or fail. He gave me the chance both ways. That day I learned to depend on myself. I have thanked my coach many times, over the years, for what he helped me to discover that day."

It is amazing how the grace of God works. God invites us to have a consistent, solid spirit of self-reliance and self-sufficiency, to depend upon the resources God gives us. God encourages us to do so with creativity and improvisation. We discover that the more we depend upon ourselves and on God, and the more we give away in God's mission, the more community resources come to us to help with the mission. God blesses us with reasonable pastoral resources to help us advance our mission and life together. We live in the grace of God.

6

Worship and Hope

Everything done in humankind is done on the basis of hope.

—Martin Luther

With quiet enthusiasm and deep appreciation, Thelma and Harold came up to me after the worship service and said, "Dr. Callahan, we thank you for what you have done to improve our pastor's preaching."

I had helped their congregation two years before. At that time, on a scale of 1 to 10, their pastor's preaching was a 4. Sunday after Sunday, the sermon, albeit well intentioned and sometimes well prepared, became the stalling point in the service. It was as if the service simply came, slowly and languidly, to a standstill. That Sunday, two years before, when I was there the first time, I watched it happen.

Individually, on that earlier Sunday, a number of people took me aside and said words such as: "Dr. Callahan, if you can't help us with anything else while you're here, at least help our pastor with his preaching. We like Walter. We want him to stay. However, his preaching isn't helpful to us, and it's an embarrassment to him." I lost track of the number of people who were genuinely concerned for their pastor and his preaching.

They were not being petty or gossipy. They loved Walter and wanted the best for him and for themselves in worship. It was simply that they could take it for only so many years, and with time Walter's preaching grew weary and tiresome. With a well-intentioned spirit, he would drone on Sunday after Sunday. He was not quite buried in his manuscript, but almost. Sometimes, a sermon would contain a helpful insight. Mostly, the sermons felt like a scissors-and-paste collection of sayings and illustrations, almost but not quite having some connection with one another, tediously and piously stated.

Walter and I invested considerable time, in that early consultation, puzzling through how he could advance his preaching. We discussed his gift for shepherding. I helped him become more fully a shepherd with the congregation and the community.

Sometimes, part of the way forward is in a nearby area of ministry, as well as in the area of focus. His strongest gift is shepherding, but Walter was allowing himself to become bogged down in administration, which is not one of his gifts. He was neglecting his strength and focusing on his weakness. We worked out an active visiting and shepherding plan on which he could focus each week. He would love, listen, and learn with his people as a shepherd. He would discover his people more deeply. They would come to know him more fully. A pastor whose preaching is a 4 and who is a good shepherd is heard as a 7.

I helped Walter advance his preaching. We looked at the material in my book *Preaching Grace.* From the eight areas discussed there, he selected two for his own growth and development. We developed an action plan whereby he could grow those two forward in the coming two years. We discussed the resources he could draw on as he did so. We put in place specific steps that he could take to advance his preaching.

We invited three people to be informal greeters before and after the services. They would help with welcoming new people. They would encourage informal conversations among the people who came regularly. The congregation's sharing before and after the services was already rich and full. The three informal greeters would simply deepen and enrich one of the strengths of the congregation.

Importantly, we improved the music in the worship service—especially the congregational singing. We also advanced the contributions of the special choirs to the service. We surrounded the sermon with moving, encouraging music. We made certain that the music immediately before and after the sermon was stirring and inspiring.

Frequently, the music would be congregational singing. Sometimes, it would be music by a special choir, soloist, or ensemble. Whatever the nature of the music, we developed the practice that the music before and after the sermon would be especially stirring and inspiring. Whenever we do so, the preaching improves both in the vitality with which the pastor preaches and in the spirit with which the congregation hears the sermon.

Over the two years that came and went since my first time of helping the congregation, Walter improved his preaching some. One could not say that he made giant strides forward, but his preaching was better. Importantly, his shepherding with the congregation advanced. He built well on one of his key strengths.

Equally significant, the music developed remarkably. What happened with the music before and after the sermon was a marked advance over what had been previously. The combined impact—of the shepherding, of the informal greeters' welcoming, of the music, and some improvement in the preaching per se—was that Walter's preaching, in the experience of the congregation, advanced.

So Thelma and Harold wanted me to know of their appreciation. Individually, and in twos and threes, many people quietly expressed their appreciation. They loved Walter and they were glad to see the growth that had happened. They were at peace that Walter and they could be pastor and people for many years to come.

Warm and Welcoming

One of the qualities present in small, strong congregations is their services of worship. Consistently, eight out of twelve Sundays and often more frequently, the services are:

- Warm and welcoming
- Stirring and inspiring
- Congregational and sacramental
- Helpful and hopeful

Tim and I were discussing his hopes for his congregation. He was concerned to help his congregation be warm and welcoming. He wanted his people to share deeply, with one another, in a spirit of community and belonging. He expressed his frustration that his people seemed to have no interest in the small groups he wanted to organize for them. He felt it very important that each person in his congregation be in some small group. He wanted me to help him figure out how he could get them into small groups.

I said to Tim: "Help me with this puzzle. Help me to understand why you're trying to do what you have already done."

He looked at me with an enchanting frown on his face. He was curious as to what I meant. We have been good friends for many years. He is a most competent, compassionate pastor. He was beginning to see what I meant, even though I had not yet fully suggested the insight toward which I was heading.

"You've been here for five years. You're having fun. Your congregation loves you. Your kids are thriving in their schools. Your wife is doing well in her vocation. Your congregation is strong and healthy."

Tim nodded with a sense of satisfaction. The five years had gone better than he expected. He was looking forward to the years to come.

"When you try to 'prod' your people into small groups, for their 'welfare and betterment,' you confuse them. They already have their small group. They're at home in their small group. They share a spirit of being warm and welcoming in their small group. They discover community and belonging. They're growing and developing in their lives."

He still did not fully understand, but the light was beginning to dawn.

"For your congregation, their small group is their service of worship. They're warm and welcoming with one another and with new people. They've found home and community, belonging and growth with the group of people with whom they worship. Look more closely at what happens during the service. Look at what happens before and after the service. People are visiting with one another. They're sharing love and concern. They're having fun. They're encouraging each other. They're being family.

"For a small, strong congregation, worship is the gathering of the family. It's not that worship is a function, and that small groups are another function. Small, strong congregations don't think in a program, function, and activity manner. They don't view worship and groups as separate functions and departments. Worship is the gathering of the household, the family, of God.

"When you ask them to organize into small groups, their spirit is that they already have done so. They already have a small group. It gathers as a family in worship. Worship is not one function. Small groups are not another function. We are family in worship."

I went on to suggest: "Your service of worship has about it a spirit of being warm and welcoming. Each Sunday, the worship leader who helps you lead the service is relaxed and genuine. As a whole, the team of worship leaders, who rotate from Sunday to Sunday helping lead the service, are warm and caring, and this spirit shows in how they lead the service when it's their turn. They relate well with the congregation.

"The people who greet before and after the service help people feel at home. The couple of ushers do their work with a joyful, happy spirit. The various orders of worship you use communicate this same spirit. They're not cold and formidable, austere and distant. People experience the grace of God in the liturgies they share as God's family. Your people find home in the worship service."

Tim saw the insight.

Earlier in his ministry, he was an associate pastor in a large, regional congregation. That particular congregation organized itself and its staff into rigid departments. Worship and music was one department. Small groups and Christian education were another department. These two departments, as well as the other departments, thought and functioned primarily in a separatist manner. They met weekly to share with one another what was happening "in their own area." Occasionally, they would cooperate on some project. However, most of the time, each department's thoughts, plans, and actions were individualistic and compartmentalized.

In the course of our conversation, Tim discovered that he had brought that earlier way of thinking and planning with him to his small, strong congregation. He reflected, looking back on his five years with his congregation, on how he had pressed his people to think and behave in that same way. He now understood the occasional perplexed looks on the faces of his people. He was asking them to do something that they had already achieved. With new insight, he began to focus on helping his people deepen the spirit of warmth and welcome in the service of worship.

Small, strong congregations are warm and welcoming with one another, and with new people. They are gracious and generous in their spirit of being family with one another. There are many door openers, and virtually no gatekeepers. They like one another and they welcome new people. There is a good-natured spirit of being family together, and this spirit is central to their services of worship.

In one congregation, Jim welcomes people before the service and visits with them afterwards. Cheryl, Bob, and Margie do the same. From the warmth and welcome of these four people, the whole congregation becomes a warm, welcoming family. The spirit of these few stirs the spirit of the whole. First-time worshippers, occasional worshippers, and regular worshippers feel at home.

In innumerable worship services each week, a few people share their warmth and welcome, and, thanks to their graciousness and hospitality, the service has a spirit of being warm and winsome, welcoming and family. It is not needful for a whole congregation to be immediately welcoming. The biblical principle is that there is diversity of gifts. Not all people have the gift of being welcoming. Moreover, for first-time worshippers, that would be overpowering and intimidating. What helps is for a few people to have this spirit of generosity and graciousness, of warmth and welcome.

In countless small, strong congregations across the planet, people find the service of worship to be warm and welcoming. They have the feeling that the service includes them in open, encouraging ways. There is a sense in which there are no strangers in this service of worship. The feeling is that the service is the gathering of a warm, caring family.

Stirring and Inspiring

George is the volunteer worship and music leader for his small congregation. He is the librarian for the local public library. He loves books, and he has developed many library programs to help people discover their own love for books. There is the children's story hour. A remarkable number of children, parents, and grandparents participate. The youth research club has been one of his best projects. The reading group for senior adults is a recent, promising addition.

George became the interim worship and music leader eleven years ago. He was to lead just until the congregation could find the right person after the former leader was transferred, by his company, to another state. George found it so much fun and so satisfying that he stayed on—for eleven glorious years.

After the first six months, the congregation saw how well he was doing and how well his sense of worship and music matched with the congregation. They slowed down their search for a new leader. Finally, the search committee quietly disbanded, and the post was offered, informally and unanimously, to George. He accepted on condition that it be an interim post. He has been the best worship and music leader the congregation ever had.

George does it this way. One group of people has fun helping him with the worship and music during September through December, essentially from the start of the fall program through Christmas. Another group has fun during February through April, beginning with Lent through to Easter. Another group of people has fun with May through August. Bill, George's good friend, leads this group. Each group has a retreat one or two months before their season. They have fun together. They pray and plan together. They develop the music, prayers, and liturgy helpful for their season. They gather a few times during their season. Mostly, they move forward from the sense of community and planning they discovered with one another on their retreat.

The congregation appreciates the variety and richness of music, prayers, and liturgy that the three worship and music teams bring. They are not large teams. They gather additional people as appropriate. Some in the congregation participate in the Christmas choir, some in the Easter choir, and some in the July Fourth choir. Each worship and music team seeks to include as many people as possible in the music, prayers, and liturgy during its season.

The congregation is grateful that George has developed the three worship and music teams. His predecessor had a tendency to do everything by himself. Because a broader base is involved in developing the music, prayers, and liturgy, more people participate deeply and fully in the worship services.

Leroy, their pastor, serves two other congregations and is especially grateful for George and his three worship teams. Leroy is essentially with them on Sunday to share the sermon and, during the week, to be a shepherd with the congregation. He frequently says that the worship, music, prayers, and liturgy are most helpful to him personally because of George and his three teams.

Sandra is the secretary to the president of a local retail company. Before she had her children, she worked in a doctor's office. Then, some years later, as her children found their way to school, she worked for one of the banks in town. In due course, she became the head teller. The president of her current company had done most of his business with her bank. When his secretary retired to Florida, he hired Sandra away from the bank.

Over time, as she worked in the retail company, she became friends with several of the people there. She discovered they were active in a small congregation in the area. They invited her one Christmas to their special Christmas Eve service. She was hesitant to go. They encouraged her. She went, and that Christmas Eve she found home with the congregation. They welcomed her warmly.

Sandra has always had a love for music. Eventually, she joined the choir. It became her family. When the long-term, legendary choir director decided to retire, the choir asked her to become their new choir director. She was overwhelmed with joy and humility. At last, she would be able to fulfill her hopes.

The choir has done well under her love and leadership. People say the music is more stirring and inspiring than before. Her choir sings nine months of the year. Because of the worship and vacation patterns in that part of the country, the choir takes off January, July, and August. They sing September through Christmas. Then, they begin again in February and sing through Lent, Easter, Pentecost, and July Fourth. They are off for the rest of July and August. For the community and the congregation, this pattern works well. It matches the rhythm of life in the area.

Sandra has developed a team of volunteers who work with her. Doris leads the fall children's choir. They rehearse in September, October, and November and sing once a month during that time. Many of the congregation's children bring their friends to participate for this short-term, good-fun choir as they learn wonderful music.

Sam leads the Lenten children's choir. They have a rehearsal gathering during the Christmas break. Some years it is held at the church. Some years it is held at one of the many good-fun retreat centers near the community. Many children come. They get a good start on the music for that specific Lenten season. Sam's choir usually sings three or four times during Lent.

Sandra, Doris, and Sam have seen much greater participation by the children of the church and the community because of the fall and spring choir possibilities. Some children participate in both the fall and the spring choirs. Most children choose, given their varied schedules, to be part of one choir or the other. Over the year, more children than ever are participating in the music and worship life of the congregation.

Beth and Robert met in college, became good friends, began to date, fell in love, and married. They have shared twenty remarkable years of marriage. They are blessed with three children, two sons and a daughter. The oldest, their daughter, is in high school. One son is in elementary school, and the other son has started junior high. They are a close, caring family.

Robert is a manufacturer's representative and travels the state. He has been with his company a long time and they respect what he has achieved in building up his territory. He is gone two or three days a week in two to three weeks of the month. Fortunately, much of his business is in the community in which they live.

Beth has all she can do, taking care of their home and the children, looking after her elderly mother, along with all her volunteer responsibilities outside the home. She is active and widely respected in the community.

Beth volunteers as the music leader for their small, strong congregation. With her leadership, the singing of the congregation is more stirring and inspiring. The congregation has discovered the joy and meaning that their singing brings to the worship service. Through their singing together as a congregation, they participate, richly and fully, in the service. Her primary focus has been on advancing the spirit of the service through the congregation's singing.

She also gathers a wonderful group of people who rehearse together three to five times and are the Christmas choir. She gathers another group of people—some overlap and some are new—who have three to five rehearsals and are the Easter choir. She gathers another group of people for a major community Sunday sometime during the year. There may be four or five occasions during the year when Beth gathers and leads short-term choirs for these major services of worship. As he can, Robert helps her with them.

Once a year she invites the high school choir to come and sing with the congregation, and they do. There are three excellent community ensembles in her town. She invites each of them to come and sing, and they do. She has several good friends who are gifted soloists, and from time to time one of them comes to be part of the service of worship.

About five years ago, Julie and I took up the hammered dulcimer—the string instrument one plays with wooden hammers, not the Appalachian dulcimer that one picks. We have enjoyed learning to play it. We have had the fun of attending several workshops across the country. We have learned there is a considerable network of people who enjoy the hammered dulcimer.

I shared this with Beth in one of our conversations. This stirred her memory of several people in her community who play the instrument. They have been glad to come and share their gift of music with Beth's congregation. They play during the congregational singing and during the special music times. She has found a further resource for community music that strengthens the music during the worship service.

Beth's predecessor spent several years, valiantly and with considerable frustration, in trying to build a weekly choir for the worship service. Sometimes she would try to entice people to come to weekly rehearsals. Sometimes she would bludgeon them with "If you were really a committed Christian, you would sing in the choir." Her alternating pleas and demands did not work.

A few people would come to the weekly rehearsals. She would have them practice music that was beyond their current abilities and was meant for a much larger choir. On Sunday morning, they would help the congregation with its singing during the hymns. However, the anthem became a point in the service where people would cringe and shrink in their seats. It was embarrassing. People would pray that it would be quickly over. Finally, Beth's predecessor quit in disgust.

Beth has good wisdom. She loves music and knows how helpful it is in a service of worship. She decided her primary focus, as music leader, would be on helping the congregation to advance and deepen the congregational singing during the service. For her, the "special music" would be the congregation's singing. She saw herself as music leader rather than as choir director. She realized that her small, strong congregation did not have—in and of itself—the resources to have a choir each Sunday. More important, she had the wisdom to know that a weekly choir is only one way of encouraging a service to be stirring and inspiring.

For Beth, encouraging congregational singing is central to advancing the stirring, inspiring spirit of the worship services. She also develops short-term, intensive choirs for special Sundays. She invites school and community groups. Her good friend is choral director of the high school choir. She draws on the ensembles and soloists from the music networks of which she is very much a part. This plan works.

Given her community network and her congregation's participation in their community mission, remarkable music resources show up. There is the children's choir that grows out of vacation Bible school and sings the Sunday after it is over. There is a community children's choir that she gathers as the congregation heads toward Christmas; they usually sing the Sunday before Christmas Sunday. There is a choir of children that sing on Palm Sunday. Short-term, well-planned, well-rehearsed choirs contribute to her congregation's services of worship. Mostly, the congregation's singing has helped the service become more alive, more stirring and inspiring.

In small, strong congregations, their sense of community and belonging encourages a natural, primary focus on congregational singing. The singing is encouraging and heartening. The music touches our hearts and stirs our deepest longings and yearnings. As the whole congregation sings, people are moved by the singing and led to the sense of the presence of God. This is especially so on the key Sundays of the year. Moreover, it can be so on eight out of twelve Sundays.

Sarah Polster is a good friend. She has sound wisdom. She has served as senior editor for this book with Jossey-Bass. When Sarah and I were discussing this chapter and the dynamic of worship and music in small, strong congregations, she shared with me her own experience. She said, "In my own small, strong Jewish congregation, we never have a choir, but we accompany our own a cappella singing with hand clapping and percussion instruments, like tambourines, drums, maracas, etc. That is about as simple as you can get! No music director, no rehearsals! For two or three special occasions in the year, we hire a band. I'm sure there are analogs to this within Christian congregations."

I thought about her wisdom. It came to me that small, strong congregations around the world, in their own distinctive ways, have comparable simple, stirring, inspiring music. The dynamic of their music leads them to the grace of God. It is not true that "if we don't have a choir, we are not a church." Small, strong congregations are the church as they share mission, compassion, community, self-reliance, hope, leadership, and generosity. Moreover, in small, strong congregations, the congregation *is* the choir. The congregation is the primary source of music in the service of worship.

The art is to select music that matches the congregation's gifts for singing. Consider the hymns, choral responses, anthems, or choruses. Look at the music at the beginning of the service. Do the same for the music at the end of the service. Consider all of the music, in whatever form, throughout the whole service. In a stirring, inspiring worship service, the kind of music we sing is decisive for helping people participate in the service.

The art is for the music to match the message and the congregation. At least, you should do this for eight out of twelve services. When the message matches the congregation, and the music matches the message, then the music matches the congregation. Sometimes the message does not match the congregation, and the music therefore may not match the congregation.

Sometimes, the message does match the congregation. However, on occasion, a music leader, believing he or she knows what is best for the congregation, regrettably decides that the music must focus on what the congregation "should" have as music. The music leader tries to force a personal musical preference on the congregation. With wisdom, competent music leaders know that the art is for the music to match what the congregation can sing well, not what someone thinks they should sing. They match the music with the singers, and, in doing so, help the congregation to grow forward.

Congregations especially look forward to learning new music that builds on the music they know and the musical gifts they currently have. Many music leaders find creative ways to help their congregations discover new music. Sometimes, the music leader introduces a new song at a good-fun, fellowship gathering.

On occasion, the music leader gathers a one-time, good-fun gathering of the congregation at the beginning of Advent or Lent. We share good times; we pray for the coming season; and we learn some new music for the worship services to come during the season. Sometimes, the music leader

introduces a new song during a worship service and frequently precedes it and follows it with a familiar song. The
art is to discover creative ways to help the congregation worship, drawing on the kinds of music that are stirring and
inspiring for *your* congregation.

You can develop special music and prayers for the worship services for Easter and Christmas. These two remarkable
events in the life of the Christian movement are decisive for
our lives. With Christmas, we discover the wonder and joy,
the closeness and the nearness of God's grace and love for us.
With Easter, we discover an open tomb, a risen Lord, new life
and hope. These two worship services, Christmas and Easter,
are among the most remarkable occasions for worship during
the year.

In these two services, small, strong congregations focus
primarily on congregational singing. The worship service
gives even richer and fuller opportunities for the congregation to sing the hymns and songs that inspire them and draw
them closer to the grace of God. It is not accidental that many
people come to worship on Christmas and Easter. Intuitively,
they sense that these two times of worship can touch their
lives with the decisive, stirring, inspiring grace of God.

Sensing the significance of these two events in our lives,
we naturally seek to be at our best in each worship service.
The art is to be at our best in our congregational singing. Yes,
for Christmas, we could have a short-term Christmas choir.
For Easter, we could have another short-term Easter choir. For
these significant services, we could include an appropriate
range of soloists, instrumentalists, ensembles, etc.

However, the mistake that sometimes happens is that a
music leader, wanting the music to be at its best, decides to
have a great deal of special music during the worship service.
The intent is laudable, but unfortunate. Too much time is
given to choirs, instrumentalists, ensembles, soloists, etc. The

consequence is that the amount of time given for congregational singing is substantially reduced. The congregation becomes spectator rather than participant. On these two consequential occasions, the art is to advance congregational singing and *also* to have some special music.

Further, for Christmas, you can invite two or three people who have gifts to do so, to develop special prayers and liturgy for the worship service for this Christmas. They can draw on the vast liturgical resources that the Christian movement has developed over the past two thousand years. Likewise, they can draw on their creativity and imagination, and their sense of what would be helpful and timely now, for this congregation. You can invite another team of people to do the same for Easter. Many people teach me they discover deep meaning and helpfulness in the prayers and liturgy of the service.

Moreover, you can develop the music, prayers, and liturgy for what I call the major-major services of worship. In addition to Easter and Christmas, you can select (your choice) five to eight services to be major-major services. These five to eight may vary from one year to the next. In my *Dynamic Worship*, you will discover a helpful chapter on major community Sundays.

For our present purpose, I encourage you to advance the congregational singing for these services and to develop some form of special music. For a given major-major service, it could be a short-term children or youth choir. You could have special soloists, ensembles, instrumentalists, or visiting musical groups. Likewise, you can invite several people to develop the prayers and liturgy for these services.

In small, strong congregations, the art is to focus on Christmas and Easter along with the five to eight major-major Sundays. The mistake would be to try to focus on all fifty-two weeks of worship and to try to have extraordinary music, prayers, and liturgy every Sunday of the year. Yes, you can have that with congregational singing. However, I am encouraging you not to follow the efforts of some small congregations that mimic large, regional congregations by having a regular choir every Sunday *and* a grand variety of special music.

If you can have, with solid excellence, a regular choir each Sunday, that is fine. However, trying to have a regular choir and a great variety of special music each Sunday is more than what is needed. This is not what small, strong congregations do. It is not a matter of lack of resources. Small, strong congregations have a very participatory spirit of worship. They shy away from anything that has too much of a spectator sense to it.

The art is to develop stirring, inspiring worship for Christmas and Easter, and five to eight major-major Sundays. This is the simplest way to advance the dynamic of worship in your congregation. The effort to do better worship every week is rooted in a compulsion toward perfectionism. To try to do everything well in every worship service is to end up doing nothing well in most services. Do your major-major Sundays well. Spillover impact helps your other services be stirring and inspiring.

If you want to do something more to advance worship in your congregation, look at what I call the major services. This may be give or take twenty services a year. Christmas, Easter, and five to eight more are your major-major services. Now, think of the next twenty that have significance for your congregation. The focus of these major services varies greatly from one congregation to the next. The essential point is that small, strong congregations do not try to deliver special music, prayers, and liturgy, or for that matter stirring congregational singing, every Sunday. This would be our old friend, a compulsion for perfectionism, showing up yet another time in our lives.

You can resource some of these twenty major services with special emphasis on congregational singing. You can draw on special music, such as a soloist, ensemble, instrumentalists, or a visiting musical group. You can invite people to contribute to the prayers and liturgy for these services. The consequence is that these services will be stirring and inspiring.

Small, strong congregations do well what they do well. They focus on their major-major services and also their major services in the year. They think and plan, behave and act with this focus. It is not that they do not care what happens in the remaining services of the year. Rather, they have the wisdom to know that if they focus on Easter and Christmas, five to eight major-major, and twenty major services, the others will come along. The spillover impact is invaluable.

The result is that, in the course of the year, more often than not the worship services are stirring. The services touch people's lives, arouse their best longings and instincts, draw them to their strengths, and help them discover the grace of God. The music, as well as the prayers and liturgy, contribute to the service of worship being inspiring.

People discover how God is present, moving, and stirring in their lives, inviting them into the future God promises and prepares for them. The services lead people closer to the sense of the grace, hope, and promise of God. The congregational singing is strong. The kind of music matches with the congregation. People share their creative special music and prayers. People experience the congregational, sacramental spirit of the service.

Congregational and Sacramental

In one small, strong congregation that Julie and I had the privilege of serving, it was common knowledge why Mrs. Smith sat where she did. She sat one seat in from the aisle, on the second pew from the back, on the left side. For more than fifty years, Mr. Smith sat on the aisle. This is why Mrs. Smith sits one seat in. Even though he died of a heart attack five years ago, we can still "see" Mr. Smith sitting there, with his arm propped on the pew end, smiling and glad to be with the congregation.

Next to Mrs. Smith, on the inside, we can still see Bobby sitting there beside his mother, even though now everybody calls him Bob, and he lives in another part of the country and has his own successful business. We can still see Nancy sitting there beside her brother, even while she lives in another city, finishing a Ph.D. at a major university and looking forward to teaching there or at another university.

When we gather, the "empty" pews that visitors might see are—for us—not empty. We can still see the people who worshipped in this congregation for all those years. In Hebrews 12:1 (RSV), the text says, "Since therefore we are surrounded by so great a cloud of witnesses. . . ." The people who have gone before are part of the cloud of witnesses. The cloud of witnesses includes the encouragers, nurturers, and mentors who mean much to us in our lives. When we gather for worship, they are with us.

The worship service is the gathering of the whole congregation—some on this side of the river, some on the other side of the river. It is the gathering of the whole of God's people. It includes all who have gone before in the Christian movement and all who are living now, around the planet. In this service of worship, on this occasion, we are all gathered in the grace of God.

We experience the congregational, sacramental spirit of worship. We experience worship as a great banquet of God's grace, a wedding feast of God's hope. It is like gathering around a table for a wonderful meal. It is like a family re-union, sharing the richness of community and looking forward with hope. It is the gathering of the congregational family of God, knowing that God's sacramental grace is in our midst, and we are family in the midst of God.

In our time, people increasingly feel a dislocation of power. That is, they feel that the decisions shaping their lives and destinies are made somewhere else by someone else, and they can't quite figure out who or why or what to do about it. Moreover, they feel that decisions once made at local levels have moved to the district level, then the state level, the national level, and now the international level.

This trend toward dislocation of power has caused people to feel a pervasive sense of powerlessness in their lives. They long to recover some sense of power in their own lives. They long for and look for some grouping of people that is congregational, not hierarchical, that is grassroots, not top-down.

The service of worship has about it a congregational spirit. The spirit is "We are in this together," not a sense of "I am telling you how to do it." The spirit is "Glad we can worship God together this morning." It does not have the sense, sometimes said by a minister, of "Glad you could be here with me this morning." The service feels more grassroots and less top-down. People discover a sense of purpose and power for their lives.

Among the mundane, the distractions, the details, the confusions and complexities of life, we discover that the service of worship is sacramental, that life is sacramental. We discover that the strengths, gifts, and competencies with which God blesses our lives are sacramental gifts in our lives. We sense the presence of holiness. We sense the presence of the One who blesses our lives with sacramental signs. We discover worship is the sacramental sign of God's grace, compassion, community, and hope with which we live through this life into the next.

As we experience the sacrament of worship, we are more at peace; we are less fearful. Our anxieties lessen; our anger dissipates; our rage is less frequent. We are blessed with the sacramental spirit of the service, and our despair, our depression, our despondency turn into signs of grace, compassion, community, and hope. We live life more fully, because we know we are loved more richly.

In our time, people are not drawn to a service of worship that is frills and fancy, gimmicks and gadgets, tricks and trivialities, fads and foolishness. What people are drawn to is a sense of the holy, a sense of sacrament, a sense that this service shares with them the sacramental grace of God. They know their lives are helped, and they move forward to the week ahead.

The service is simple, strong, and stirring. It feels more like basic math than advanced trigonometry. It is basic and foundational, not complicated and convoluted. It is simple, not complex. It may be simple high-church liturgical, or a simple contemporary service. It may be a traditional, alternative, gospel, or jazz service. The service is not a manifold conglomerate multiplicity of enigmatic steps. It is simple.

Some congregations have long discussions about whether to have a traditional or contemporary service. Unchurched people, and for that matter many grassroots people in congregations, do not know what a traditional, contemporary, alternative, jazz, gospel, high-church, low-church, middle-church, blended, seeker, or liturgical service is. Those are "inside the church" typologies that inside-the-church key leaders and pastors discuss and debate.

What most people know is whether the service:

- Touches their hearts
- Stirs their longings for a whole, healthy life
- Advances their understanding of life
- Helps them discover hope for the week to come

What they know is that a simple service, with a few steps, resonates with them where they are.

Simplicity takes many forms. It can mean having a service with a few steps: singing, praying, preaching, singing, and blessing. The more steps to a service, the more complex it feels. At Bethel, they had a service of worship with twenty-plus steps. Some ten years before, a pastor brought that order of worship with him. He had grown up in a congregation with a complex, multiple-step service. Every where he served, he established that order of worship, whether it fit the congregation or not. He was at Bethel for two years before he moved on. The next two pastors continued the complex order he had implemented.

Then the new pastor invited me to come and help the congregation. In the interviews, one of the interesting discoveries I made was that person after person shared with me that they did not feel at home in the service. In the group discussion, I invited the group to share examples of worship services that were especially helpful to them. The response was interesting. People mentioned the Easter sunrise service and the Christmas Eve service. They spoke of the children's service and the youth service. They talked about the Maundy Thursday service, the All Saints service for persons who had lost a loved one during the year, and the special service for families having a new child during the year.

We looked more closely at each of these services. To be sure, they were special services. More important, they all had in common the same few steps for a service: singing, praying, preaching, singing, and blessing. What had happened was that earlier pastor, with his complex service, left the planning of these special services to various people in the congregation. There was a sense that he did not have the time to fool with these services. He was focused on seeing to it that, during the regular service, the congregation "benefited" from the kind of worship they were supposed to have.

The result was that the special services became gathering places for the simplicity of worship that matched well with this congregation. The services were special in two senses. First, they had a special focus. Second, more important, they were special because they matched the congregation.

I suggested that we learn from our experiences of worship. I said to them, "It makes sense that we do, each Sunday, the order of worship we have found meaningful in our special services. Our regular services can have the simplicity of singing, praying, preaching, singing, and blessing. From time to time, we can explore other orders of worship. Our regular services will have a spirit of simplicity about them." In the time come and gone, the pastor and people of the Bethel congregation have shared with me, again and again, about how they now feel at home in worship.

Simplicity can mean having a very leisurely service, rather than rushing from one step to another. Some worship services are slow and plodding, dull, deadly, and boring. More often, I discover congregations where the service is a rushing from one step to the next. We have crammed too much into the service. We are trying to do too much in too little time. We are rushing, rushing, rushing so we can finish on time.

A stirring, inspiring service can be a very leisurely service. Some people think that worship should feel like a high school pep rally. As a counter to that, some people go out of their way to be sure the service is dull and boring. Their excuse is, "Well, at least it's not a pep rally." One poor excuse does not excuse another poor excuse.

There is no excuse for a dull, boring service that plods deathly and pathetically to its end. The merciful part of such a service is that it is finally over. By contrast, there is value in having radiant enthusiasm and excitement in some services.

We sing with power and spirit. The music is vibrant, resounding, almost deafening. The prayers are energizing. The sermon is animating and galvanizing. The service has an active, vigorous spirit. The service is powerful and moving.

Similarly, a leisurely service can be powerful and moving. Many people find a gentle, leisurely service has a quiet power in their lives. For many, in this time, life is rushing from one activity to another. We feel the rushing, rushing, rushing of life. We come to worship and discover one area of life where we can reflect and pray, meditate and relax. I have lost track of the number of people who have said to me, "Dr. Callahan, worship is the only time of the week where I feel I can slow down and think about what I am doing and where I am heading." For many people, a service with a thoughtful, purposeful leisurely pace is a gift of grace in their lives.

Some services can move quickly from one step to the next with an energizing, active spirit. Some services can have the simplicity of little structure, with lots of quiet time for prayer and reflection. For many people, worship is the one quiet moment in their week. The pace and fury of the activities of the week are both exciting and exhausting. The service helps them discover what is enduring and lasting, what is of value and significance in life.

The structure can be loose enough to allow for spontaneous contributions from participants. This is one possibility present in small, strong congregations that is difficult to bring off in large, regional congregations. The size of a large congregation makes spontaneous contributions less likely. When they do happen, they are much more time-consuming because there are so many.

In a small congregation, spontaneous contributions are easily and naturally shared. Participants can suggest a hymn or song we sing together. They can share a personal word about some event happening in their life, or some new insight for living that they have discovered. They can invite the congregation to be in prayer in some special way, and they can share their prayers on behalf of the people in the congregation.

Further, the structure of the service can be loose enough for spontaneous contributions from God. Some services are so fixed, inflexible, and unbending that God has trouble getting into the service. It is as if the service is happening in lockstep fashion, with no openness to the stirring, moving, living grace of God. The service is too tense and tight, stiff and rigid. What the service does is to help people become tense and tight, stiff and rigid in their own lives. A service that is open to spontaneous contributions helps people live life with a spirit of flexibility and openness, creativity and spontaneity. They live life open to the stirrings of God's grace.

The mistake many congregations make when they launch a new service to reach occasional worshippers and people in the community is that they launch a *complex* service. They know how to do a complex, traditional service. They launch a complex, contemporary service. Why it does not work is not because it is a contemporary service. It does not work because it is too complex. To be sure, it is a contemporary service, but it has too many steps in the order of worship, the music is too complex, and the service is too wordy. They would have been better off launching a *simple,* traditional service.

Now, this is not a discussion of pop-gospel versus classical music. (One of the simplest, most stirring and inspiring pieces of music ever written is Beethoven's "Ode to Joy." It was even sung at the 1996 Olympics in Atlanta.) Rather, this is a discussion of the texture and tone, the spirit and focus of a worship service. For some of us who are longtime Christians, what we think of as simple is really both familiar and complex. We have experienced it for so long that, for us, it seems simple.

This is a first-century time. This is a twenty-first century time. This is a beginning time. We have taken virtually two thousand years to develop the forms of worship that are practiced in congregations. It is not that we cease doing these practices. Rather, it is that we begin anew, building on the beginnings of the Christian movement. This is a time for basic math, whether that is high-church liturgical, traditional, contemporary, alternative, or whatever. The art is for the service of worship to match the yearnings and longings, gifts, strengths, and competencies of both the congregation and the community the congregation seeks to serve.

Early one morning as I was in my study writing, this phrase came to me: "The millennium begins with the manger." We celebrate the millennium because of God's gift in the manger. There is no millennium without the manger. We are the people of the manger. It is not accidental that Christ was born in a manger, not a mansion. Christ was born in a cradle, not a castle. Christ was born in a stall, not beneath a steeple. God could have chosen whatever place God wanted Jesus to be born. God wants us to know that God's grace is for *everyone*—poor and rich, of the grass roots and at the top, shepherds and wise men.

God's grace comes to us in the common events of life. In our desire to worship God and give God the praise we want to share—coupled with our compulsion toward perfectionism and our long history of liturgical practices—we sometimes complicate worship in ways God likely never expected. What helps in our time is a service that has about it a spirit of simplicity. This is especially important on major Sundays such as Christmas and Easter. On such key Sundays, it is vital that the service share the grace of God in rich, full ways and *with a spirit of simplicity.*

Regrettably, some congregations, in an effort to be at their best, make the Easter and Christmas services too complex.

There are too many steps in the order of worship. The music is too complex. The service feels busy and hurried. The service tries to do too much. If the Easter service is too complex, it is not accidental that some people do not come back until next Christmas. They have had all the help they need for some time to come. They have had more than they can handle and absorb on that Easter Sunday. It takes a while before they muster their courage to try again.

Around the world, many small, strong congregations worship God in a simple service with no bulletin. Some congregations choose to have a bulletin. I encourage congregations, if they choose to have one, to have a simple bulletin. The bulletin has on it only those pieces of ink essential for people to participate in the service. A simple service with a simple bulletin is fine.

However, bulletins have become filled with stage instructions. In a simple bulletin, there are no stage instructions for the leaders of the service. For example, people are perfectly capable of figuring out this is the welcome and these must be the announcements. The words *welcome* and *announcements* do not need to be in the bulletin. Likewise, the word *opening* is not needed right before the word *hymn*. We are wise enough to know that, since it is the first hymn, it opens the service. Look for all the places you can leave out unnecessary verbiage and black ink. The more open space the bulletin has, the simpler the bulletin feels.

Most of the time, it helps to have a simple service and, if you choose, a simple bulletin. On those occasions when you have a complex service of worship, I still encourage you to have a simple bulletin. A complex bulletin makes a complex service feel even more complex. If the bulletin is simply stated and organized, the complex service of worship is easier for people to follow. A simple bulletin helps a complex service feel simple.

For many people, the most helpful service of worship is one of rare, genuine simplicity. This service of worship mirrors the manger. This service of worship lives out the incarnation, the way God chose for it to happen in long-ago Bethlehem. Through the remarkable magnificence of Jesus' birth and the simplicity with which it takes place, God is seeking to teach us how God's grace comes to us. Regrettably, we often make too complex what God makes very simple. Let your services of worship live out the simplicity of the grace God reveals in the manger. Let them have a congregational, sacramental spirit.

Helpful and Hopeful

In small, strong congregations, the whole service of worship is helpful and hopeful in people's lives. *The whole service touches the whole person with the whole Gospel.* The music, the prayers, the scripture, the preaching, the liturgy, and the blessing all help us discover the whole of God's good news for our lives today and in the days to come.

We start strong and grow stronger. If only one part of a service can be helpful and hopeful, I encourage congregations to let it be during the first three minutes. We can never make a first impression the second time. The art is to start the service of worship with a stirring, inspiring spirit of hope.

In the first three minutes, we do not need to hear a call to worship that is more like a call to despair. We do not need to hear an announcement that we are behind in our budget. Healthy congregations are always giving away more money than they have, confident that God will supply resources to match the mission. We do not need, in the first three minutes, to hear that some committee needs to meet. We do not need to start the service in a dull, deadly, boring manner. Worship is not routine. We have come to worship God. We have come here this day to discover, helpfully and hopefully, the grace of God in our lives.

If a second part of the worship can be helpful and hopeful, let it be the last three minutes. Start strong. End strong. End with hope. We can never make a last impression a second time. The people have gone. There will not be another opportunity to end this service on a note of hope.

It does not help to use the last three minutes of worship to scold and rebuke people. It really does not help to scold and rebuke people anytime. Nor does it help to end with a faltering lack of confidence, with the service sort of trailing away to nothing. Quit while you are ahead. End once, not three times. End well. What helps in the last three minutes is for people to experience the blessing of the grace of God in their lives and to leave with that sense of hope for the time to come.

I encourage congregations to have many warm moments in their service of worship. The reason people are drawn to warm moments is that—in them—we discover the sharing of help and the sense of hope. It can be baptizing a child. It can be receiving people into God's family. It can be someone, with a spirit of helpfulness, sharing her wisdom, strength, and experience for day-to-day life. People are drawn to those warm moments.

There are enough cold moments in life. Loneliness and lostness visit us. Despair and depression try to do us in. Sickness and death are not strangers to us. Resentment and bitterness come over us. We know life is more than such experiences. We identify with warm moments. They touch our hearts and stir our souls. They are sacramental signs of hope in our lives. We experience the hope of God in these moments. We are drawn close to the promise of God, the good news of the Gospel.

A helpful, hopeful service helps people discover one strength for living. Richly and fully, people discover some one way forward, some one insight, some one clue, some one possibility to help them directly with their lives. The strength of one service may be that people discover handles of help and hope in their search for individuality—for identity, integrity, autonomy, and power. In another service, the strength may be that people discover, deeply and generously, their search for community—for roots, place, belonging, family, and friends. In another service of worship, the strength may be that people discover handles in their search for meaning—for value, purpose, and significance in life.

I encourage congregations to have many services where the strength that people discover is hope—for that which is lasting and enduring, for that which helps them live with hope in the coming week. Our longing for hope is expressed well by Luther in the saying that opens this chapter: everything done in humankind is done on the basis of hope. The same sentiment, in words of my own, is that hope is stronger than memory. Memory is strong. Hope is stronger. We live on hope.

We bring our memories to a service of worship. We remember tragic events that mar and scar our lives. We remember sinful events for which we ask God and others for forgiveness. We remember events of disappointment, despair, and disaster. We remember incidental events. We do not know why we remember them, and yet they are with us. We remember celebrative events, of good fun and good times: birthdays, anniversaries, graduations.

We bring our experiences of change to a worship service. The pace of change is swift. Kingdoms rise and fall. Civilizations come and go. Some people are born. Some die. Some come into our lives. Some leave. Some people grow and develop. Some things stay the same. Much changes around us— and within us.

We bring our sense of conflict to a service of worship. We experience conflicts of priorities and power. We have differences of opinions. We displace our anxieties and our fears into anger, and sometimes rage. We feel powerless and defenseless. We feel the decisions that affect our lives and shape our destinies are made somewhere else, by someone else, and we cannot find who, where, or why. We feel helpless and conflicted.

Yes, we bring memory, change, and conflict to a worship service. Most of all, we bring our search for hope. We bring our longings and yearnings, our anticipations and our expectancies. We long for hope. We live on hope. Luther said it well: "Everything done in humankind is done on the basis of hope." Both the service and the sermon help with hope.

Frequently, the strength of the service, lived out in the whole service, is gathered in the sermon. People look for sermons that are helpful and hopeful. They are not looking for great sermons—polished and published, with phrase, rhyme, and alliteration. Fancy and frivolous sermons do not interest them. They are not looking for dull, boring sermons. Nor do they long for stern, solemn, strident sermons. They look for some clue, some insight, some bit of wisdom and experience to help them live with hope in the week to come.

There is a myth afoot, regretfully, that suggests the primary way to develop a strong, healthy congregation is to find a great preacher. The few people who promulgate this myth happen mostly to be fairly good preachers. In effect, they are saying that the primary way to be a healthy congregation is to do it the way they did it—with preaching. Sometimes, we who are pastors also make the fatal assumption that the only way a congregation can be strong and healthy is if we, who are pastors, take center stage in the effort.

There are many ways to win football games. There are a remarkable number of possibilities to paint a picture, or create a work of art. There are many ways to make a wonderful quilt; or sail a boat; or play stirring music; or be a small, strong college; or build a house; or be a family together. There is no one way.

Small congregations become strong and healthy as they share:

- One excellent mission
- Compassion and shepherding
- Community and belonging
- Self-reliance and self-sufficiency
- Worship and hope
- Leaders and team
- Just enough space and facilities
- Giving and generosity

These resources help a small congregation be strong and healthy. God blesses small, strong congregations, richly and fully, with these remarkable qualities.

Do they have gifts and strengths in worship? Yes. Their strengths can be in a service that is warm and welcoming, music, prayers, and liturgy that are stirring and inspiring. Their strengths can be in a service that delivers the spirit of congregation and sacrament. The service can share hope—for living life in the grace of God.

Does preaching help? Yes, when the preaching is helpful. Through worship, we help people grow whole, healthy lives in the grace of God. The helpful sermon touches people's lives and genuinely helps them grow forward a whole, healthy life in the grace of God. Is preaching the primary way to create a small, strong congregation? No. Am I for preaching? Yes.

I am a preacher. I have spent much of my life preaching. I have listened to countless sermons in my travels. I have coached many, many pastors in their preaching. Out of these experiences, I wrote *Preaching Grace*. The book is helping many pastors and congregations. To me, preaching is virtually a sacrament of grace.

Importantly, it is *among* the resources for developing a small, strong congregation. However, it is not the only one, nor even the most important one. If it were the only one or the most important one, then congregations would roll over and play dead, waiting for a preacher to show up and save the day. They would think their future was in someone else's hands. In so doing, they would lose the future they can grow forward, whether they have solid preaching or not.

The art is to build on the strengths God gives you, not the ones you wish you had, or the ones you think you should have. There are many small congregations that are strong and healthy but that, for a variety of reasons, do not have helpful preaching. Sometimes the preaching is adequate. Sometimes the preaching is dismal. However, they so well deliver some of the other qualities of small, strong congregations that they are healthy and vibrant, solid and effective.

The purpose of worship is to discover the grace of God, the compassion of Christ, and the healing hope of the Holy Spirit. Worship serves to help us know that God is stirring and moving, present in our lives now. Because of this, we can live the day and week to come, confident, with a spirit of hope. We live, knowing the grace of God surrounds us, the compassion of Christ encourages us, and the hope of the Holy Spirit leads us forward.

We live on hope, not on memory. We look for hope in the present, and when we cannot find hope in the present we look for it in the immediate future. When we cannot find hope in the immediate future, we look for it in the distant future. When we cannot find hope there, we look for it on the other side of the river, with God in the next life. We post-pone our hopes down the road.

One reason some congregations are drawn to hymns such as "We Shall Gather at the River" or "In the Sweet Bye-and-Bye" is because these are hymns of hope. There are a lot of old hymns that nobody sings anymore. The reason some hymns endure is because they offer people sources of hope.

We come to a service of worship to discover hope for our lives. We look for worship experiences that have the qualities of being stirring, helpful, and hopeful. In such a service as this, our lives take on a new spirit of hope. The door to the future is open. We live with confidence today and in the days to come. We experience the tragedy and travail, the sickness, the sins (both simple and tragic), the endless difficulties and complexities of life. We live with assurance that God's grace is with us, Christ's compassion stirs us, and the power of the Holy Spirit lifts us. We live with hope.

In small, strong congregations, people discover hope in the worship services. In weak and dying congregations, people experience a service of worship that lacks hope. Oh, in dying congregations, there may some posturing and prancing that tries to pass itself off as hope. There may be glib statements, loquacious verbiage, and voluble assertions. However, these are like a person in the dark, talking to himself, nervously and anxiously, quickly and loudly, with a stuttering and stammering of words, trying to reassure himself.

Hope is simple, confident, assured. Hope does not prance and posture. Hope comes in a manger. Hope lives on a cross. Hope opens a tomb. Hope is present with us now. Our hope is in God, not ourselves. Hope is not of our own doing. Hope is the gift of God. Small, strong congregations live with this spirit of hope. Their worship services are services of hope.

7

Team, Leaders, and Congregation

Imagination is more important than knowledge.

—ALBERT EINSTEIN

Donald and Harriet are a remarkable couple. They did their training in a distinguished seminary. They did advanced training in a mission school. Their lifelong work is training lay pastors for mission work on one of the richest mission fields on the planet. They are legends for what they do. They have busy schedules and many traveling commitments across the vast area they serve.

Their sponsoring group provides them with a large home, with wonderful gardens in the English tradition. Because of their commitments and because of the size of the house and the gardens, their sponsoring group has arranged for them to have a housekeeper who comes three days a week. They also have a gardener who comes once or twice a week.

One day their housekeeper said to Harriet, "Miss Harriet, would you teach me the Bible? I have watched how you live, and I want to know more about God." They agreed to a one-hour Bible study each week from nine to ten on Monday morning. They had good sessions together.

Time passed.

One day the gardener asked if he could join the Bible study. They welcomed him. From then on, the gardener, the housekeeper, and Harriet gathered each Monday morning at nine o'clock for one hour of Bible study.

Time passed.

One Monday, as Harriet was walking into the room where they met, she heard the gardener say to the housekeeper, with quiet enthusiasm, "I have founded my own church now."

Harriet was interested, and she inquired of the gardener, "Oh, you have found a church to attend?"

"Oh no, Miss Harriet," he said. "I have started my own church."

Harriet, trained in established ways of doing church, was slightly taken aback, but she did not allow it to show on her face.

"What do you mean, you have started your own church?"

"Oh Miss Harriet, you remember when we were studying in the Gospel of Matthew, Christ said, 'Go and make disciples.' I thought that is what you wanted me to do. I thought that is what Christ invites us to do. That is what I am doing. With the help of two of my friends, we started a new congregation. We have a wonderful congregation. We worship together each Sunday."

"About how many attend?" asked Harriet, a bit more perplexed and interested.

"We have about 120 who come now. We have a wonderful time worshipping God. We can feel the grace of God there with us."

"Who comes to do the preaching for you?" asked Harriet, with a searching, troubling concern.

"Why, Miss Harriet, I do the preaching."

Now really amazed, Harriet asked, with a halting, hesitant concern, "And what do you preach?"

"Why, Miss Harriet, I preach on Sunday what you teach on Monday!"

These days, when Harriet and Donald share the story of how their gardener founded a congregation, they do so with eagerness and enthusiasm. They have learned from their gardener. Their faces glow, their smiles broaden, their eyes light up. They value deeply what they have discovered from their gardener.

Throughout the history of the Christian movement, countless congregations have come into being in this way. In the coming century, in this country and all over the planet, many more small, strong congregations will come into being this way. They will do so with the help of people from all walks of life: gardeners, grocery clerks, ditchdiggers, bankers, waiters, doctors, manufacturer's representatives, dentists, airline attendants, secretaries, college administrators, recreational directors, and more.

Mostly, it will happen the way it did with Harriet and Donald's gardener. One person, with the help of someone like Harriet, discovers the grace of God. One person discovers the richness of the Biblical message. God's grace stirs in that person's life. He or she shares the good news with two or three friends. They live what they have learned.

They become a team. They discover they can be leaders. They share their good news with their friends and family, people with whom they work, and strangers who become family in Christ with them.

Time passes.

A congregation is born. People in the congregation share their good news of the grace of God. The congregation flourishes.

Team

One of the qualities present in small, strong congregations is their gift for living and sharing together as:

- Team
- Leaders
- Congregation

These three are a seamless unity. They are virtually insep-arable qualities present in their life together. Team, leaders, and congregation: these qualities help small congregations be strong and healthy. They think and act, plan and practice—indeed, they live with these three interactive dynamics as central to who they are together. They are competent as a team, as leaders, and as a congregation.

The ability to live and share as a team is one of the important competencies of small, strong congregations. These factors contribute to their being a team:

- Their capacity to see the whole, not the parts
- Their understanding of the diversity of gifts
- Their appreciation of the gifts of a pastoral leader

They see the value and importance of working together. They work naturally together. They see the congregation as a family, and they lead as the team leaders of a family. They count on their pastoral leader to be part of the team. They work hard to close any gap between themselves and the grass roots of the congregation.

The Whole

Small, strong congregations have developed their capacity to focus on the whole, not the parts. One of the advantages small, strong congregations offer is the ability for people to participate—whether children, youths, or adults—in the whole of the congregation, not just the parts.

The spirit of a small, strong congregation is that everybody participates in the whole. There is no effort to divide people into parts. Oh, there may be specific activities for different needs, but the genius of a small, strong congregation—the genius of the leadership team in a small, strong congregation—is its capacity to nurture the whole, not the parts.

Dostal Valley, as a small, strong congregation, has an excellent youth program. Their youth program includes their worship service, where young people, children, and adults worship together as God's family. The service is both child- and youth-friendly. The youths are included in the service, as participants and leaders. They are not disconnected into a separate service for youth. The music groups develop along interest lines, not age levels.

The youth program includes family Bible studies, where youngsters and adults learn together the richness of the Christian life. The congregation's mission projects are shared, youths and adults together. The fellowship events are for the whole family. There is a youth retreat in the fall, and there is a family retreat in the spring. There are a number of one-time events specifically for youths, and there are many such events for the whole family.

Small, strong congregations offer a youth program built on the principle of the whole. Youths are included in the whole, not set apart from the whole. The belief is that it is important and valuable that they participate in the whole congregation, not just in their own part. Young people experience considerable compartmentalization in other sectors of their lives. Given this fragmentation and isolation, small, strong congregations offer the advantage that youths can experience the whole. Worship, music groups, Bible study, mission projects, fellowship events, retreats, and one-time events give them the opportunity to participate in the whole of God's family.

I was visiting with Glenn and Cynthia. They were sharing with me their pilgrimage. They had been active leaders in a large church in the community. Glenn grew up in the church, albeit at a time when it was somewhat smaller. When the two of them married, they joined the young marrieds' class. There were about thirty to forty couples in the class. It was the up-and-coming class in the church.

Over the years, Glenn and Cynthia, as well as many in the class, gave birth to children. Together, the class helped one another and their kids through preschool, kindergarten, and elementary school. The class continued to flourish. The children thrived. The time for confirmation came. The parents had their confirmation class. Their children, now emerging youths, had their own class.

Glenn and Cynthia said, "It was at this point that we became ill at ease. We were told about all of the activities to which our kids could look forward in the youth program. Once confirmation was completed, they would be 'promoted' to the youth program. It felt like we would never see our kids again. The vast array of activities would keep them busy every spare minute. They were already busy enough with school activities."

They smiled, looked at one another, and continued. "We had a family gathering. We shared our interest in being a family together. We know that each of us has our individual activities. We want our church to be a group where we can participate together, and not be split up as we are in virtually every other sphere of our lives. Our kids want the same."

They went on to describe how they had asked around, among friends, work associates, and acquaintances. Cynthia happened, one day, onto the topic over lunch with Doris, a relatively new friend. Doris said, "Clint and I had the same concern. Three years ago, we discovered our present congregation. We're small, and we do things together as a whole congregation. Our kids like it. We invite you to come."

Glenn and Cynthia went on to share with me that they visited the congregation. They found home. It was tough to give up the young marrieds' class. It was difficult to give up the leadership positions they had in the large church. But for them, the gains and the advantages far outweighed what they had given up. Cynthia said, "We are happier here. It is the one group in which all of our family can share together." Glenn said, "This congregation is more like what I remember when I was growing up, before our former church got so big."

In a small, strong congregation, the whole family participates in the whole congregation. Departmentalized churches talk of doing an intergenerational event, now and then. They talk this way because they have fragmented and compartmentalized their congregation. Small, strong congregations do not talk of doing intergenerational events because they have never thought departmentally. They simply live life together as a whole family. The focus is the whole.

This does not mean that all small, strong congregations have people of all ages, cradle to grave. There are small, strong congregations with no one under sixty-five, because there is no one in the community under sixty-five. Similarly, I recently helped a small, strong congregation where the volunteer pastoral leader is in his late thirties and virtually everyone in the congregation is fifteen to thirty years old. It is a remarkably young congregation, because the area in which it is located has a remarkably high density of young people.

Whatever the makeup of the congregation, what distinguishes a small, strong congregation is its focus on the whole. It is in this way that small congregations are strong. They deliver a sense of the whole of life, the whole of the Gospel, the whole of the grace of God. In this way, people discover a sense of wholeness and integrity in their lives.

Indeed, small, strong congregations are teaching larger congregations that what many people want to do is to participate in the whole, not the parts. In other sectors of their lives, people experience sufficient compartmentalization and departmentalization, fragmentation and segmentation to last them four lifetimes. They long for and look for a grouping where they can participate in the whole, not simply the parts.

Consequently, a new kind of large, regional congregation is emerging, where the focus is on the whole, not the parts. In an earlier time, as congregations grew larger, they tended to become increasingly compartmentalized and departmentalized. As the church grew ever larger, there emerged departments upon departments, compartments upon compartments.

Recently, in one large congregation, we gathered all of the leaders and staff who have anything to do with youths. The focus of the gathering was, "How can we help the whole person and the whole family? How can we help the whole youth and the whole family discover the whole Gospel in their whole life together?" It was not a gathering to coordinate individual department calendars between the youth department, the music department, the Sunday school department, the recreation department, and the scouting department. That is what they had been doing.

The purpose of the gathering was to begin to work together as a whole team in serving the whole youth and the whole family with the whole Gospel. It was the first such gathering in the congregation. The leader of the Sunday school said, "This way is better. We have been so caught up in our individual parts that we lost the whole. We are headed in a stronger direction now." More such gatherings will happen. A new day has come in the congregation.

The genius of small, strong congregations is their natural capacity to serve the whole person and the whole family.

They do not think in parts. For them, it is a foreign, strange way of thinking and living. They seek to see life as a whole, not a collection of separate parts. Thus they see their congregation as a whole.

The Diversity of Gifts

The biblical principle is that there is a diversity of gifts, not a hierarchy of gifts. This understanding is a second factor that contributes to small, strong congregations' living and sharing as a team.

God blesses equally all of the gifts that God gives. No gifts are better than other gifts. There are no higher or lower gifts. No gifts are more favored of God than other gifts. There are no greater or lesser gifts. Just as God loves all of His children, God loves all the gifts He bestows on His children.

David serves as pastor of a small, strong congregation. He has been with the congregation for ten years. The first few years were tough. Then, it was as if David and the congregation came into their own. It was during David's tenth year that I was there helping. Informally, I asked what they liked most about David. Person after person said such things as "David brings out the best in us." "Until David came, we never knew what we could do." "He is one of us." "He helps us discover what we do best."

David is a quiet, gentle, almost shy person. He loves his wife, his children, and his congregation. He does not talk a lot. People sense his love for them more in his presence than in his words. He shares simple acts of kindness and thoughtfulness with many people in the community. People sense the quiet confidence and deep assurance he has in them. He values each person. He cherishes a rich, full relationship with them.

He is interested in them and in their lives. He listens well. When he is with people, he is fully attentive with them. His mind is not somewhere else. He is not distracted. Somehow, in the conversations with David, people discover their gifts. It is not that he tells them. It is hard to describe what happens. Person after person, almost intuitively, comes upon personal strengths as he or she visits with David.

David has the spirit that he is grateful to be a pastor. The thought stirs his gratitude and humility. He is amazed that God invites him to serve as a pastoral leader in this way. He is grateful God gives him this congregation to serve and the gifts to serve it well. Precisely because he feels so blessed, he is confident God gives each person gifts, strengths, and competencies to live well in the grace and mission of God. He is convinced of the diversity of gifts.

Robert is like David in many ways. He, too, is quiet and shy. They are about the same age and share many similar interests. He manifests his love for his wife and children. He is glad to be, as he puts it, "a servant of his congregation." He talks much about being a servant leader and the priesthood of all believers. That sounded good for a while. Now, some say he talks too much.

Robert, at first, seemed interested in the people in the congregation. He listened to the stories of their lives. He seemed intent on coming to know them better. He frequently talked of his desire to visit and share with them. But he had difficulty remembering their names. He talked much of the role of the pastor. His sermons were heavy and academic. He seldom visited.

Whenever Robert met with the congregation's leaders, rather than inviting their suggestions he would share his ideas. Usually, he had a number of ideas that he thought they should do "for their own good." He tended, in an unobtrusive, almost low-key way, to talk down to them. He insisted frequently on his own way. He treated the part-time church secretary decently enough, but it was as though she were a hired hand in a lesser position. With Robert, she never sensed that her gifts and all that she did were fully appreciated.

Gradually, over several years, people pulled back. Robert seemed to know what *he* wanted to do, and what he thought they should do. He waved aside many excellent ideas and good suggestions. He did so politely enough. He avoided arguments. He simply continued on the way he thought best. But it began to dawn on people that he was not really interested in their ideas and suggestions. The next conclusion came: "He is not really interested in us."

Somewhere, Robert had learned the subtle assumption of a hierarchy of gifts. Without thinking about it consciously, he simply behaved as though some gifts were better than others. In his dealings with the congregation, he acted as though there are higher and lower gifts. Mostly, he thought he believed in the diversity of gifts. At least from time to time he said he did. However, he also had the belief that being a pastor was being *the* pastor. He felt that his calling and his training made him the professional. Therefore, he knew best what to do.

Even though they seldom speak the words aloud, a few pastors still cling to these mistaken assumptions. "Some gifts are better than others." "Some people are better than others." "Some positions are more important than others." "The position of the pastor is more significant than any other position in the congregation." "My training gives me a better sense of what to do." "My ordination makes me the more qualified person." You will find this set of mistaken assumptions in weak and declining, and dying, churches.

A hierarchy of gifts creates division and separation. It may feed the misplaced ego needs of a pastor, but it does not create a team. It creates an upper and lower class division in the congregation—mostly between the pastor and everyone else.

It causes people to *not* discover their own gifts and strengths. It fosters passive aggressive behavior, low-grade hostility, subliminal resentment, and eruptive forms of anger. People do not feel valued. They do not discover their best true selves.

David lives the diversity of gifts. Robert sometimes talks it, but he lives a hierarchy of gifts. Robert was asked to move at the end of four years. David has had a happy pastorate for ten years, and he looks forward to many more.

The Gifts of a Pastor

In small, strong congregations, there is deep appreciation for the gifts of a pastoral leader. Key leaders, and the congregation as a whole, have a sense of gratitude and recognition for the strengths and competencies that a pastoral leader brings to the congregation. Likewise, the pastor has a clear understanding of both the diversity of gifts and the specific gifts that he or she shares with the congregation and the community.

I have deep appreciation for ordained ministers; I am one. I have invested my life in being one. Over the years, I have had the privilege of knowing, sharing, and working with thousands of ordained ministers. The vast majority of ministers do excellent work. *Indeed, pastors frequently do better work than they think they do.*

Most ministers have received solid training. They have deep compassion, work hard, love their congregation, and serve well. I am amazed at the compassion, creativity, and competence most ministers bring to the mission. Sometimes, we become preoccupied with the few ministers who have difficulty, or who seem to lack the gifts and competencies to be a minister in our time. Most congregations are fortunate to have the minister they have.

The goal, however, is competencies, not credentials. Credentials can be, and frequently are, a clue to competence. I am known to have said, "When someone has a master of divinity degree, I do not hold that against them, but it is not a point in their favor. What *is* in their favor are the competence and the compassion they bring to the congregation and the community they have come to serve."

I have four degrees: B.A., M.Div., S.T.M., and Ph.D. I am *for* education and training. I have given many years of my life teaching in a highly distinguished seminary. I founded the continuing education program in that seminary and led it for ten years, working with countless pastors to help them enhance their competence.

I do many advanced seminars across the country to help ministers grow and develop their competence. What counts is how well a pastor has the competency for serving congregations in our time. Education and training can do much to help in this nurturing, but it is, finally, what one brings to the mission in competencies—not credentials—that counts.

Harriet's gardener is doing solid work. Because of God's stirring grace and the gifts of a gardener, a small, strong congregation is serving God's mission. People's lives are touched and made whole. They are discovering the gifts with which God is blessing them. The congregation, thanks to Harriet's Monday morning Bible studies, is growing in its understanding of the Christian life and mission.

Countless thousands of congregations across the planet are like the one Harriet's gardener is leading. He brings the competencies and compassion Harriet has helped him discover. He may be shy on credentials, but the gifts and competencies he shares are making a difference in people's lives.

In our time, particularly in small, strong congregations, the primary competencies important for a pastor to develop and share are these:

- Good shepherd
- Helpful preacher

- Wise, caring leader
- Community pastor

I discuss these competencies in depth in my recent book *A New Beginning for Pastors and Congregations.* I encourage you to benefit from the research and resources shared in that book. For our purposes now, I want simply to confirm the competencies helpful for pastors to have. Frequently, people say to me, "We're looking for a minister who will come and love us and whom we can come to love." When I invite them to share more fully what they mean, in their own words they go on to say that these are the qualities and competencies they hope to find in their minister.

They are looking for a *good shepherd.* They look for someone to shepherd them in everyday, ordinary life. Someone to celebrate with them during the remarkable, happy occasions in life. Someone who is with them in sad, tragic times. They seek someone who shares rich, full compassion with them.

They are looking for a *helpful preacher.* They are not looking for great preaching on Sunday. They are not seeking fancy preaching. Nor do they long for dull, boring preaching. They look for a sermon that helps them discover the grace of God and the whole of the good news of the Gospel. They seek a sermon that helps them live whole, healthy lives. They look for a sermon that is helpful to them during the week to come. They long for a sermon that helps them make some sense of life and give them hope.

They are looking for a *wise, caring leader,* a person who is part of the leadership team, who with wisdom and caring helps the congregation advance its mission, compassion, community, hope, and generosity. They are not looking for an administrator with formal, organizational, institutional competence. They do not seek a manager with a multiplicity of policies and procedures, rules and regulations. They are looking for a person who knows how to lead himself or herself and who therefore knows how to lead with others as a team.

They are looking for someone to be a *pastor in the community*, not just in the church. Small, strong congregations have a healthy relationship with the community around them. They want a pastor who relates with the whole family of the congregation: community people, those served in mission, constituents, friends of the congregation who live elsewhere, and members. Small, weak congregations become closed, cliquish, exclusive, and cut off from the community around them. They want a pastor whose only focus is on the members inside the church. Small, strong congregations want someone who is a pastor in the community, not just in the church.

Importantly, in small, strong congregations the key leaders, the grassroots participants, and the pastor see themselves as a competent team together. They understand, think, and live as a whole. They value the diversity of gifts with which they are blessed. They appreciate the gifts of a pastoral leader, who is part of the leadership team. Together, the team shares a leadership of love, not a leadership of law. The team leads the congregation with a strong, healthy, constructive spirit.

Leaders

The *capacity to lead* is one of the important competencies present in small, strong congregations. Most small congregations have more leaders than they think they have. They look for formal leaders. God gives them informal leaders. They look for organizational leaders. God gives them team leaders. They look for committee leaders. God gives them community leaders. God blesses small, strong congregations with leaders that match the nature of small congregations and the distinctive mission they serve.

Leaders lead. These factors contribute to their being leaders:

- Their capacity for imagination and creativity
- Their gift of encouragement and coaching
- Their appreciation for the steps of loving, listening, learning, and leading

Imagination and Creativity

One of the signs of leadership is imagination and creativity. This is true of all healthy congregations, but in small, strong congregations imagination and creativity are remarkably present. In such congregations you hear "Let's try it; it will be fun." In Australia, the phrase is "Let's give it a go."

In small, strong congregations, we use what resources we have with imagination and creativity. We value flexibility, innovation, and discovery. We know we have modest resources. If we were brimming over with resources, we might be lazy and wasteful in deploying them for God's mission. Our limited resources stir our imagination and creativity to use our resources well.

We know we have strengths and resources sufficient unto the mission. Once, I had a notion that small congregations, because their resources were limited, must therefore use them carefully or they might not be adequate for their needs. The truth is that small, strong congregations have resources sufficient to the strengths and mission they develop and share.

Think of it this way. Small, strong congregations never have enough money. They never have enough leaders. With imagination and creativity, they are always giving away more than they have. The result is that God supplies new leaders and new resources to match the mission. The stronger the mission, the more leaders the congregation develops. The stronger the mission, the more generously God helps us discover the resources to share the mission.

Weak congregations conserve and hold, protect and preserve their "meager" leadership resources. As a consequence, their meager leadership resources grow weaker and more meager. Not used, muscles atrophy and weaken. Strengths and gifts not used atrophy as well.

This way of thinking also teaches everyone in the congregation to conserve and hold, protect and preserve *their* meager resources. The further consequence is that people withhold the strengths and gifts they could share to advance the mission and health of the congregation. As they withhold them, their own strengths wither. A downward spiral happens.

The Eagle Point congregation was in that downward spiral for more than twenty years. Mr. Hammond, now with God on the other side of the river, had, during his lifetime, pounded away that the church must be careful with its meager resources. Three pastors back, about twenty years before I was there to help, Reverend Thomas had come to be their pastor.

Mr. Hammond and Reverend Thomas were soulmates. They lived life carefully and cautiously. They were cautious about getting too close to people. They held their distance. They were creatures of habit. Everything had its place. They were careful not to show too much love, enthusiasm, or generosity. Their spirit was "You never know when there will be a rainy day." In subtle, insidious ways, they pounded home the thought that "Our congregation has few resources, and we must be careful with them."

Reverend Thomas left after four years. Mr. Hammond died a couple of years later. Nevertheless, their imprint and influence continued. The congregation clung to the notion that they must be careful with the few resources they had. Every decision, modest or major, was weighed against that dictum. The persistent question was, "Are we being careful enough?" The sentiment was that they needed to be more careful and cautious. The ghosts of Mr. Hammond and Reverend Thomas were strongly present.

Twenty-some years came and went. The congregation continued to decline. The decline only caused them to be more careful. The notion emerged that "We are declining because we are not being careful enough; if we are more careful, we will decline less."

The decline continued.

Steve came to be their pastor. He had not been successful in his two previous congregations. One congregation asked him to leave. With the other, he announced his leaving just ahead of their requesting him to leave. He came to this congregation with few hopes and much baggage. Eagle Point did not expect much from him. He did not count on much from them. He was careful with his love for them. They were careful with their love for him.

The death dance of decline continued for three more years. The feeling was that the decline, having gone on for so long, was now the inevitable future of the congregation. The assumption was, "We are simply one of those congregations fated to decline and die." The sense was, "We must be careful, so that we do not decline any faster than we already are."

God sent Jennifer to this congregation. This is how I think of it, and, as I shared this thought during my time there, this is how Steve and the congregation have come to think of it.

Actually, Jennifer was already there. She was the niece of one of the congregation's leaders. Her parents were not active in any church. When she was in third grade, she came several times with her aunt. She felt at home in the worship service. She thrived in the vacation Bible school. She was quietly outgoing. She did not rush up to people, but she was gently eager to love and to be loved.

Third, fourth, and fifth grade came and went. Jennifer was a likable, enjoyable person. She did well in school. She had a solid intellect. The congregation watched her grow. She became part of the family. She sang in the Easter choir. She was in children's pageant one Christmas. She and her aunt were active in the few projects the congregation still tried to do, as things declined.

The doctor said that it was not the flu. The cough was not the sign of a cold. The fever was not the symptom of a simple childhood ailment. The hacking and wheezing were not the suggestion of allergies. He did not know fully what Jennifer's dilemma was. Tests would be needed. She was in serious trouble. Her aunt had finally brought her to the doctor. He took her directly to the hospital.

She stabilized for a couple of days. Then, she started downhill. The decline was rapid. Nothing seemed to stop it. She lay there, barely breathing, pale, and dying. The doctor called in a friend who was a leading internist in the area. The congregation prayed and visited. Jennifer's mother and father, so long absent from her life with their own problems, were present hour after long hour in the waiting room. The congregation came to know them.

Jennifer's father worked one full-time job and two part-time jobs. He was a carpenter with a small construction firm that hired him by the project. In what spare time he had, he worked with a person who installed drywall in homes and at a nearby nursery on the weekends. Her mother worked two jobs, one three-quarter-time as a waitress, and the other half-time as a clerk in a store. They did not earn a lot of money at any of the jobs. They were decent, hardworking folk, just trying to make ends meet.

They thought an operation would help. It would take the best surgeon in the area. The parents had no medical benefits. Years before, the construction company had told Jennifer's father it did not need to provide any since they hired him by the project. The part-time jobs offered no benefits. There were no savings. Jennifer's aunt had already done what she could.

Steve and the congregation did not easily catch on. Days passed. The operation was delayed. The congregation was like a person, slowly, sluggishly waking from a deep, fitful sleep. They could not quite get their minds around the idea that Jennifer was dying. Her youth and promise seemed so strong. She reminded them of their own early years. She reminded them of their long-ago, thriving years as a congregation.

They prayed. They passed the hat. "Careful" money was given. A little money, not a lot. After all, children are resilient. She will come through. But she was not coming through. The breathing was slower, more strained. They passed the hat again. A "generous" pittance was given. From the viewpoint of careful people, it seemed a lot. It was not enough.

There was no clarion call. There was no sudden insight. There was no decisive gathering. These were careful people. Gradually, it began to dawn on the congregation that they could be careful and Jennifer would die, or they could be generous and Jennifer might live. Her dying began to stir their imagination and creativity.

Two people discovered a project that would raise money. Three other people came up with the idea to contact friends of the congregation who lived elsewhere. Two others visited the principal and the teachers at Jennifer's school to get the school to help. Six people came up with the idea of putting on a benefit concert. Five people began to contact their friends, work associates, and acquaintances in the community. Their imagination stirred. A flurry of creativity occurred. Many people gave money they "could not afford to give."

The creativity of the congregation stirred even more. Someone remembered a fund of $30,000 that had been tucked away and almost forgotten about. They had not talked about it for years. It was their rainy-day fund, should the building need major repairs.

Actually, $25,000 had come to the congregation in the will of a longtime beloved member, Mrs. Johnson. Mr. Hammond and Reverend Thomas quietly put the money away in a separate fund. It was almost by accident that the congregation even learned of the gift. Mrs. Johnson's son called to be sure the congregation had received the money. Mr. Hammond and Reverend Thomas failed to send a thank-you note. Thus, the son did not know whether the congregation had received his mother's gift. He called a friend in the congregation, and that is how the congregation learned of the gift. Mr. Hammond and Reverend Thomas then persuaded the congregation to let the money sit in an account, earn interest, and be there for a major building emergency.

Once the congregation remembered the money, there was no immediate rush to use it to help Jennifer. These were careful people. They had practiced that pattern of behavior for twenty-plus years. As they gathered to discuss it, the dire echoes of Mr. Hammond and Reverend Thomas, now departed, whispered warnings of caution.

It came down to this: "We can help Jennifer, or we can have a nice church building. We can keep the ghosts of Mr. Hammond and Reverend Thomas and have a pretty church— and we will add the ghost of Jennifer. Or we can share the money, deliver the operation, and hope that Jennifer will live." There was no resounding movement. The discussion was careful. Fears and anxieties were expressed. Second thoughts were shared. What-ifs were explored.

They knew Jennifer had run out of time.

They decided.

They talk now of how freeing the decision was. Jennifer's gift was that she awakened the imagination and creativity of the congregation, so long slumbering. The creative projects that emerged to help Jennifer created a spillover impact. People began to see new possibilities in many areas. A cloud of caution lifted. The operation was successful. Jennifer is healthy and alive. The congregation is healthy and alive.

We do not expend our leadership resources foolishly and frivolously. We do not squander God's gifts; these are sacramental gifts. We exercise a spirit of imagination and creativity, flexibility and discovery, wisdom and discernment as to where, how, when, and why we invest the leadership resources with which God blesses them. We invest them with a spirit of generosity, graciousness, and self-giving. As we do so, we become stronger.

Small, strong congregations give *positive recognition* for excellent mistakes. They do not encourage people to make mistakes. Rather, what they affirm is that in all areas of our lives, we will make our fair share of mistakes, some simple and some serious. An excellent mistake is one from which we *learn something* that enables us to share God's mission richly and fully.

A congregation may adopt the attitude that no one should make a mistake. The best way to avoid making a mistake is to do nothing. As they say in the Bahamas, "A skipper who says he has never run aground is a skipper whose ship has never left the dock." Negative reinforcement for mistakes freezes people at the dock. It lowers the level of imagination and creativity in the group.

The more *positive* the recognition for excellent mistakes, the higher the level of imagination and creativity in the group. In this way, we encourage people to be creative and flexible, to discover new ideas, to make excellent suggestions, and then to try them out. Of eight new ideas we try, five may work and three may be excellent mistakes. We learn from those mistakes.

In healthy congregations, we do not frequently say "We've never done it that way" or "That won't work" or "We've already tried that, and it didn't work." Indeed, in healthy congregations, we hardly ever hear these words. Yes, from time to time, we say, "We've already tried that, and it didn't work. We affirm it as an excellent mistake!" Mostly, as a leadership team of key leaders, grassroots people, and pastor, we work together with imagination and creativity, and trust and confidence in one another to discover new ways in Christ.

Encouragement and Coaching

One of the signs of leadership is the capacity to encourage and coach people to develop and grow. An encouraging spirit helps people have confidence in themselves, to trust themselves that they can grow and develop. Coaching helps people discover what they can do. Correcting tells people what they cannot do.

In small, strong congregations, we encourage one another to live our lives at our very best. The spirit is one of encouraging and coaching, not one of discouraging and correcting. We encourage people to discover new possibilities for living whole, healthy lives. We do the same in encouraging people to develop new ways forward for sharing their competencies to advance the mission of the congregation.

The spirit is encouragement-giving leadership. This is not the old permission-granting leadership from the top down. That regrettable way of thinking assumed authority is at the top and permission is benevolently granted to the bottom. In small, strong congregations, there is no top or bottom. The sense is that we are all in this together. We are a congregation, not a hierarchical organization. The focus is with the whole of the congregation.

We have the confidence that everyone in the congregation in fact has strengths, gifts, and abilities. We know, in the end, that authority is internal, not external. We have the assurance that we all have the internal authority and power to grow and develop ourselves. We encourage one another to *claim* our strengths, to *expand* some of our current strengths, and to *add* new strengths with the grace of God. We encourage those in the congregation to develop their own abilities, richly and fully.

We live out this coaching encouragement in informal relationships and mentoring. We know that being a constructive person in life, and in the congregation, is more than a matter of the person being willing. It is a matter of intentionally growing and developing one's competencies. It is both willing and growing.

When we think of specific leadership possibilities in our congregation, we look for who will do it well, not who is willing. We do not make the mistake of simply emphasizing who is willing. We encourage people whose competence matches the specific leadership possibility, who are willing to grow their competence, *and* who are willing. We actively encourage people to advance their competence.

Mary has been the church treasurer for longer than most people can remember. She is getting older and beginning to weaken in various ways. She knew Sally had competencies that matched being treasurer for the congregation. She took Sally under her wing. Informally, for the past three years, Mary has mentored Sally to be the new treasurer of the congregation. Sally is knowledgeable, is trained, and helps Mary now. She is fully able to serve as church treasurer once Mary retires.

Sam led the vacation Bible school in his congregation for many years. Years ago, he took Judy under his wing. He knew that she was head and shoulders above anyone else. He informally coached Judy over a number of years. Finally, Sam retired and Judy became leader of the vacation Bible school. Years passed. Judy did excellent work. Then she took Doug under her wing and began to encourage and coach Doug along. When you and I go to that church twenty years from now, we will find Doug has given much of his life to leading the vacation Bible school in ways he learned from Judy, who learned from Sam. Each advances and improves the vacation Bible school of the congregation during his or her time as leader.

As a teenager, Phil began to serve as one of the informal ushers in his small, strong congregation. He would welcome people and help them feel at home. He would also help with taking up the offering. Harold informally coached him. Years came and went. Phil is in his sixties, and now he mentors Jim, a young person who is likely to serve as usher for years to come.

In small, strong congregations, we have a spirit, a climate, of informally encouraging and coaching leaders on the job rather than doing training workshops. Yes, from time to time, we do participate in seminars, workshops, and training events to discover new ideas and excellent suggestions. I have had the privilege of leading countless seminars. The seminars help greatly, and at the same time informal coaching is one of the primary ways leaders develop in small, strong congregations.

The reason for this practice is important. People learn how to live the Christian life as they experience the encouraging example and coaching mentoring of persons in their small, strong congregation. This truth is aptly described in the remark by St. Francis of Assisi cited earlier in this book: "Go and preach the Gospel. Use words if necessary." People learn how to live whole, healthy lives in the grace of God as they experience the encouragement and coaching of those long in the life of faith.

Just as this is the process by which we learn how to live the Christian life, this also is the process through which we primarily learn how to share and give leadership in small, strong congregations. Life is learned by example. Leadership is learned by example. People lead the way they experience being led. Encouraging, coaching leaders create encouraging, coaching leaders.

Loving, Listening, Learning, Leading

One of the signs of leadership is the capacity to love, listen, learn, and *then* lead. The sequence of the steps is crucial. Some try to lead before they have loved, listened, and learned. It does not work. On the other hand, when we think and plan, act and live these steps, they make a difference in our lives. You will discover helpful resources in *Twelve Keys for Living* and in *Effective Church Leadership*.

For our current purposes, I want to confirm that the foundation of leading is *loving*. The first step in becoming the leader of a group of people is to fall in love with them and give them the opportunity to fall in love with you. Long ago, I created two helpful sayings to illustrate the principle:

1. The team plays well for the coach who loves
   the team.
2. Congregations care about what leaders know,
   when they know the leaders care.

When I help pastors and leaders who are in difficulty with the grass roots of their congregation, the first thing I look at is whether the leaders and pastors have a genuinely loving and caring relationship with the grassroots people. The more loving, the less bickering. The less loving, the more bickering. Sometimes, key leaders and pastors get so busy with one another that they neglect the grass roots. People follow a leader team that genuinely loves and cares for them.

Leaders listen. People who love one another listen to one another. The second step in leading is *listening.* As you listen, you show your love, respect for, and interest in the person and the group. The leader team in a small, strong congregation listens well. We are family. Healthy families listen to one another. We listen to our ideas and suggestions, our anxieties and our expectancies, our fears and our hopes.

We are not that many people. There is no excuse for not listening. We are not that busy. We take time to listen. We listen at three levels: we listen to what is said; we listen between the lines; and we listen to what is not said. *We learn as much from what is not said as from the other two.*

Leaders learn. The third step in leading is *learning.* We learn when we listen. We cannot learn when we are talking. Excellent leaders listen a lot, and they learn a lot. They do not do much telling. They do not scold, rebuke, admonish, or threaten. They are not so busy telling what they know. They listen for the imagination and creativity of the group. They listen for excellent ideas and good suggestions. As a consequence, they have an extraordinary learning curve.

The old notion was that the leaders know, and the grassroots folks should learn what the leaders know. In fact, the grassroots knowledge is considerable, and it is incumbent upon leaders to learn what the grassroots folk know. To be sure, the learning-knowing relationship is mutual and reciprocal. This is precisely why the leader takes the initiative to learn. Leaders who do not learn create congregations that do not learn. Leaders who learn create grassroots people who learn.

Leaders lead. Through loving, listening, and learning, you are in the strongest position to lead. The fourth step in leading is *leading*. I encourage you to let it be your fourth step. Do the first three steps first. You will discover how to lead as you do them. Now, you are in the strongest position to lead.

Mr. Gordon said to me, "Dr. Callahan, I have seen them all." Mr. Gordon is the longtime respected leader of the Mountain View congregation. Graying of hair, tanned from the outdoor work he does, in his seventies, married to Betty for forty-nine years, with three children and five grandchildren, he was sharing with me his wisdom on the pastors who had come and gone over the years.

He went on to say, "Ian is the best pastor we've had. I don't agree with him on a number of matters, and yet I know where he stands, and he's honest and fair with me. Years ago, we had Reggie, who seemed always to want to boss us around. I don't know how he got that way. He was nice enough. But he was forever reminding us that he was the pastor. He insisted that we should do things his way. We were glad when he left after four years.

"Somewhere along the way, I don't quite remember the order, we got Alfred. He got us into the project of developing a policy manual for our congregation. At first, it sounded like a good idea. We probably did need to firm up our guidelines on a few matters. But we did not need to spend a year on the fool thing, and Alfred dragged it out for more than a year. It seemed like every time we got together, he had another policy he wanted to put in the manual.

"He was a stickler for detail. Betty tells me I'm a little like that myself, but Alfred wanted to run the whole church that way. Someone would come up with a new idea and he would talk about policies. He was forever saying, 'That's not in our policies.'

"Some of us got to thinking. He did not visit. His preaching was marginal. He spent a lot of time at his computer, working on the policy manual, and who knows what else. He was more like a manager. He didn't participate in some of the congregation's activities. He hardly spent any time in the community.

"A couple of us went to him, and, as best we could, we suggested that we put further work on the policy manual on hold. This would give him the chance to come to know the people in the congregation and the community better. He agreed. He thought it was a good idea. But he continued in his same old way and then announced that he was leaving in July. I hope whoever got him likes to work on policy manuals.

"After Alfred, we got Edwin. He and I became good friends. We enjoyed fishing together, and occasionally we played golf together. When Betty was in the hospital for her surgery, he visited regularly. He was a good preacher. He had a good family. His kids seemed to be doing well in school. We liked his wife. She was a good spirit, and people enjoyed being with both of them.

"When Edwin suggested we have a planning retreat, we were all for it. It turned out to be the best planning retreat we've ever had. In my own business, I've been to many planning retreats. Edwin led our retreat better than anyone I've ever seen. It was something to watch him. We came up with more ideas and suggestions than we thought possible. It was a great time.

"After the retreat, a month or two later, he suggested we get together for an evening to go over what had come out of the retreat. That made good sense to us. We had a covered-dish dinner at the church. We invited everyone. We're not that big of a congregation, and we do most things together. Betty baked her special pumpkin pie. We had a wonderful evening planning.

"Edwin continued his visiting. His preaching seemed to get better. The congregation was moving along. We delegated several of the ideas we had come up with to a couple of project teams. Each team had its first get-together and was about ready to begin work on their projects when Edwin suggested we do a bit more planning to be sure these two projects were what we wanted to do. That sounded reasonable enough to us. We remembered Reggie, who bossed us around. We remembered Alfred telling us what was and was not in the policies. It sounded pretty good that Edwin wanted to plan and consult with us.

"However, two years went by, and that's all we ever did: plan. We couldn't figure out whether Edwin simply couldn't make up his mind on something, or whether he was trying to please everyone so much that he never did anything but plan. It finally got to the stage that everyone would have been pleased if he'd just done something, or at least let us do something. After another year, he left.

"Then we got Roland. He was something. He just went ahead and did what he wanted. He didn't consult with anyone. He was not certain he wanted to be here. His second Sunday in the pulpit, he informed us that he would only be here a short time. Despite his dictatorial ways, we liked him, and once he came to know us, he seemed to like us. We celebrated the one-hundredth anniversary of our church while he was here, and he went out of his way to be certain it was a great celebration. Even though he acted like a dictator much of the time, we will remember Roland for a long time because of his special efforts for the celebration.

"After Roland, Ian became our pastor. We hope he stays a long time. The last six years with Ian have been the best we've had in a long time. Ian doesn't boss us. He's happy we have some policies, but he doesn't want us to spend a lot of time on them. We have a planning retreat once a year, and then we encourage the project teams to move forward. We accomplish a lot for a small congregation.

"He visits. His preaching, most Sundays, is helpful. He's a good leader. When we ask Ian what he thinks about something, he shares his wisdom. He loves us and listens to us. He's a good shepherd. When he and I disagree, and we sometimes do, we try to see one another's viewpoint. We try to work it out. He leads, and he lets us lead. We're having a good time with Ian. Dr. Callahan, we want you to help us keep him a long time. "

As leaders, we do not boss, manage, enable, or dictate. We do not manufacture rules and regulations, policies and procedures, conditions and stipulations. We do not create neverending, complex, intergalactic, planning processes. We do not waver and waffle. We are not hesitant and ambivalent. We do not dominate and dictate. We are a healthy family. We love, listen, learn, and lead.

Congregation

One of the most important competencies in small, strong congregations is the capacity to be a congregation together over the long haul. The members see the value and importance of living and sharing together. They cherish the present together. They look long-term at the future to which God invites them. The following factors contribute to their being a congregation, a family living in the grace of God:

- Their spirit of continuity
- Their appreciation of being informal
- Their ability to pass the power

Continuity
Small, strong congregations have a continuity of key leaders and pastor. It is not possible to be a small, strong congregation

and at the same time rotate leaders and change pastoral leadership every three or four years. Just about the time they begin to know and do their work well, they are rotated away. They do not get the satisfaction of fulfilling their objectives richly and fully. After the frustrations of experiencing this a couple of times, they usually decide to decline being part of a leadership team again in this congregation.

Rotating leaders may be helpful in one or two areas of your life and mission together. Some congregations have a nominating team that thinks of possible leaders for the coming year. Many small congregations simply have an informal gathering of the whole congregation. If you have a nominating team, you may want to rotate some of the leadership on that team from one year to the next.

New people on a nominating team contribute much to advancing the leadership of the congregation. Their wisdom and experience bring fresh new ideas as to who could be part of this or that team from the grass roots of the congregation. Their insights and perspective help congregations discover new leaders for the mission. They also help us discover new possibilities for our present and our future.

Likewise, if you have a personnel team, some modest rotation of people may be helpful. This helps encourage the growth of the current pastoral leadership—and whatever other modest staff a congregation may have (possibly a part-time music leader, a part-time custodian, or a part-time secretary).

Years ago, some denominations wanted to give new people a turn and also wanted to prevent the problems created in a church dominated by one "boss." In that effort, they created a structure of rotation. The dilemma is this: people may rotate leadership positions within the formal organizational structure, but in small congregations the *informal* organizational structure tends to prevail. The boss may have rotated off all the formal committees but may still be running the congregation through the informal relational networks of which he or she is the boss.

Rotating is not the solution to a boss-run church. The solution to a boss-run church is a three-step process:

1. Develop and encourage competent leaders.
2. Add new people to the leadership team (you can add people without rotating anyone off).
3. Advance a shared understanding of *congregational leadership*.

We develop competent leaders by encouraging them as they move through the four stages of creating a healthy team. In any project, the stages are:

1. Learn the possibilities for the team and begin to picture accomplishing some of them.
2. Discover the match of strengths the leader brings and the few key objectives to accomplish.
3. Develop and mobilize a team to achieve these few key objectives.
4. Let the leader and team come into their own.

In stage four, the leader and team accomplish and achieve their objectives. They discover sources of satisfaction in having done solid work. They grow and develop as they learn from excellent mistakes along the way. They look forward to continuing and growing in their leadership as a team. If these leaders are rotated off, just as they are coming into their own, neither they nor the congregation receives the full benefits of their growth and achievement. They also do not show much interest in coming back to do it all over again.

Many leadership teams, in our time, may want to achieve a one-time project. They may want to accomplish a seasonal project, or a short-term project. Whether it is a one-time, seasonal, or short-term project, each team goes through the four stages of possibilities, matches, team, and accomplishments. They do so in a short-term, highly intensive manner. Given the opportunity, and having achieved its objectives, the team is glad to tackle another set of objectives.

Although the team does the work in terms of a series of one-time, seasonal, or short-term projects, given time it develops a sense of continuity. Take the team whose focus is with children. They lead a one-time project for children and their families: a field trip to the city zoo. They may lead the seasonal vacation Bible school. They may lead the Christmas children's choir, which has three rehearsals and sings the Sunday before Christmas. Some people will help with one of these projects, some with another, etc. What develops is the continuity of an informal group of people. With a series of projects, over time, they come into their own in helping children and their families.

If we look closely at small, strong congregations, we may find that the formal organizational structure has rotated people on and off. Nevertheless, what is really happening is that an informal grouping of people with competence and compassion are delivering the key objectives of the congregation. They welcome new people to the team. They achieve this project. They accomplish that project. They come into their own. They become the legend.

Likewise, many pastors tend to come into their own as they are given the opportunity for continuity. Frequently (if we assume a healthy match with the congregation), pastors begin their most productive time in their fifth, sixth, or seventh years. There are three reasons. First, the *shepherding* reason: it takes several years to develop the relational networks of sharing, caring, and shepherding that help one be a leader.

The reason the productivity curve soars in years five, six, and seven is that the shepherding curve soars.

Second, there is the *learning* reason. A pastor who stays at a given church for five or six years has made enough mistakes to begin learning from them. It was said of one pastor, "Oh, he's been in the ministry over twenty years." The reply was, "No, he's been in the ministry for four years. He's just done it in five different places."

People who move too frequently tend to simply turn over the barrel of sermons, start again at the top, and work their way to the bottom. They tend to repeat in this church the same things they did in the previous church. If a pastor is with a congregation long enough, he or she makes some mistakes. By learning from them, wisdom and experience increase. *The reason the productivity curve soars in years five, six, and seven is that the learning curve soars.*

Third comes the *leading* reason. It takes some time to move through the steps of loving, listening, and learning to reach the step of leading. It takes some time for the person to develop a sense of confidence and assurance about his or her own leadership with this group of people. It takes some time for this group of people to develop a sense of mutual trust, respect, integrity, confidence, and assurance about this pastor being among their leaders. *The reason the productivity curve soars in years five, six, and seven is that the leading curve soars.*

What I have just said in relation to pastors is equally true for key leaders. It takes time for a key leader to develop the shepherding relational networks. It takes some time for the leader to develop the learning curve. It takes time to develop a sense of leadership. In many congregations where pastors and leaders have shared, lived, and worked for five, six, or seven years, the productivity level is so strong because the shepherding, learning, and leading curves have soared during the first three or four years.

To be sure, if there is clearly not a match of strengths between the person and the post, there is no reason to leave the leader hanging out to dry. Sometimes, in the early stages, a leader or pastor discovers that what he or she has been invited to do does *not* match competencies. With honor and integrity, affirm this and move on to a post that more fully matches one's gifts.

However, if the promise of a match is there, give the leader or pastor time to come into his or her own. This is especially true if:

- The competencies of the person match the objectives of the task
- The person is doing solid work and having fun doing it
- The person is developing a team to help with the work
- The person is growing in the work
- People are being richly helped

Then, leave the person alone in the leadership post. If you want to do something, encourage him or her, and thank the person. Continuity counts in developing a strong, healthy congregation.

Informal

In small, strong congregations, the spirit, the custom, the way of life is primarily informal. This is true whether the congregation is in a rural area, a town, or a major city. It is not that rural congregations are informal and city churches are formal. Some rural churches function in a formal leadership fashion, and by contrast some city churches function in an informal leadership manner. For the most part, small, strong congregations, regardless of where they are, live and lead informally.

It is more a matter of spirit than of size. Living and leading with an informal spirit is not so much a matter of location or size. We simply choose this way to live with one another in this congregation. We choose to live together as a family, not an organization. We choose to be a community, not a collection of committees. We choose to be a congregation, not an institution.

Increasingly, among larger congregations, the spirit and way of life is informal. It is not the case that the larger the church, the more formal its leadership style. Yes, as some churches grow larger, their style of leadership becomes more formal. The organizational structure becomes complex, hierarchical, and rigid. By contrast, notably in our time, as many congregations grow larger, they continue to share their leadership informally, simply, flexibly, with the grass roots.

This spirit of informal and flexible leadership is especially the case in small, strong congregations. One of our advantages is our spirit of a simple, grassroots, natural manner of leadership. Informally, we discuss many decisions with one another as in a large, extended family. We may visit after church, under the large oak tree out front. We discuss some emerging decision. We touch base with one another at the fellowship supper. We have a conversation before or after the bible study. We run into one another at the grocery store or at work. We have lunch together. We talk about it as we watch our kids at the elementary school soccer match.

In the naturally informal spirit of a congregational family, we consider, analyze, and examine the matter under consideration. We weigh the pros and cons. We discuss the advantages and disadvantages. We explore all the options and possibilities we can discover. We think about it, and then we think about it some more. We deal with our second thoughts. We consider our fears and hopes, our anxieties and anticipations.

From the viewpoint of some one who is committed to a formal, organizational, committee structure of making decisions, it looks as if we are gossiping on the grapevine. Their view is that the matter should be discussed primarily in committee meetings. Frequently, they want the discussion and the decision to be limited to the formal structure with which they are comfortable. However, families do not function formally and institutionally.

We arrive at our decision informally.

A developing sense of direction emerges. We have the feeling that the decision we are heading toward is the helpful way forward. We began to picture what we will be and what we will do as we move toward our decision. We visualize the constructive results of our decision.

We reach a point in our thinking and discussions where we say, "Why didn't we think of this before? This is the obvious way forward." Then, we may formalize our decision in some explicit organizational gathering—but even that "formal" gathering has about it the spirit of being informal, simple, grassroots, and flexible.

Small, strong congregations have a streamlined approach to leadership. It does not take them several months to make a simple decision. Nor does it take passing the decision from one committee to the next. In some large congregations, the labyrinth of committees is such that it takes months to make simple decisions. By contrast, in small, strong congregations, many of these simple decisions are delegated to one, two, or three people in the family, people who have wisdom and experience and who make such decisions promptly. We have a high frequency of delegating the simple decisions.

We have a gathering of the whole family for major decisions. We usually have a grassroots annual planning gathering. Everyone is invited. Every person's ideas and suggestions are considered. Our annual planning session looks much like the informal gathering of a family for a reunion. We have a good-fun, good-times gathering. Usually, there is too much to eat. We laugh and share with one another.

We pray and plan. We look one to three years ahead. We gather excellent ideas and good suggestions from everyone. We seek to advance God's mission. We look forward to living together in the grace of God during the coming one to three years. We look at our strengths. We claim our strengths. We decide which one or two to expand. We decide which new strength to add. We discover a few key objectives that advance our mission.

We do not always agree on everything. There are differences of opinion. There are times of conflict. Sometimes, the conflict has to do with priorities; sometimes it has to do with process; sometimes it has to do with power. Sometimes the conflict has to do with a feeling that we are not yet certain that a proposed direction is the best way forward.

We share a healthy spirit and high capacity for mutual trust, respect, and reconciliation. We know, with honor, that from time to time we who dearly love one another will disagree. We find ways, informally, to move forward. We share a healthy track record of conflict resolution. There is little conflict repression, conflict domination, or conflict avoidance. What counts is advancing the mission of God, sharing the grace of God, the compassion of Christ, and the community of the Holy Spirit in ways that help people live whole, healthy, hopeful lives.

Pass the Power

Small, strong congregations pass the power well. They have learned the capacity to pass the power. A congregation that has been in existence for 120 years has had several opportunities to pass the power to the next generation of leaders. They have learned, usually through fits and starts, and excellent

mistakes, how to do it well. If they had not learned how to
pass the power, they would no longer exist.

A congregation that has been in existence for twenty to
twenty-five years is learning how to pass the power for the
first time. Sometimes, they pass the power with generosity
and graciousness. The new generation helps the congregation
move forward.

Sometimes, the group with the power only reluctantly
and begrudgingly passes it on. They learned somewhere to
hold on to power. They try to convince themselves that the
younger generation (who may be in their forties and fifties)
are not yet "ready for it." Frequently, the people in that
younger generation are their own children. If the older generation reluctantly shares power, the congregation is heading
toward becoming a weak and declining congregation—or a
dying one.

A given congregation may have a group of people who
are in their sixties and seventies. They may have another
group of people in their twenties and thirties. However, there
is a gap; the people in their forties and fifties are missing. Frequently, they are missing because the older generation did
not pass the power to the next generation.

Sometimes, what has happened is that the older group,
when they were in their forties and fifties, seized power. For
whatever reasons, the power was not passed to them, but
they were able to seize it. Because they worked so hard to
seize the power themselves, they hold on to it. They actually
recapitulate what their older generation did to them. They
keep the power. They fail to pass it on. The result is that the
next generation vanishes.

In our congregation, we find home. We include everyone.
We share power. We help one another. We affirm a diversity
of gifts. As we share and pass the power, we grow forward our

distinctive strengths and gifts. We find that some people have gifts of mission, some compassion, some community, some hope, some leadership, and some generosity; many have gifts other than these. God's grace blesses us.

We discover that one of the qualities present in our congregation is our gift for living and sharing together as team, leaders, and congregation. We share the quality of leadership well. With compassion, continuity, and competency, we are a small, strong congregation. We will be healthy for years to come.

As the epigraph for this chapter tells us, Albert Einstein was wise about imagination being more important than knowledge. Harriet's gardener is doing well. His small congregation is doing well. He did not know enough to know what he did not know. He did not know enough to know what he could not do. With imagination and creativity, he has followed the clues he discovered in the scriptures, and in Harriet's bible study.

With the help of two friends and the grace of God, he began a small congregation. The congregation is strong and healthy. It has a gift for living and sharing together as a team, as leaders, and as a congregation. Naturally and informally, they think, act, practice, and live these three interactive dynamics. Countless thousand of congregations around the world have discovered this grassroots way of living and being a small, strong congregation together. Countless thousands more are discovering this way forward.

8

Space and Facilities

A bigger house does not make a better one. People do.
Joyce and Bob are generous. They opened their home
to their small, strong congregation. It is not a large group, but
it filled their house. The service together was amazing. Sally
led the singing and it was wonderful; it stirred our souls.
Andy led the time of sharing and praying, and we were
greatly helped. Jim shared the sermon; it made sense and
gave us handles for the week to come. Carol gave the blessing, and we left in peace.

During our time together, the spirit of compassion and the
sense of community were remarkable. We sensed the stirring,
moving, living presence of the grace of God in our midst. In
that gathering for worship, we were grateful to be alive, to be
together, and to share in the worship of God. We discovered a
sense of help, hope, and home. The congregation is thriving.
The mission it shares in the community moves forward in
ever-increasing ways.

The small, strong congregation that Sam leads meets in
his apartment. He has an L-shaped living and dining room.

Some people gather in the living room area; others gather in the dining room area. The people who lead the service of worship stand in the one corner so that everyone can see them. Mostly, the people who come are in their twenties and thirties. There is much fellowship before and after the service. There is singing and praying, a sermon and blessing. People's lives are helped.

Roberta leads a small, strong congregation that meets in the office building where she works. She has worked in the building for a number of years. She knows many of the people who work there. The building has a reasonably large atrium area, and on Sunday mornings the congregation gathers there to worship God, share fellowship, and encourage each other for mission. Some of the people who work in the building and the two office buildings on either side have been drawn to stop in on Sunday morning and join the service of worship.

The small, strong congregation of which Richard is the leader meets in the community center. It is among the major gathering places for the whole community. The congregation began in the small meeting room. As they grew, they moved to one of the larger rooms. The community center also includes two basketball courts, a swimming pool, tennis courts, and a baseball diamond. It is the focal point of many people's lives, and every week more of these people find their way to the congregation.

Tom is the leader of a small, strong congregation that meets in the auditorium of the local high school. Their first plan was to meet in an auditorium at one of the elementary schools. However, they wanted to be a small, strong congregation serving at least three elementary schools. They realized that if they met at one school, they would be likely to serve only the families of children attending that one. By meeting in the high school auditorium, they are able to serve more fully the families of children in the three elementary schools, the junior high school, and the high school. Their services have drawn a number of people for whom education and the schools are central in their lives.

The strong, small congregation of which Merle is the leader meets in a local business facility. On Sunday mornings, the congregation gathers for singing, sharing and prayer, the sermon, and the blessing. It's amazing to Merle the range of people who attend. Some of the people who come are vendors and customers of the business. The owners of the business have also found their way to the congregation.

Around the planet, an amazing number of congregations meet in homes, apartments, office atriums and lobbies, community centers, schools, local business facilities, warehouses, or wherever they feel drawn to share the grace of God. In the course of the two thousand years of the Christian movement, congregations have been extraordinarily creative in discovering space and facilities to serve God's mission.

Adequate for Their Mission

Small, strong congregations are healthy and vital because their facilities are:

- Adequate for their mission
- Both sacred and shared
- A blessing, not a burden

These principles inform their mission and their mortar. They think, act, practice, and live their mission, with just enough facilities to serve their mission.

One of the most important strengths of small, strong congregations is that they have space and facilities adequate for their mission. These congregations focus on delivering mission, compassion, community, self-reliance, hope, leaders, and generosity. They discover the mission to which God is inviting them. Then, they discover *just enough* of a facility to assist in the mission. Mortar follows mission, not the reverse. The blueprint for mission determines the blueprint for meeting.

Small, strong congregations do not have lots of programs and activities. They do not have a multiplicity of staff and therefore the need for offices. They may or may not have open accessibility or high visibility. They do not have acres of land. Their parking may be barely adequate. They do not have large facilities.

A house does not make a home; people do. A building does not make a congregation; people do. The search is for roots, place, and belonging; the search is not for walls, windows, and doors. The house is not the mission. Can a family be a family without owning a house? Many families are warm, caring, healthy families without owning a house.

Can a congregation be a congregation without owning a building? Some think that if they don't have their own building they are not really a congregation. *The truth is that when they discover their own mission, they are a congregation.* They may or may not own their building. Sometimes, house owners want to be church-building owners. They own their houses; thus, they think it is naturally the case that they should own their church building. However, people who own their houses discover that there is more to being a family than owning a house.

A few years ago, I was working with a new congregation. They were interested in the steps that would help them become a strong, healthy congregation. I suggested four steps to them: mission, team, future, service.

1. Mission: discovering the people with whom
   God is inviting you to be in mission

2. Team: developing the mission team of leaders, congregation, volunteer staff, and pastoral leadership, whether lay reader or lay or ordained pastor (volunteer, part-time, or full-time)

3. Future: building your future blueprint for mission, compassion, community, self-reliance, hope, leadership, and generosity

4. Service: helping, richly and fully, the community that God gives you for mission

"As you bring about these four steps," I said, "you will grow a strong, healthy congregation. People will find help, hope, and home with you. They will look forward to sharing in your mission. They will want to contribute their own strengths and competencies to the mission."

Someone in the group asked, "But, Dr. Callahan, where will we meet?"

I said, "First, we discover our mission. Once we know where we are heading in our mission, God will lead us to a place to meet that matches with our mission. First, we think through and pray through who God is giving us to serve in mission."

I went on to share with them that it is not that we find a place to meet and then let that meeting place determine our mission. The regrettable result would be that the meeting place would shape the mission; we would decide on a mission that would be convenient to the meeting place. Rather, we discover our mission and the strengths and competencies God gives us; then, we look for a place to meet. We decide on a meeting place that is convenient to our mission. Our mission shapes where we meet.

In the few years since I helped them, they have grown forward an extraordinary mission in the community. They have discovered that new people look forward to being part of their mission. They have found that who they help is more important than where they meet. Moreover, they have been able to focus their competencies, their volunteer time, and their generosity on their mission, not on a building.

Now, I honor the fact that, years ago, I contributed much time and energy to what I affectionately call "the big bucks" approach to starting new congregations. That approach has four steps: land, minister, members, building.

1. Land: buy land, hopefully an excellent location for a reasonable price.

2. Minister: find a full-time, ordained minister who knows how to start a new church, and, with help from the denomination, support his or her salary for the coming five years.

3. Members: recruit members to this new congregation.

4. Building: build the building, or at least build the first unit of what might be a three- or four-stage building program.

The underlying assumption is that once we achieve the land, the minister, the members, and the building, then we can figure out more fully what we need to do as our mission. Unfortunately, with this approach the mission sometimes becomes getting the land, finding the minister, recruiting the new members, and building the next new building.

On the one hand, I want to confirm that this way of beginning new congregations "works." Land is bought. A competent pastor is found. We recruit new members. We build stage one, stage two, and stage three of our master plan for our buildings. We sponsor many programs and activities for our members. On the other hand, I want to confirm that these four steps seem preoccupied with "us." The preoccupation seems to be church growth rather than mission growth.

I have helped a number of congregations at about the time of their twenty-fifth to thirtieth anniversaries of starting as a new church. They were begun with the four steps of land, minister, members, building. With one congregation, I was there to help them at the time when they were celebrating twenty-five years as a congregation.

Over that quarter of a century, they secured land, had three different ministers, recruited about six hundred members, and completed their three-stage building master plan. They finished building the buildings. These steps were all complete. Everything on the land now looked exactly like the architect's master plan, created twenty-five years before. That drawing hung in the entryway for the whole of the twenty-five years. Ministers and leaders pointed to it. It was a source of pride and accomplishment.

However, as they neared their twenty-fifth anniversary, they slowly began to realize that now they had a real identity crisis: "Our identity has been in completing our buildings. What do we do now? What is our new goal?" For twenty-five years, their focus was on finishing their master plan. They labored long and hard. They achieved all the planned physical facilities.

Intuitively, they knew they needed to discover a new sense of direction, a new understanding of their identity as a congregation. They contacted me and asked me to come and help them. We shared a remarkable time together. They are a congregation with many gifts, strengths, and competencies. I helped them discover four steps: mission, team, future, service. They are thriving with their newfound blueprint for mission. For them, this is their new master plan. Their spirit is: "This is the mission to which God is inviting us."

There is nothing in the New Testament that suggests the first priorities should be buying land and constructing buildings. The first priorities have to do with people, not plants; mission, not mortar; service, not steeples. In Matthew 26:19 (KJV), Jesus invites the disciples to "go, therefore, and teach all nations. . . ." He invites the disciples to go and share the Gospel, not go and build a building. Jesus invites them to go, teach, encourage, and develop new disciples.

When John the Baptist hears that his head is now in Herod's wife's hands, he sends two of his disciples to Jesus to ask, "Are you the one who is to come, or are we to expect some other?" Jesus answers, "Go and tell John what you have seen and heard: how the blind recover their sight, the lame walk, the lepers are made clean, the deaf hear, the dead are raised to life, the poor are hearing the good news . . ." Luke 7:20–22 (NEB).

Jesus does not say, "Go and tell John that committees are meeting, land is being bought, pastors are being hired, members are being sought, architects are being consulted, money is being raised, buildings are being built."

Jesus describes the mission: concrete, effective help is being delivered to specific human hurts, now.

In Matthew 25:34–36 (RSV), we discover these words: "Come, O blessed of my Father, inherit the kingdom prepared for you from the foundation of the world; for I was hungered and you gave me food, I was thirsty and you gave me drink, I was a stranger and you welcomed me, I was naked and you clothed me, I was sick and you visited me, I was in prison and you came to me."

The text suggests that God's passion is that we help people with specific human hurts and hopes—that we deliver concrete, effective help, and live a life of mission.

We learn as much by what the New Testament does not say as by what it does say. The text focuses on mission with people. There is nothing in the text that suggests "For I was hungered, and you bought a piece of land, I was thirsty and you hired a pastor, I was a stranger, and you held a committee meeting, I was naked and you sought out an architect, I was sick and you raised money, I was in prison and you built a building."

Land, minister, members, and buildings have their appropriate and relative place in the order of priorities. Some try to make a feeble case that the land, minister, members, and buildings are necessary before we can do the mission. The difficulty is that by the time the land is bought, the minister hired, the members acquired, and the buildings built, amnesia has set in and we have forgotten why we did all of this in the first place.

The first priority of your congregation is to discover the mission to which God is inviting you. The central question is *"Who is our mission?"* Who are the people who are our mission is the key question, not where is our land. Who is our mission team is the significant question, not who is the minister who will build this church for us. What is our blueprint for mission? What is our blueprint for compassion, community, self-reliance, hope, team, and generosity? The question is not how we recruit members to give us money to pay for the land, the pastor, and buildings he or she will help us acquire.

Years ago, a wonderful colleague and I taught a course together entitled Planting New Churches. It was an excellent course. We had a wonderful time together. We encouraged the students toward mission growth. We invited them to discover the blueprint for mission to which God was inviting them. We helped them focus on mission more than mortar.

Many of the students have gone out and planted more than one new church. However, in the time come and gone, I have reflected on the title for the course. Our focus was on mission, but the title, Planting New Churches, regrettably had a connotation that suggested a focus on a place and a building. These days when I teach seminars on beginning new congregations, I use the title Beginning a New Congregation. Sometimes, I use the title Developing a New Congregation, or Starting a New Mission. The focus is on people and on mission.

Some new congregations are too eager to build a building. In our time, it only works in baseball, and it only works in Iowa when the voice says, "Build the stadium and they will come." *Field of Dreams* was a wonderful movie, but that concept does not work for churches today. Buildings do not draw in our time. If people want to see a beautiful building, there are lots of them around.

Remember the little game and the words and hand motions that went with it?

Here is the church,

and here is the steeple.

Open the doors

and see all the people.

The focus of the poem is on the building, and on the people *inside* the church.

In our time, I would use this phrasing and gestures that fit:

Here is the love,

and here are the people.

Open your hearts

and serve all the people.

Sometimes, we are drawn to large, grandiose spaces. We look at high mountains and tall buildings. We go on vacation to see them. We stand in awe of their grandeur, bigness, and splendor. Sometimes we prefer small, intimate spaces. Sometimes we prefer one; sometimes we prefer the other, depending on the occasion. There is value and room for both in our lives.

Increasingly, given the bigness around us, we are drawn to family spaces and places, to the kind of place where we feel at home. We know that a house is not a home. A home is where we feel like family and share in the grace of God.

Around the earth, many congregations meet in brush arbors, near wells, or at village circles. Many meet in apartments or homes. Many gather in office buildings, warehouses, or local business facilities. Countless congregations meet in schools and civic and community centers. Some meet in their own building. They are family. They share in the grace of God.

These are the seven primary possibilities for a congregation to find a place to worship. There are four possible arrangements it can have in relation to those spaces: volunteer, rental, lease, or own. There are, then, twenty-eight possibilities for congregations to creatively and flexibly discover a place where they can share in worship and in service.

Many times people volunteer their apartment, home, or local business facility as a meeting place. There are also civic and community groups that offer the use of space in their buildings for a small congregation. The first step is to explore what facilities can provide a volunteer arrangement where use of the space can work well for your congregation.

You may want to rent space. Sometimes, this is the appropriate, helpful way forward. You may decide to move to lease. This can ensure that you will have the space for some period of time to come. You may then want to own your own land and your own building.

One of the churches with whom I have worked met for fifteen years in a local junior high school before they even considered buying a piece of land and building a small building. Their focus was on their mission and their service in the

Space Possibilities for Congregations

	VOLUNTEER	RENTAL	LEASE	OWN
Brush arbors, wells, and village circles				
Apartments				
Homes				
Offices, warehouses, local businesses				
Schools				
Civic and community spaces				
Traditional church buildings				

community. Across the planet, many congregations use volunteer, rental, or leased space.

We know a house does not create a family in closeness, generosity, bonding, and love. Some families own a house and do not have a home. They are not really a family in that house. They imagine that if they get a bigger house they will become a better family. They simply end up with a bigger house. Many families do well as family without owning a house. The spirit of the family counts, not the size of the house.

All sorts of successful groups meet in space they do not own. The space is donated, or they rent it or lease it. Service clubs have this practice. Quilting groups, Boy and Girl Scouts, Campfire, community music groups, AA and Al Anon—lots of long-term, continuing organizations find this plan for meeting space totally satisfactory. The group's focus is on the purpose to which they feel called, rather than finding a place they can own.

People in castles build cathedrals. People who own their own house sometimes want to own their church building; it is an extension of their values. The key point, as we begin the twenty-first century, is this: *people who own a mission build a congregation.* A group of people is a congregation because it owns a mission, not because it owns a building.

Sacred and Shared

In small, strong congregations, we live sacred, shared lives together. The grace of God makes our lives sacred. It is not of our own doing. It is the gift of God. We are born, blessed, and made new by the grace of God. We live holy lives because we are surrounded by the holiness of God. Our lives are sacramental as a gift of God. We are grateful and amazed to discover the sense of the sacred in our lives.

We live shared lives together. We do not live in isolation. We do not live apart from one another. We sense we are meant to live together as God's family. We share everyday life. We celebrate good times. We are with one another in tough, tight times.

We do the same with our spaces. A sacred space is a shared space. A shared space is a sacred space. Our spaces reflect the way we live our lives. We value the sacred, shared quality of our life together. We know that living a sacred life, with humility and gratefulness, is more helpful than visiting a sacred building. The *building* stays put. It does not move with us. We cannot carry it with us. Yes, we can remember the sacred feeling we had when we were in the building, but the building does not go with us. It stays put where it is.

Significantly, we can remember, we can realize now, this moment, the presence of God's sacred grace with us. Which is more helpful: to remember the feeling of sacredness we had when we were in a building, or to experience *now* the sacred grace of God? We live, move, and have being; we are surrounded, uplifted, supported, and helped, wherever we are, by the grace of God.

The grace of God makes a space sacred. The source of its holiness is the grace of God. God is sacred and holy, and it is the presence of God that causes a space to have the sense of the scared. Nothing inherent in a space makes it sacred. A space is a space. A space by itself is not sacred.

A building by itself can do nothing. It is like a ship sitting dead in the water. It is lifeless. It cannot sail itself. It wobbles back and forth, the victim of the waves and currents. It takes the wind of grace, the crew of compassion, the course of mission to stir the idle ship. With these forces, the ship then becomes a moving, breathing, living thing that races across the water to the future that God is promising and preparing.

Do we have a need for sacred spaces? Yes. They remind us of the grace of God. Do we have an even deeper need to live a sacred life? Yes, yes, yes! A sacred life is a richer, fuller sign of the grace of God. Sometimes, a sacred space can point us toward a sacred life, and sometimes it can distract us. It is true that—sometimes—a little bit of something can immunize us from the real thing.

A place of worship is sacred not because it is a certain shape or size. It is sacred because the congregation senses the moving, living, stirring grace of God. The building, in itself, is like the idle ship. It takes the wind of God's grace, the crew of compassion, and the course of mission to stir an idle ship. *God's grace* makes a place sacred.

The art is to sense the sacred in our lives, not our buildings. We sense the stirring presence of God's grace in our lives, and we experience the sacred and the holy in our lives. It is not that we build a space and then *we* make it holy. In ancient times, unexpected places and spaces became sacred because God's presence was overwhelmingly there; *for that reason*, the place was holy. It is the same in our time.

All the architects, building committees, and dedications we can think of cannot make a space holy. A space becomes holy not from anything we do; it is the gift of God. A space is sacred when it is filled with the grace of God; it is holy when it is filled with the compassion of Christ; it is hallowed when it is filled with the hope of the Holy Spirit. A space is blessed when it is filled with the mission God sends to us.

In living day-to-day life, we have those places and spaces that, for us, are sacred. The kitchen may be a gathering place for our family, a friendly, compassionate place, full of love, sharing, and hope. The picnic table in the backyard, or in a nearby park, where many happy family celebrations have taken place, may be sacred. The sacred, special place for some may be by a lake, where a marriage proposal was shared; she accepted; and the long years of a rich, full life for your family began.

For some, a sacred place is a cabin on a lake, or a farmhouse in the country—the gathering place of good fun for the whole family. A sacred place may be a school where as children we discovered our gifts and talents, where we were filled with hope for a full, successful opportunity to use them throughout a good life. We go back, drive by, and remember the promise that the school gave for our lives. The school may be the one where our children discovered the same hope and promise.

We share our lives. We share our spaces. Small, strong congregations do both. These days I think of it this way. A sacred space is a shared space. Indeed, the act of sharing a space helps to make it sacred. We share our lives in a sacramental spirit. We share our spaces with this same spirit. What is shared is sacred; what is sacred is shared. We share because God first shared with us.

A few people say, "The parlor is sacred; it's off-limits!" What they really mean is that the parlor is off-limits and *not* sacred. By definition, spaces that are not shared are not sacred. Small, strong congregations know this truth well. We are most creative in sharing what few spaces we have.

In small, strong congregations, we have just enough square feet to advance the mission and, as family, share the use of what space we have. In a large church, there may be a separate parlor, library, bride's room, and classroom. Each has a designated, single purpose or use. In a small, strong congregation, one room may serve all these purposes.

In one church, there was a parlor with one key. The president of the women's group had the key. There was a desire among the women in the group to have a space they could call their own. Thus, only the women used the parlor. Their children grew.

Time passed.

Grandchildren came along.

When you go to that church today, in one end of the parlor the formal furniture remains in a nice, methodical arrangement. At the other end of the parlor, there is a rocking chair, a crib, a playpen, and an area for toys, which are sometimes scattered and sometimes put up. Now the women share the space with their grandchildren, and they teach me that the room has become much more special because of this sharing.

In many small, strong congregations, we have a large gathering room that serves as a place for fellowship and meals together. We use it as a classroom and a meeting space. Our children, young people, and adults use the space to share together in a wide range of gatherings. Vacation Bible school benefits from the use of the space. It is a work area for volunteers. It is the location for our fun, yet exhausting, October bazaar. It is the place where we do the quilt show. People come from miles around for our spring quilt show. Each year the quilts seem to become more beautiful and awe inspiring.

Our large gathering room is one of the key places where we share in bible study. Each week, there are bible studies to help our congregation grow in the Christian life. Teachers share in training here. Wonderful, joyous wedding receptions are held here. Creative teams do their planning here. After funerals, families gather here for fellowship, food, and encouragement. Community groups benefit from the space. It serves a multiplicity of activities and purposes across the years. There are no distinctive, separate spaces for each of these purposes.

We have the same spirit with all of our spaces. The more people who can benefit from them, the stronger we are as a congregational family. Although we have only a few rooms, the wonderful result of our shared use of space is that our rooms do not stand empty most of the week. We use our space twenty to forty hours a week, and sometimes more. In some large, regional congregations, the spaces that have been built are so specialized—so "single usage"—that they get minimal use during the week.

Small, strong congregations know how, generously and efficiently, to share space. The space they have is well planned and well kept. The facility is well done. It offers a sense of warmth, welcome, and invitation. The space feels inclusive, rather than closed and exclusive. The facility has about it the spirit of family and community.

The facilities are clean, not cluttered. A good friend of mine, Merrill Douglass, once said, "Clutter expands to fill the space available." I have been in church buildings where they have built more and more rooms. They have only created more and more clutter. The purpose of a church building is not to store stuff. Frequently, no one can remember how we got it, where we got it, or what its current purpose is.

Small, strong congregations do not have a lot of space. The purpose of what little space we have is to serve people, not store stuff. At least once every ten years, it helps for a team of people to go through the space. We discover the things we have not used, touched, or even seen over the last decade.

We keep those things that are precious family memorials for the congregation. We give the rest away to someone who can use it. I grant that this is difficult for some of us. We have this same dilemma at home. Somehow, we are able to move forward. There is no point in the stuff sitting, unused, untouched, and unseen for another decade. We want to use our space to help people, not to be storage closets for stuff.

Well-kept facilities send a message of life, energy, vitality, and hope. The message is that "our congregation is strong and healthy." Faded facilities teach a faded, withering, declining church. The message is, "Our best days have been."

I helped a congregation that owned its building. However, they had not cared for the building for many years. Nothing had been done to maintain it, inside or out. It had become one of those faded buildings that we drive by every day of the week, never notice, and could not remember where it is located if we were asked.

When I was there, it was clear to all of us that this small congregation did not really have the money to make repairs and paint the whole building. Wisely, what little money they did have was being invested in their mission. Sometimes, you grow forward where you can grow forward.

I discovered Dave, whose hobby is gardening. He has a friend, Richard, who enjoys gardening as well. I suggested to them that one of the best gifts they could share with the congregation would be to plant a patch of flowers somewhere in front of the building. I mentioned to them that as people drive by, their eyes will be drawn to the beauty of the flowers and not to the faded, declining building.

Dave and Richard planted three patches of flowers, one at each front corner and one in the front center. The road made a slight curve in front of the church so they matched the plantings to the longest line-of-sight visibility. They placed one patch so that it was highly visible on the "going to work" side of the road. People could see it as they drove to work. They placed one patch so that it was highly visible on the going-home side of the road. People could see it as they drove home.

The flowers blossomed.

The congregation became visible for the simple planting of three patches of flowers. Some people began to say, "Where did that church come from? I didn't know it was there." Some people could now give directions to the church: "Oh, that's the church with the flowers." The three patches of flowers became signs of hope for the congregation.

A couple of people in the community looked up Dave and Richard. They too were interested in gardening and wanted to know how Dave and Richard had been able to achieve the exceptional health and beauty of the particular flowers. These inquiries led to new friendships and common interests. Dave and Richard shared a one-time community event for interested gardeners. A new sense of worth and value, vitality and hope came to the church.

Sometimes, when we are limited in what we can do, we do what we can. We can ensure that the exterior of our space and facilities is warm, welcoming, and inviting. This may mean new signage out front that is inviting, constructive, and helpful. Sometimes it means new flowers. Sometimes it means improving and advancing the landscaping by pruning the bushes or trimming the trees. If nothing else, it may mean that the entryways are well kept. It may mean that our main space of gathering is well done. A space that is well done and well kept communicates the spirit of being strong and alive. It invites people to discover and share God's grace in this place.

Shared space is sacred space. Sacred space is shared space. The sharing of space is a sacred act. Space that is not shared is not sacred; it is selfish. We are a small congregation. We cannot afford to have single-use, unshared space. We do not have the resources to build, maintain, and repair a collection of single-use, unshared spaces. We do not plan to have so busy a collection of bustling programs and activities held so frequently to warrant such spaces.

Most important, we do not want single-use, unshared spaces even if we can afford them. We are wise enough to know that single-use, unshared spaces regrettably push a tendency toward compartmentalization and fragmentation, thereby undermining the family and community spirit that is central to the strengths of our small, strong congregation. Sacred and shared space draws us to together as God's family.

Blessing, Not Burden

One of the important strengths of small, strong congregations is that their facility, whether it is volunteer, rental, lease, or owned, is a blessing, not a burden. Too many facilities can be a burden. We become preoccupied with trying to get people to come to our building rather than taking the mission to them. We spend too much of our time cleaning them, maintaining them, and repairing them. We become concerned with filling the building rather than filling people's lives.

Too much debt can be an even more difficult burden. We are always making our decisions based on "How can we pay off the debt?" Mostly, we are asking people who did not participate in the decisions to acquire the debt to help us pay it off. Facilities in poor condition can be a burden. They teach us (as well as the people in the community) that we are a fading, declining church.

I was helping one congregation that was a wonderful group of people. We were praying and puzzling about the future of their small congregation. They owned three buildings. Their sanctuary and worship center was built sometime in the 1860s; their social and fellowship hall was built sometime in the 1870s; and their modest one-floor education building was built sometime in the 1880s.

Not one drop of new paint had been applied to those three modest buildings since about 1925. The Great Depression came. They could not afford to fix them up. Then, World War II quickly followed. Many of the men went off to service. Times were lean. They put everything into winning the war. Years went by. The condition of the buildings worsened. Their depression over the state of the buildings deepened. The expenses to fix them up soared. They postponed action.

I was there around 1985. They called and said, "We would really appreciate your help in discovering our mission. We also need your wisdom in deciding what it makes sense to do about our buildings. The outside of them creates a poor impression. When people come inside, they're even more turned off by their condition."

This is a wonderful group of people. We had a grand time together. We put considerable thought into their mission and their buildings. I discovered that one of the people in the congregation is an interior designer. She and I spent two or three hours together looking carefully at the facilities. Then, we spent two hours with the key leaders of the congregation. Together, we put in place a seven-year, preventive-maintenance, ongoing restoration and major-emergency repair plan.

In year one, the narthex of the worship center and the vestibule of the social hall were repaired and updated. It was a low-dollar investment. Now, the entryways looked fresh and new. We achieved two highly visible quick wins. The first impression was warm and welcoming.

In year two, one corner room in the education building was made into a nursery. Another corner room, where lots of the gatherings were held, was redone. It's a principle I call "cornering the building." People say, "This corner looks really nice and this corner looks really nice, but now everything in between looks a whole lot worse!" It builds the momentum and the money for years three, four, and five.

Year seven brought us to the climax: updating and refurbishing the sanctuary, so that it would look like a warm, welcoming, and inviting space. What did we do in year eight? Start over!

The art with buildings is to *show something new each year.* I pointed out that even if we had the money to fix everything up all at once, we would not do so. I said to them, "You could fix everything up now, and it would look really nice for a year or two. However, then you would face twenty years of fading and declining until you have to conduct another capital campaign, and the whole thing would start again."

The reason for meeting with the interior designer and the key leaders was to put in place a seven-year, ongoing restoration plan. We created an integrated design where the colors and textures went well together. In year eight, we could change our theme, if we chose: add new colors and so on, but during the following years everything we did would enhance the things already done and still to be done.

For some congregations, the buildings have become a burden. Sometimes, they have too many buildings for the mission they are now sharing. For whatever reasons, over the years they "added on." They built one addition after another. In an earlier time, many congregations had a few very creative, shared, multiple-use spaces that were used frequently during the course of a week.

In more recent times, congregations began to build single-use spaces. Instead of one space serving four functions, they now had four separate, single-use spaces. The catch was that sometimes the four together were less used during the week than the one had been. Further, these single-use spaces caused fragmentation in the congregation.

Moreover, as time passed, they found themselves spending more time and more money on cleaning, maintaining, and repairing the spaces than made good sense. The solution then may be to match the mortar to the mission, by selling the buildings that have become a burden and developing new space to match their current mission.

Some people move into a large house, excited and enthusiastic with all the vast space they now have. But after living there awhile, they discover they are really using only a few rooms in the house. They simply have found they do not need all the space they thought they did. They prefer not to spend their time cleaning space they do not really use. They move to a smaller house.

Some people, as their life circumstances change, move to a smaller house. Their children may be grown and gone, or the activities they now do require less space. They decide to move from the old homestead that has been home for years. It is too big. It is now too hard to keep up. Thus they move to a space that matches who they are now.

Some congregations, as their life circumstances change, move to a smaller house. In the heyday of the churched culture of the 1940s and 1950s, some congregations got caught up with the enthusiasm of the times and the building booms all around. Everyone was building. They decided to build too. They overbuilt. They built too many single-use spaces. Even back then, if they had practiced more fully the principle of shared space, they would have found they had more space then they needed.

It is difficult to leave a church building that we have had for many years. It is even more difficult to leave a house in which we have lived for many years. People do. Now, I am not suggesting you do so. Your building is a blessing, not a burden, when these key principles are central with respect to your space and facilities:

- The focus of our congregation is on the mission.
- We have just enough facilities, but not too many.
- We sense the sacred in our lives more than in our building.
- We practice shared, multiple use of our facilities.
- Our facilities help our mission, not hinder it.
- We develop the wisdom and generosity of enduring gifts.

With respect to the last principle on the list, I encourage you to develop generous enduring gifts. These enduring gifts will free up your giving to the annual budget to focus on advancing your mission.

Enduring gifts are helpful for all small, strong congregations. I encourage congregations to identify five to eight projects that have enduring value. Congregations that own a building are wise to have, as one of their five to eight projects, an enduring gift endowment of their building. Congregations that use rental or leased space can include this specific enduring gift project to assist with rental or lease expenses.

For congregations owning a building, one of our important enduring gift projects is to endow the building. That is, we have an enduring gift fund that covers the expenses for our preventive maintenance, ongoing restoration, and major emergency repairs of our building. This frees our annual giving to focus on our mission and our staffing to serve people in their lives and destinies.

This means, among other things, that we no longer use our annual budget to maintain our building. Yes, the annual budget sweeps the floors, washes the windows, and mows the lawn. That is, our annual budget does routine cleaning, but it does not try to paint the walls and fix the roof.

In forty-plus years of ministry and helping the thousands of congregations with whom I have shared, I have never yet found a single one whose annual budget can cover the long-term costs of a building. If the annual budget tries to cover preventive maintenance, ongoing restoration, and major emergency repairs, the congregation may cover these areas but it does so at the expense of the mission and staffing parts of the annual budget. Essentially, neither the mission nor the building is well covered. The consequence is that *both the mission and the building suffer.*

In the chapter on enduring gifts in *Effective Church Finances,* I offer a full discussion of how congregations successfully go about developing enduring gift endowments. For our purposes here, I want to affirm that enduring gifts focus on more than buildings. I help many congregations develop endowment funds that, above and beyond their yearly budget funds, help to advance the congregation's mission.

These enduring gifts advance the congregation's mission with children, with young people, with senior adults, with worship and music, with the poor in their community and across the world, and with those who benefit from the shepherding of the congregation. These enduring gifts also fund the ongoing care for the buildings. I commend to you the chapter that I have just mentioned. You will find that people are perfectly willing to give you enduring gifts.

An important question people have in this life is, "What endures; what lasts?" "What is lasting, what is enduring?" People want some of their giving to endure and last. They want their generosity to continue in enduring, lasting ways. Therefore, I encourage congregations to develop, among their several enduring gift projects, one that delivers sufficient funding to cover the preventive maintenance, ongoing restoration, and major emergency repairs for their building.

Preventive maintenance is less expensive and more effective. Deferred maintenance is more expensive and less effective. Ongoing restoration is central in most congregations. The older the building, the more important it is to show something new each year. What I would not do is wait until the paint is virtually falling off the walls and then try to do a hurried cover-up paint job. Both the disrepair and the hurried repair communicate the wrong message. If your congregation has five rooms, I encourage you to paint one each year. If you have eight rooms, you might paint two a year. Something will look new each year.

Major emergency repairs are needed. Doing the first two tasks—preventive maintenance and ongoing restoration—lessens the need for this one, but it still happens. A large tree fell on the roof of one church building. They were immediately involved in a major emergency repair job. Some things such as this are simply going to happen.

The way to puzzle through enduring gift endowments for your facilities is to take the value of your facilities, not counting the value of your land. Find 3 percent of that value. For example, if the value of your facility is $200,000, then 3 percent is $6,000.

Principle of $100,000 or so can yield annual interest of about $6,000. What we want, therefore, is enduring gifts of $100,000 in place. This covers much of the preventive maintenance, ongoing restoration, and major emergency repairs that come along. The principle is never touched. If you invade the principle, for whatever emergency reason, it just costs you the loss of future enduring gifts. People give to causes where they are assured that the principle is left intact.

Now, with the enduring gift endowment for the building in place, your congregation is free to focus the generosity of your annual giving on your mission and staffing, your outreach and service in the community. The building is not a burden. In terms of the annual budget, it is off line and cared for by the enduring gift endowment.

Small, strong congregations have sufficient space and facilities for their mission. They have almost enough space to be helpful, but not so much space that the space becomes harmful and detracts from the mission. They know that a bigger house does not make a better home; people do.

Their space and these facilities have about them a sense of being both sacred and shared. They serve as a blessing to the congregation, not a burden. They focus on building their mission, their spirit of compassion, their sense of community, their self-reliance, their confidence in hope, their leader team, and the generosity of their giving.

There is a time for tents. There is a time for temples. This is the time for tents. There is a time for community. There is a time for castles. This is the time for community. There is a time for congregations. There is a time for cathedrals. This is the time for congregations. There is a time for homes. There is a time for houses. This is the time for homes. This is the time for hope.

Small, strong congregations remember that Jesus was born in a manger, not a mansion, in a cowshed, not a cathedral; and that Christ came to a stable of simplicity and grace. The message of the Christmas narrative is not that there was no room in the inn; the message is that the grace of God enables us to do well with whatever space can be found. The message is that in nontraditional ways, space was found where Jesus could be born.

In the days and years to come, God invites us to focus on the grace of God, the compassion of Christ, and the hope of the Holy Spirit. God invites us to find sufficient space with simplicity and grace, so that Jesus can be born anew in the hearts and minds of the people we serve in mission.

Small, strong congregations have a passion for a mission, not a mansion. They focus on the family more than the facility. They focus on living sacred lives more than on building sacred spaces. Small, strong congregations have a people-centered, person-centered, grace-centered understanding of the mission and the life to which God invites them.

9

Giving and Generosity

We love God, because God first loved us.

—I John 4:19 (KJV)

I was leading a seminar on generosity and giving. There were about six hundred people in the seminar. We were having a good time together. We were discussing whether people give because they can afford to give. I shared two suggestions with them. The first was that we live life out of our generosity, not from what we can afford to do. The second was that we give out of our generosity, not from what we can afford to give.

A woman stood—I can see her now—with graying hair spotlighted by the sun shining through the stained-glass windows. The light gave her hair a shining spirit of its own. She was simply dressed. Her smile taught us she was having good fun. Her nature was warm and gracious. She was about halfway back on the right side of the church. Her husband, beaming and smiling, was sitting beside her.

With quiet enthusiasm and genuine pleasure, she said, "Dr. Callahan, you are exactly right. Today, my husband and I are celebrating our fiftieth wedding anniversary."

We all applauded.

259

She continued happily, "We have often said, across the years, that if we had based our decisions on what we could afford to do, I would still be wearing my wedding dress!"

We all applauded. We all laughed. We knew she was sharing the truth.

Informal Giving

Small, strong congregations share a remarkable spirit of generosity and giving. This is among the qualities deeply present in our congregation because:

- We share our generosity through informal giving
- We make available all six sources of giving
- We are alive with the strengths for giving
- With the grace of God, the spirit of giving is present with us

We give as we live. We share our generosity through informal giving. We live with a generosity about life; we give with that same spirit of generosity. How we live shapes how we give. How we give shapes how we live. We live the nature of giving that matches with us. As a small, strong congregation, we live an informal life with one another. Thus, the nature of our giving is informal, not formal. We live out our informal giving in three ways:

1. Spontaneous giving
2. Seasonal giving
3. Major project giving

Spontaneous Giving

We give the way we live. In small, strong congregations, giving is informal and spontaneous, not formal and planned. Informal living is informal giving. Spontaneous living is spontaneous giving. It is impulse giving. We do many good things on impulse. The Samaritan shared help on impulse and, in the centuries come and gone, has become known as the Good Samaritan.

Many acts of generosity and charity happen on impulse. If people thought about it for too long, they might talk themselves out of it. The fellow races to save a buddy on the battlefield; it is impulse helping. Someone shares a gesture of goodwill for his or her neighbor; it happens virtually on impulse. Another shares an act of kindness with a stranger. All of these gifts happen with a good-natured, generous spirit of impulse.

People give on impulse, not planning.

On a Sunday morning, or in a gathering of the congregation, someone identifies a worthwhile cause. It may be a major advance in mission; it may be a sudden need or emergency— a family in a desperate plight, people in need because of hurricane, flood, famine, etc. The need is immediate, critical, and worthwhile.

The person sharing the invitation has the mutual trust, respect, integrity, credibility, and confidence of the congregation. Those hearing of the cause see that their gift directly helps people. The person inviting the congregation to their best generosity does so with confidence and assurance, in neither a weak and timid nor a harsh and demanding manner. The consequence is that the invitation touches people's compassion, and we give generously.

When Julie and I receive an invitation to give generously, we do not look at our budget to see whether we can afford to make this gift or not. We look at whom we are helping. We look at the team that does the helping. We look at who is inviting us to give. We want to know their spirit of confidence and assurance about the cause. Then, we decide to give generously.

Much of the charitable giving on this planet is through spontaneous giving. Informal, spontaneous giving touches the longings of people to share in an informal and spontaneous spirit. Further, spontaneous giving appeals to both "excellent sprinters" and "solid marathon runners."

Excellent sprinters do what they do in short-term, highly intensive ways near the time at hand. Solid marathon runners do what they do in steadfast, routine, regular ways weekly, monthly, year in and year out. Annual budget giving, as it is currently practiced, appeals primarily to solid marathon runners. It does not reach excellent sprinters. It does not touch the informal, spontaneous spirit of the sprinters. Nor, for that matter, does it stir the impulse giving of marathon runners. Both excellent sprinters and solid marathon runners give generously to spontaneous giving causes.

Seasonal Giving

Seasonal living is seasonal giving. People who live in a harvest economy give in a "harvest" way. We saw this in the nineteenth and twentieth centuries in rural, agricultural America. It was a barter economy. We gave through seasonal giving. Most of the giving happened at the time of the harvest. The emphasis was on "give as the Lord prospers."

We passed the offering plate Sunday after Sunday as the sacramental symbol that "all we are and all we have are gifts from God." Almost no money was placed in that offering plate. There was no emphasis on weekly giving. There was hardly anything to give each week. Virtually all the giving happened at the time of the harvest. We still see this in harvest economies today.

It is a simple point. People give in direct relation to how they receive their income. That is the only way they can do it.

When, in some parts of the planet, we moved to a cash economy, people began to receive their income in cash weekly.

They began to pay their grocery bill weekly. Insurance premiums were paid weekly. Rent was paid weekly. The emphasis shifted to weekly giving. The focus was much more on a weekly offering to the mission of the church.

Weekly envelopes were invented. People received their pay in cash in a little brown envelope each week. The offering envelope is really the little brown envelope turned white, with the flap shifted from the end to the side. In fact, God's mission moved forward on this planet for more than one thousand nine hundred years without ever knowing what an offering envelope was. A gift of the Lord's acre or the gift of a cow does not fit into an envelope.

Then we moved, in some parts of the planet, to a check-and-credit-card economy. People began to receive their income once or twice a month, and the pattern of giving for many people moved to once or twice a month. They would write a check to the church at the same time they received their income, writing checks to pay their utility and credit-card statements. They would share their generosity as they both received and expended their income.

It is significant to note that *cities have a seasonal, harvest economy* as much as rural areas do. In many cities, the period from Thanksgiving through Christmas provides a harvest season for stores, shopping centers, and other retail businesses. The vast majority of their business for the year is done in that short-term, highly intensive, seasonal time. Part of what drives this pattern is the seasonal spirit of the time. Another factor is that many people receive more of their income toward the end of the year.

Similarly, we find seasonal patterns, at varied times of the year, in the hotel and restaurant industries, in sales and service businesses, in computer and manufacturing groups. We find seasonal patterns in residential and automobile sales, in medical and helping professions, and in construction and building trades. The work is seasonal. The income is seasonal. The giving is seasonal.

People in a significant number of vocations receive their income on a varied, seasonal basis. Regrettably, just enough people get on a finance committee who do receive their income in equal amounts each month—year in and year out. Sadly, the presumption of the committee therefore is that most all people are like them and receive their income in equal amounts each month. They conclude, then, that the church should also plan to receive its income in equal amounts each month. In fact, healthy congregations receive much of their giving seasonally.

People give as they receive. They cannot do otherwise.

Many people in cities receive their income in seasonal patterns. For waiters and waitresses, there are high and low seasons of income. For manufacturer's reps and sales people, there are high and low months of income. For surgeons, there are high and low seasons of income. Few people have elective surgery in August. They go on vacation, have fun, and then come back and have their elective surgery in the fall. Lawyers, real estate people, plumbers, electricians, builders— we could go on and on naming the vocations whose income pattern constitutes seasons of high and low income over the year.

It is a mistake to assume that seasonal giving was a reality only in rural, agricultural America during the last century. It is a myth to assume that, in the twenty-first century, giving will be regular because income is in equal, regular amounts, weekly or monthly. Both rural areas and cities continue to have a seasonal economy, and in a seasonal economy people give their gifts seasonally. The biblical principle for giving is that "people give as the Lord prospers." They give the way they live.

In strong congregations, two major sources of seasonal giving are Major Community Sundays and special planned giving. Major Community Sunday giving happens on our seasonal, high-worship-attendance Sundays. Christmas and Easter are examples. The loose plate offerings and recorded contributions are significant. People who worship with us tend to give. People who are members but do not worship with us have a tendency not to give.

The art is to develop, seasonally, throughout the year, eight to ten Major Community Sundays, including Christmas and Easter. A major service may focus on a life stage, a specific human hurt or hope, or a community interest or concern. In a way, it is like having Christmas and Easter several times during the year. The more seasonal Major Community Sundays we have, the more people who attend, the more people we help, the more generous people are with their giving. People give because they are helped, and being helped, they want to help. They give spontaneously without being asked.

Many congregations have a Major Community Sunday for all the families in the community that have been blessed with a new child during the past year. Some congregations, in Florida, Arizona, and New Mexico, have a special Sunday for everyone in early retirement. Many congregations have a Sunday with the focus on education, because in their community it is a major interest and concern. Many congregations have a helpful, major Sunday for persons in the community who have lost a loved one during the past year. Many have a major Sunday for people who have a friend or family member wrestling with some form of addiction.

Look at the loose plate offerings and recorded contributions that people give on your one Sunday with the highest attendance. Now, do eight Sundays a year where the attendance is virtually equal to that Sunday. Your loose plate offerings and recorded contributions for each of those eight Sundays will be virtually equal to your one current Sunday of highest attendance.

On a Major Community Sunday, we have an extraordinary turnout. We do not take up a special offering. We do not push people to give. They give with generosity because of the special nature of the Sunday. People give generously because the service and the sermon, the music and the message touch their lives profoundly and helpfully. You will discover further resources on Major Community Sundays in both *Dynamic Worship* and *Giving and Stewardship.*

Special planned giving happens when the congregation and the community are invited, usually seasonally, to support some special cause that has ongoing, long-term significance in God's mission. These special causes are supported year after year, on a regular basis, by the generosity of the congregation. They usually happen on the same Sunday, from one year to the next. Some congregations have a special planned offering on Worldwide Communion Sunday. Some do the same on Mother's Day, or Pentecost, or Christmas Eve.

Small, strong congregations look forward to special planned offerings that share their giving across the planet; they do so with *considerable generosity* when four things are true:

1. They feel they have participated in choosing the causes.

2. There are clear people pictures as to who is helped.

3. They can see that what they give goes directly to the people they seek to help.

4. They are encouraged to give in a way that matches the way they live and give.

Small, strong congregations support special planned giving causes *less generously* when:

1. They do not feel they have really participated in the choice of the cause.
2. There are no clear, compelling people pictures.
3. It is vague as to whether their giving goes directly to the people they seek to help.
4. They are pushed to give in a way that does not match the way they live.

People give to people. People give to help the "poor." People give to help "children." These are compelling people pictures. They are mission-centered, person-centered pictures of who we help. Functional, organizational pictures of some budget or fund are not compelling. We do not give as generously to such. We give far more generously when we can see the people we directly help. We give with enthusiasm and generosity when the people pictures are straightforward and clear. We are giving to help the poor and to help children. We are glad to help.

We give to special planned giving causes when we are encouraged to give *generously* in an informal, seasonal spirit. We live an informal life together. We give with an informal spirit. When you help us give with an informal, seasonal spirit, we give with considerable generosity. We do not give as generously when we are encouraged or told to give in a formal, planned manner.

I have come across a few finance teams in local congregations that, from time to time, have been known to push the congregation to give to a special planned giving cause. They press the matter with a habitual spirit rather than encourage them in a seasonal, harvest spirit. They turn special planned giving into formal, routine giving.

They lose sight of the people being helped through this special planned offering. They urge their congregation to give to the special cause because "we've done it every year."

In defense of this practice, a finance team leader once said to me, "Dr. Callahan, people make house payments and car payments because they are supposed to. They should do the same with their special giving."

I shared two helpful suggestions. First, I noted that the family has personally decided to buy the house or purchase the car. It was actively their decision. They invested thought and time in their decision. They shopped and compared. They looked at a considerable number of houses before they made up their minds. They visited several car dealerships, drove various cars, compared prices, and then they made their own personal decision. They have clear ownership for their decisions.

When the finance team lets the congregation participate in deciding what the special planned giving causes are for a given year, the congregation has strong ownership for the causes and gives generously. By contrast, when the finance team selects the causes and presses them upon the congregation, the congregation has no ownership and gives less generously.

Second, I suggested that when we reduce giving to an obligatory payment, it does not invoke people's generosity; it invokes their resentment. People do not give *generously* out of obligation. They may give out of obligation, but they do not give generously. They may give just enough that we think it works, but what happens is that they give the rest of their generosity to causes that invite them to do so in an informal, spontaneous, seasonal spirit. Given half a chance, people give with a generous spirit.

Paul says it clearly in II Corinthians 9:7 (RSV): "Each one must do as he has made up his mind, not reluctantly or under compulsion, for God loves a cheerful giver." The Phillips translation says, "Let everyone give as his heart tells him, neither grudgingly nor under compulsion, for God loves the man who gives cheerfully." The emphasis is clear. Do not give out of duty or obligation. Give with a cheerful spirit. We look forward to giving cheerfully and generously.

We give generously. We give in the way we receive our income. We respond to spontaneous invitations and to seasonal possibilities. We look forward to Major Community Sundays and to special planned offerings. We seek to help people through our giving. We are grateful for God's blessings in our lives.

Major Project Giving

A small, strong congregation decided to launch a mission with children. The congregation wanted to do a summer program as their gift to the children of their community. They were specific. They shared details about how they planned to help and serve the children. They were concrete about the volunteers who would be helping. They were explicit about who was on the leader team and what they would do. They were clear as to the part-time staffing they would include.

They had two spontaneous offerings, one in October and one at Christmas. These two offerings generously secured the up-front money needed to launch the program the following summer. Then, during the spring before their first summer program, they invited people to give generously to this major project to ensure all of the needs would be covered in launching the program for the children.

The first summer program was well done. It greatly helped many children and their families. During the spring, before the second and third summer programs, they took a spontaneous giving offering. The second summer was successful. Generous giving begin to come from community persons, several businesses, and one civic group. The seasonal support for the yearly summer program began to come from members, constituents, community people, families helped in the summer program, and friends of the church who now live elsewhere; it came from businesses and several civic community group. The vast majority of this giving came informally and spontaneously to support this major project.

Another small, strong congregation wanted to advance the strength of worship through music. They decided the way forward was to secure a part-time music leader and director. They identified the competencies needed. They identified the objectives, the programs, and the services to be accomplished during the first three years. They outlined the role of the new person as part of the congregation and the worship team.

They launched an informal search committee to discover the most competent person who would match well with the mission of their congregation. They were clear about the competencies for which they were looking. They were concrete about the objectives they expected this person to achieve. They created a substantive search team that had the trust and respect of the congregation and the community.

For this major project, they had a spontaneous one-day giving invitation in the fall, and a second spontaneous one-day giving invitation in the spring. Because the grapevine communicated so well the thoughtful spirit in which the search team was going about its work, the spring offering was extraordinary.

These two spontaneous offerings were held to raise the up-front money to cover the first year of salary for the part-time music leader and director. They invited community persons to contribute. They invited friends of the congregation living elsewhere to contribute.

The spirit was that this is a major project. It advances both our congregation and our community. We plan to do it well. We have been specific and concrete about what we want to accomplish. We invite you to give generously. They found an extraordinary match in a part-time music leader. The music grew and flourished. The giving to that major project continues informally, spontaneously, and seasonally. People are happy to give to that major project.

Short-term major project giving can focus helpfully and successfully on a major mission and outreach project. It can focus on a major project for a new program and future staffing, say, a part-time music leader. From time to time, churches have used major project giving to build a new building, to make capital improvements, for debt retirement or debt servicing. Small, strong congregations successfully use major project giving as a way to raise funds to launch a specific mission and outreach or to bring on board a new program and future staffing.

People want to do something that is specific and concrete. It is not true that they want to give money only to build buildings. Show people a generalized mission statement: "We plan to help everybody with everything all the time." Now, show people a picture of a building with all the plans and details, specific and concrete. Many people will give money for the building. It is not, however, because it is a building. It is because the plans are detailed, specific, and concrete. People do not give to generalized statements of glowing sentimentality.

Be specific and concrete when you identify a mission or a staffing project. Clearly state what you plan to accomplish, the competencies, the objectives, the values, the amount of funds needed, and where they will go. You will find that people give major project gifts. They give precisely because you have given them evidence of thoughtful planning and careful attention to detail in all areas needed to accomplish the project. What they see and hear is specific and concrete. They give generously.

Sources of Giving

Small, strong congregations make available all six sources of giving:

1. Spontaneous giving
2. Major Community Sunday giving
3. Special planned giving
4. Major project giving
5. Annual giving
6. Enduring giving

These are the six ways people share their generosity and give money for God's mission. These six sources are discussed in considerable depth in *Giving and Stewardship*. Earlier in this chapter, we have briefly discussed the first four.

Annual Giving

Annual giving is the fifth source of giving. This way of giving is lived out as a number of small, strong congregations create an annual budget. It is helpful to observe, as we look across the planet, that many small, strong congregations have an approximate idea of what they hope is their annual budget. This is also the case, in this country, with many congregations that are strong and healthy. We find the notion of a fixed, rigid, line-item, annual budget in some congregations.

Many people, in their own lives, have an approximate idea of their own personal financial budget. They see it as a guide. They do not plan to be the slave of it. They have the same spirit with their congregation. Sometimes, a person on the finance team says, "We've got to get organized. We need a line-item budget, and we need to stick to it." Sometimes, that person does his or her own personal finances that way.

However, I have met more such people who want their congregation to do what they, themselves, are not doing.

I encourage you to have an approximate-idea annual budget. I encourage you do develop your annual budget in a *mission budget* format. I share more about this in the next section of this chapter, and you can discover fuller resources on this in *Effective Church Finances*.

Sometimes, with an annual budget, people are invited to give, regularly and systematically, weekly or monthly. Some people do give this way. It is especially true of people who receive their income in regular, systematic, equal amounts each month. However, do not get your hopes up that most of your giving will come to you in this accountant-friendly manner.

Enduring Giving

The sixth source, enduring gifts, is important. We have discussed this earlier. People want their lives to count in enduring ways. People look for ways to give enduring gifts that have lasting value. When you do not make enduring gift possibilities available for your congregation, all that happens is that your people give their enduring gifts to some other group, a college, a community group, a nonprofit group, etc.

I encourage you to identify five to eight enduring projects that have balance, integrity, and broad-based appeal. These projects can include something for mission and something for mortar, something for others and something for us. They have lasting value. They are sufficiently compelling so that people are drawn to give spontaneously and generously to one or more of these enduring gift projects.

You can identify specific enduring gift projects, such as these:

- Our mission with children
- Our mission through worship and music

- Our mission with the poor
- Our mission through our space and facilities
- Our mission through scholarships
- Our mission through general projects

Once you have identified the projects, then set a helpful goal for each one and the date you plan to achieve the goal. Now, create an enduring gift team, to give leadership to this possibility for giving. In a good-fun, good-times annual gathering of the congregation, share a brief progress report on how you are doing and thank the people who are giving. I encourage you to study the chapter on enduring gifts in *Effective Church Finances*. You will grow enduring gifts forward.

Total Giving

Small, strong congregations think *total giving*, not annual giving. They are wise enough to think of these five sources of giving (in addition to annual giving):

1. Spontaneous-giving causes
2. Major Community Sundays
3. Special planned offerings
4. Major projects
5. Enduring gifts

They encourage these sources, knowing these ways of giving stir people's generosity informally and spontaneously. They know people tend to give to the annual budget in a more formal, planned way.

People give all six ways. This is simply a listing of how people in fact give. I call these "six giving doors." You can open all six giving doors. You can allow, encourage, and make it possible for people to share their generosity all six ways.

When you open all six doors, a few annual givers may switch to some of the other five ways. Mostly, you discover new giving households, while the current giving households increase their total giving.

With all six doors open, congregations find that annual giving accounts for about one-third to one-half of their total donations. When a congregation does spontaneous giving and Major Community Sundays well, has a healthy enduring gift endowment in place, and is wisely making special planned offerings and significant major project giving available, then annual giving is about one-third of the congregation's total giving for the year. When these five sources of giving are present, though to a lesser extent, then annual giving is about one-half of the total giving for the year.

Over time, with all six giving doors generously open, we can develop a 1:2 or a 1:3 giving ratio. That is, the giving to our annual budget becomes one-half to one-third of our total giving. This is especially the case when spontaneous giving, major project giving, and enduring gifts are well in place. Three examples help.

In one congregation, which we will call church A, the giving to its annual budget is $20,000. The total giving to all six sources is $51,000. Then, we add $5,000 for what I refer to as service income. This includes special gifts not otherwise anticipated, which come from community people and friends of the congregation who live elsewhere. It encompasses income from facility rentals to various groups, from weddings, etc. It includes any special fundraisers such as bazaars, car washes, community dinners, etc. Thus, for church A, total giving and income is $56,000.

Church B is giving $50,000 to the annual budget. All six sources of giving generate $138,000 in contributions, with service income of $15,000. Their total giving and income is $153,000.

With church C, giving to the annual budget is $80,000. Their total giving, with all six giving doors open, is $224,000. Their service income is another $20,000, with their total giving and income being $244,000.

The ratio of annual giving to total giving varies from one congregation to the next. What is true in all cases is that if a congregation opens only the annual giving door, the total giving results are less than if it makes available all six giving possibilities.

Regrettably, some small congregations think they should close their church because they do not have sufficient money to continue. However, they have focused only on annual giving. They do not have the money because they have closed five giving doors. If a church closes too many giving doors, the church may very well close, too.

I am simply confirming that people give money to a congregation in all six ways. If you limit them to one way, you lose the money they would give in the other five ways. They continue to give that money, but they give it to the Salvation

Giving Door	Church A	Church B	Church C
Spontaneous	5	15	24
Major Community Sundays	1	4	8
Special planned offerings	2	4	7
Short-term major projects	18	45	75
Annual	20	50	80
Enduring gifts	5	20	30
Total giving	51	138	224
Service income*	5	15	20
Total giving and income	56	153	244

NOTES: AMOUNTS ARE IN THOUSANDS OF DOLLARS.

* SERVICE INCOME INCLUDES SPECIAL ONE-TIME GIFTS, RENTAL INCOME, AND SPECIAL FUNDRAISERS.

Army, the American Heart Association, etc. They give to groups that are wise enough to have all six giving doors open.

The Strengths for Giving

In small, strong congregations, we are alive with these strengths for giving:

- Giving is compassion-driven.
- It is marked by solid financial leadership.
- It is developed with positive reinforcement.

Compassion-Driven

Small, strong congregations are high-compassion, high-community congregations. They know people give out of a spirit of compassion and a sense of community. They understand people give money to people. People do not give money to line-item budgets. These are useful for accounting and auditing purposes. They do not raise money. They do not stir generosity.

Reasonability is a motivation for giving among those of us for whom reason and logic are major factors in our day-to-day lives. We have high analytical abilities and want to look at a line-item budget. We enjoy and gain satisfaction from doing a thoughtful analysis, comparing this year's line-item budget to last year's, and to the proposed line-item budget for the coming year. We want to be certain that the proposed budget is reasonable, and we enjoy our study.

There are five major motivations out of which people share their generosity:

1. Compassion: sharing, caring, giving, loving, serving
2. Community: good fun, good time, roots, place, belonging, friends, family

3. Challenge: attainment, accomplishment, achievement
4. Reasonability: data, analysis, logic, "it makes good sense"
5. Commitment: duty, vow, obligation, loyalty

Giving is compassion-driven; it is people-driven. For our current purposes, I want to confirm this foundational principle. You will benefit from the fuller discussion of these motivations found in *Giving and Stewardship* and in *Twelve Keys: The Leaders' Guide*. For now, I want simply to confirm that the motivations of compassion and community stir the vast majority of giving. People have a real longing to be of help to other people. If a cause touches people's compassion and stirs their sense of community, they give with extraordinary generosity.

A "people budget"—a "mission budget"—helps greatly with the generosity of giving in small, strong congregations. It is usually on one sheet of paper, and it says simply and straightforwardly:

- We plan to help these people during the coming year.
- These volunteers plan to share the help.
- Here is our leadership team.
- We are investing this amount of funds.

Such a budget is developed around three to five—maybe eight—major projects that have balance, integrity, and broad-based appeal. For example, the mission budget categories may look like this:

- Children
- Worship and music
- Shepherding and congregational care
- Youth and their families
- Mission and outreach

Under each category, simply and clearly, we describe whom we plan to help in the coming year. We share:

- The number of people we plan to help and how we plan to help them
- Who is involved in the helping; the volunteers ready to help
- The names of those on the leader teams, including who the leaders are for each area
- The amount we plan to invest in each area during the coming year

We share people pictures. We are specific and concrete. The result is that people give generously. The focus is on people and mission, not accounting and auditing. The focus is on advancing and developing people's lives and destinies. The focus is on encouraging people to share their generosity richly and fully. The manner of giving is people-driven. People give to people.

A budget that is people-driven resonates with the compassion, community, and generosity with which people live their lives. A budget without generosity is "as sounding brass or a tinkling cymbal." Regrettably, in small and weak or dying congregations the text is something like this: "Though I speak with the budgets 'of men and of angels and have not charity, I am become as sounding brass or a tinkling cymbal.' And though I have the gift of accounting and understand all line items and all auditing and though I have all facts 'so that I could remove mountains and have not charity, I am nothing.'"

Budgets, accounting, line items, auditing, and facts are helpful. What stirs people's generosity is the sense that their gifts directly help others with their lives.

I have the privilege of working with and helping the Salvation Army around the planet. Whenever these two words, "Salvation Army," are mentioned, the people pictures that come to mind are of the poor and a Salvation Army officer. Now, ask yourself what two people pictures come to mind when the name of your congregation is mentioned. If the two pictures that come to people's minds are of a line-item budget and a picture of a committee meeting, the congregation is in difficulty with its giving.

We discover small, strong congregations to be a legend on the community grapevine for their compassion, community, and generosity in people's lives and destinies. They are a legend for having a compassion-driven, people-driven budget that demonstrates an extraordinary spirit of generosity.

Solid Financial Leadership

The second strength for giving in small, strong congregations is the presence of solid financial leadership. There is a spirit of respect and integrity present in the congregation. The leaders and the grass roots have a mutual trust with one another. It is based on how they live their lives, as well as how they lead and participate in the congregation. There is no suspicion about decisions. There is no mistrust about the handling of the money. Both the leaders and the grassroots people share and work together aboveboard, openly, and inclusively.

The church has open books. There are no hidden decisions. There is no hidden money. Unfortunately, some churches do have the practice of hiding money. They seem to feel that if people ever find out that the church is doing pretty well, they might quit giving. Those are the churches that send out "the July letter." Enough churches have sent out this letter for so many years that it is likely to make its way into the new hymnal and lectionary for the church year.

The July letter has three paragraphs. The first paragraph says, "Our church has gotten a little behind in its bills." Paragraph two says, "The utilities were a little bit more than we anticipated." Paragraph three says, "Would you please send us a little money to help us catch up?"

It is a perfectly good letter, but there are three things wrong with it. Paragraph one, which says "We are a little behind in our bills," reminds people that probably *they* are a little behind in their bills. Do you know anyone who is ahead? I do not think that the way to develop giving is to start by reminding people they are behind in their bills.

The second paragraph has reduced the winning cause of Christ to a utility bill. I have yet to find people who rush home from work, eagerly and expectantly, and dash to the mailbox hoping to find the utility bill. They sprint to the house to fill out the check. They hurry to the post office to mail their utility bill as their biggest high of the week. No, we pay our utility bill with decency and honor. So too we want our giving to go toward some cause that is substantive and satisfying. We want the sense that we are personally contributing to a strong mission to advance people's lives in the grace of God.

The third paragraph does the real damage: "Would you please send us a little money to help us catch up?" People live forward or downward in response to our expectancies of them. Regrettably, what this paragraph inspires people to do is send a *little bit* of money! They send just enough little money that we think the July letter worked.

Small, strong congregations share how well they are doing. Following Easter—which is often an extraordinary event in the life of many small, strong congregations—I suggest that they send out an "encouragement letter." This letter has three paragraphs. Paragraph one confirms that "Our church is doing solid work. This has been among the most remarkable Easter seasons ever." Paragraph two says, "The lives and destinies of many people are being helped with the grace of God." Paragraph three says, "Thank you for the generosity of your giving. God's mission moves forward." Use your own words and convey this spirit.

People give money to a winning cause, not a sinking ship. Any time a church describes itself as a sinking ship, it raises less money. People intuitively know that we are the "winningest cause" in the galaxy. But if this is not the message we send out, people back off in their giving. If we share with integrity how *well* we are doing, people give more generously.

Success breeds success. Some churches make the mistake of hiding money. They think that if people know how well they are doing, they might quit giving. Some make the mistake of opening only one giving door, namely, annual budget giving. The truth is the six sources of giving complement each other. The more successful you are, the more successful you will be.

The mark of solid financial leadership is one of trust, respect, and integrity. There is respect for the compassion and competence that key leaders and the grass roots contribute to the congregation's mission. There is no bossism in small, strong congregations. There is no pushing or prodding. There is a spirit of teamwork and family between the leaders and those of the grass roots. The integrity of the leaders and the grassroots congregation is well in place. Both live life with honesty, principles, and fairness. They share a remarkable decency with one another.

In small, strong congregations, our focus as solid financial leaders is on mission development and giving development. In this sequence, we develop our blueprints for:

- Mission
- Giving development
- Budget

Mission and giving development come first. They are steps one and two. Then comes budget development.

God invites us to grow generous givers. Giving development is more than fundraising. Some say we are not doing fundraising; they talk of fund development. We are invited to do more than fundraising or fund development. I call what we are about "giving development." We share all six sources of giving with our people. We help them live their lives richly and fully, with generosity. Growing generous givers is what God encourages us to do.

I have had the privilege to serve as founder of the National Certification Program for Church Finance and Administration. The program has trained and certified many of the church administrators across the planet. They serve in strong, competent ways in advancing God's mission.

In the certification program, I have encouraged church administrators to focus on mission development, giving development, financial administration, property administration, office administration, and personnel administration. The first two of these areas drive the other four. Where we are heading in mission and giving development shapes where we are heading in financial, property, office, and personnel administration.

I have worked with any number of small, strong congregations that have a mission plan and a giving development plan but do not have a budget. Now, I grant you that it is sometimes helpful to have all three: a blueprint for mission, a blueprint for giving development, and a blueprint for budget. Because they have a mission plan and a giving development plan (they are growing generous givers), they are thriving, even though they have only an informal budget.

I have worked with any number of small, weak and small, dying congregations that have a budget but do not have a mission plan or a giving development plan. If a church could have only two of the three, the two to have are a mission plan and a giving development plan. A budget without a mission and giving plan is a ship dead in the water. It has no course; it has no sense of direction—no wind in its sails. It sits in irons. In their desire to be organized, the leaders became too organized around budgets. It is more helpful to be well organized around our mission and our giving. Then, if we also have a formal budget, God may bless us yet again.

Sometimes, what drives the need for a formal budget is our desire to be fair and reasonable with whomever we have as our pastor. In rural, agricultural economies, pastors receive most of their income at the time of the harvest. They are paid as the Lord has prospered. They are not paid an equal amount of money in the twelve months of the year. They are paid just as everyone else is: namely, at the time of the harvest.

In seasonal economies in cities, many people receive their income seasonally. Ditchdiggers, lawyers, waiters and waitresses, accountants, salespersons, dentists, manufacturer reps, doctors, real estate people, plant workers—the list could go on and on—of people in vocations where income is received seasonally. In the same manner, pastors, especially in emerging congregations, can receive their income seasonally. There is some basic amount of income each month, but the total income matches the seasonal pattern of income and giving in the congregation.

I am deeply impressed with the range of lay pastors, volunteer ministers, and ordained elders across the planet who give their lives in God's mission, trusting God to supply their day-to-day needs. They live with the confidence that seasonal giving will deliver to them a seasonal income sufficient unto the day. They know with confidence that in some weeks and months there is less money coming to them—and it may come to them in the form of barter, not money. In other seasons and months, there may be more money coming to them.

The point is simply this. Small, strong congregations focus on mission, giving development, and budget—in that order.

Small, dying congregations focus on budget, giving development, and mission, in that order. They have put the cart before the horse. They have tried to figure out their budget needs before they discover the mission to which God invites them.

Small, strong congregations are blessed with the kind of solid financial leaders who understand that we want our money to be spent wisely in God's mission, not foolishly. Yes, we invest our money (that is the term I prefer to use) wisely and generously, not foolishly and in a squandering manner. We have the sense that we are investing our giving in advancing people's lives and destinies. We have the spirit that our leaders share solid financial leadership and work well together with our congregation.

Positive Reinforcement

A third strength for giving in small, strong congregations is the presence of positive reinforcement. You will find the leaders saying thank-you frequently. Positive reinforcement raises more volunteers and money any day than negative reinforcement every day. The art is to say thank-you.

The art is to create three dollars of goodwill for each dollar people give; people eventually give the three. The art is not to create three dollars of ill will for each dollar given. You will never see the three dollars and eventually you will lose the one dollar. Under threat, people wither; with encouragement, people grow.

In their fundraising, some congregations focus on a spirit of lamenting, whining, complaining, and bemoaning. They talk about how far behind they are. They raise less money. Yes, they raise just enough "less money" that they think this method works.

The spirit of positive reinforcement raises both more volunteers and more money. The art is to find as many ways as possible, with integrity, to say thank-you. Some congregations send out a formal or informal giving statement of contributions at the end of each month or each quarter. I encourage financial secretaries to write two words on the statement: thank-you.

The financial secretary of one congregation that I was helping asked me, "Dr. Callahan, do you really think this helps?" I said, "Try it and see what happens." I was in that church again eighteen months later, and she said to me, "You know, Dr. Callahan, I did what you suggested and was amazed at what happened. People began to write back to me, thanking me for thanking them!" In that congregation, it had been a very long time since anyone had said thank-you.

With a perspective that people are supposed to give out of duty and obligation, the consequence is that no one ever says thank-you. If the perspective is that God loves a cheerful giver, the practice is that—when people give generously—someone says thank-you.

I encourage congregations to use their monthly or quarterly giving statement of contributions as a thank-you note. You can enclose some constructive report as to what is happening with our children, with our music and worship, with our shepherding and pastoral care, with youths and their families, or with mission. Let people know that their generosity is actually counting right now in people's lives and destinies.

At the end of the year, I encourage congregations to enclose, with the summary of what each family has given during the year, a copy of the congregation's "people and mission report." It shares the results about who we helped this past year. It shares something about the volunteers who have been gracious and generous in helping. It thanks both them and the leadership team for their help. The report confirms what the congregation has given and invested in each area of mission.

The purpose of the year-end report is not primarily to help people know what charitable contributions they can claim on their tax returns. The purpose of the year-end statement is to thank people—with integrity and positive reinforcement—for what their giving has meant in people's lives and destinies during the past year, leading them to the grace of God.

The generosity of giving in small, strong congregations is compassion-driven, blessed with solid financial leadership, and encouraged with positive reinforcement.

The Spirit of Giving

In small, strong congregations, the spirit of giving is a spirit of wondrous generosity. We have an almost overwhelming sense of God's amazing grace in our lives and in our congregation. God's spirit with us is astonishing generosity; our spirit in living is amazing generosity. We live the way God lives with us.

We are generous because of *whose* we are. We are God's people. We are the Christmas people. We are the people of wonder and joy. We are the Easter people. We are the people of hope and new life. We have the confidence and assurance that we are surrounded by the grace of God, blessed with the compassion of Christ, and led by the hope of the Holy Spirit. We are in awe and wonder at these gifts of God, and our generosity flows freely.

We are generous because of *who* we are. We are created in the image of God. Who we are is not our own doing. There is no cause for foolish pride or haughty ego. We are who we are because of God's generosity. Therefore, we live life with a spirit of humility and gratitude.

Yes, fear and anxiety visit us. Anger and rage sometime overtake us. We are upset and confused. We find ourselves in conflict. Despair, depression, and despondency pull us down. We commit simple sins and terrible, tragic sin. We are not always the way God creates us to be.

Nevertheless, God stirs us, and we discover anew the grace of God. We remember once again who we are. We live as our true selves. Our generosity is the gift of God. We live generous lives because of the generosity God shares with us. We live with meekness and humility. We are almost overawed at the extraordinary generosity and grace with which God blesses our lives. We live in gratitude. We are generous because of God's generosity with us.

The spirit of giving in small, strong congregations is a spirit of "we never have enough"—and in a marvelous paradox, we are glad to never have enough! We are always giving away more than we think we have, and then we discover God supplies resources to match the mission we share.

I have a good friend who grew up in dire poverty. He developed the fear of being poor. He has extraordinary competence, leadership ability, and compassion. Over the years, he has been most successful. He has amassed a great deal of money. He has continued, however, to fear returning to that early state of poverty and once again not have enough of anything. The problem is not in the money he has, but in the fear he has.

People who live with a fear of never having enough and then do have enough find something else to fear. We all have our fair share of fear in this life. With the grace of God, the compassion of Christ, and the healing hope of the Holy Spirit, the art is to learn to deal with our fear.

Small, strong congregations have discovered that there is always a shortage of personnel, inadequate supplies, and hardly ever enough money. With a spirit of generosity, they continuously give away more than they have. What they discover is that God supplies volunteers and money to match the mission. Money follows mission, not the reverse. The stronger the mission, the more generous the money.

With integrity and hope, small, strong congregations live the spirit that "we never have enough *people* whom we can help in mission. We are always looking for more persons we can serve." We are grateful for the generosity of God's grace in our lives; "we never have enough" is another way to say "we can never do enough to express our gratitude for God's blessings in our lives."

Our spirit of giving is based on the confidence that God is growing our lives, that God is growing our mission. It is not of our own doing; it is the gift of God. God is advancing and building us in our lives and in our mission.

God teaches us that living is giving. God teaches us giving is living. God is not conserving, holding, protecting, and preserving when God deals with us. God does not hold back grace, compassion, peace, and hope from us. God shares with amazing generosity in our lives for two reasons: first, God loves us; and second, God is teaching us that a whole, healthy life is one developing the strengths, gifts, and generosities with which God blesses our lives. We give the way God gives with us.

The generosity of giving in our small, strong congregation is built on the amazing generosity of God's love and hope in our lives. We live generously because we know love lasts and hope endures. When we know what is lasting, when we discover what is enduring, we are free to live generously. We put aside our struggling and striving. We know God's love lasts. We know God's hope endures. We are at peace. We are generous.

In the act of giving, we live. We come alive like desert flowers in a gently falling rain. We know our lives count like a sunrise promising a bright new morning. We sense new life stirring in us like a cool breeze on a hot, stifling day. We are at peace, like the quiet serenity of a moment shared in the safety of God's care. We are who God intends us to be. We live generously.

10

Living with the Spirit of Promise

Yesterday is history. Tomorrow is a mystery. Today is a gift.
That is why we call it the present.

—Author unknown

God invites us to live with promise. We look for some promise in life. We can deal with the problems of life, for the most part. We do so more fully when we have confidence in the promise of life—that there is some purpose, some value, some significance to living. We look for some assurance that we can live whole, healthy lives in the grace of God. We are grateful for the promise, the covenant, God shares with us.

We know God is with us. God surrounds us with overwhelming grace, generous, abundant compassion, and stirring, compelling hope. The promise is not that there will be no difficulties, no hardships, no temptations, no sin, no disappointments, no death. These come to us. We deal with them as best we can.

God's promise is that, amidst all of the problems and possibilities of living, God is with us—fully, completely. The strength of God's grace, the gentleness of God's compassion, the encouragement of God's hope see us forward. We live with confidence and assurance because of the promise of God.

Small, strong congregations live with this spirit of promise. We know, feel, have confidence in:

- The promise of our life together
- The promise of the possibilities God gives us
- The promise of resurrection and new life

Most small congregations *are* stronger than they think they are. Most small congregations *can* be stronger than they think they can. Some small congregations, regretfully, become preoccupied with getting bigger. They miss their strengths. The art is to focus on your strengths, not your size.

I am reminded of what Patrick Henry once said: "They tell us, Sir, that we are weak, but when shall we be stronger?" Even when we are weak, we do not wait to become stronger. We build on whatever strengths we are given, however weak we may think they are. They are, in fact, the strengths, for this moment, God gives us.

Center on the strengths you do have. It is easier to center on your current strengths than to be preoccupied with your weaknesses. Indeed, the effort to overcome old weaknesses causes us to become preoccupied with those old weaknesses— and thereby to give them more power over us than they have or deserve. The art is to focus on our present strengths and to develop these gifts of God. You can advance your congregation, and your life, with confidence and assurance in the grace and promise of God.

The Promise of Our Life Together

As a small, strong congregation, we focus on the promise of our life together. We fulfill the promise of our life together as we:

- Live for who we are
- Live, richly and fully, for our present
- Look, with anticipation, to our future

In doing so, we live out the promise of our life together.

I was helping a small, strong congregation. For fifty-plus years, they had thought, planned, behaved, and lived the qualities of a small, strong congregation. Over the years, their various pastors had done the same. Excellent matches between the congregation and their pastors blessed them. In recent times, they had eleven remarkable years with their pastor who, a short while before, had retired.

The new pastor, Larry, had been there for three years when we talked. Things were not going well. Worship attendance had declined. Giving was off. Bickering had begun to emerge. Complaining was raising its head. People who used to get along with one another were having some difficulty in doing so. The spirit of the congregation was diminished. The leaders and the pastor were puzzled. They could not figure out what had happened. Larry was such a likeable, helpful person.

Larry and I visited. I invited him to share something of his growing up years. He spoke of the metropolitan city in which he grew up. He shared, with quiet enthusiasm, about the substantial university he attended, with its vast student body and the range of courses he was able to take. He valued his studies at the large seminary from which he graduated.

I invited him to share something of his ministry before coming to this small, strong congregation. He told me of graduating from seminary and going to the one of the largest churches in the state. He felt fortunate that he was invited to go there. He spent eight years as associate minister on the staff. He loved the people. His wife and he were happy living there. Their two children were born while they were there. He did well as the associate pastor.

Some of his friends encouraged him that it was now time for him to get his own church. They said that he had been an associate long enough. Thus he came to be the pastor of this small, strong congregation.

I invited him to share what he had fun doing in day-to-day life by way of hobbies and interests. He talked of the family camping trips, the family vacations in the mountains, the trips to visit with family and friends. He spoke of his enjoyment in just sitting around and sharing with his family.

We had a good conversation.

Somewhere along the way, Larry said something—I do not now remember what it was—that reminded me of Melissa, the choir director I had helped some years before. I shared with him the story.

Melissa was a gracious, warm, likeable person. Her predecessor had grown the choir from about eight people to a choir of around sixteen. This was a strong choir for that small congregation. The choir was a wonderful family together. The rehearsals were fun and lively, rigorous and hard work. The people in the choir thrived. The music matched the message and the congregation.

Her predecessor led the choir for something like fifteen years before moving to another part of the county. Both she and her husband were transferred by their employers.

From time to time, Melissa had served as the backup choir director when her predecessor was gone. She did good work. People thought well of her and of the music she helped the choir to do. Thus, when her predecessor left, the congregation asked Melissa to be their choir director. Melissa was honored. She worked hard. She tried very hard.

Within a year, she grew the choir downward from sixteen to about seven. Her experience was with larger choirs. She had the choir singing music that worked well with a large choir of many voices and four strong sections. She wanted to show everyone that she could do the job.

However, she led this choir the way she experienced the eighty-voice choir she had sung with in the university she attended. She rehearsed the sixteen as though they were eighty. In her desire and anxiousness to do good work, she fell back on her memories and experiences of the choir that meant much to her in her early years.

It was not working. The rehearsals did not go well. Choirs develop not when they sing on Sunday, but in the rehearsals during the week. She continued to press the choir. The rehearsals were not fun anymore. She would focus on section work, when there were hardly enough people to be a section. The sense of getting down to business became the focus, rather than the sense of being family together. People lost interest.

She became nervous and more anxious. She tried harder. The choir became nervous and more anxious. They tried harder. They thought, *Maybe she knows a better way.* As matters worsened, she fell back even more on her earlier, large-university choir experience. The gap between her and the choir widened. People came less frequently to rehearsals.

I helped Melissa develop a growth plan for herself, not for the choir. The issue was not how to grow the choir back to sixteen. The issue was how Melissa could grow herself as a choir director so as to learn the competencies to lead a choir in a small, strong congregation rather than a choir in a large university. Melissa began to grow herself. Her choir began to grow as she grew.

Leading a small, strong choir is an excellent gift. Leading a large, regional university choir is an excellent gift. They are distinct gifts. Neither gift is better than the other. God blesses both gifts.

Having shared with Larry the story about Melissa, there was a moment of silence. Then he said, "Dr. Callahan, what I'm discovering from you is that I've been leading this congregation the way I learned to lead as the associate pastor of the large congregation before I came here. What you're helping me to see is that I need to learn how to lead *this* congregation."

I confirmed with Larry his new insight. He had learned large, regional and had not learned small, strong. He was thinking, planning, behaving, and living the way a pastor does in a large, regional congregation.

He was likeable and helpful. He was energetic and persuasive. From him, his congregation was reluctantly learning how to think, plan, behave, and live as a large, regional congregation. It was not working. This way did not fit with this congregation. They wanted to go along with their new pastor's way of doing things, but it did not match them.

I shared with Larry the qualities present in small, strong congregations. I discussed with him the particular qualities present in large, regional congregations. He began to see the distinction. I suggested that he lead the congregation with the spirit of a family camping trip rather than the tone of committee reports in a business meeting. I encouraged him to share his leadership with the same spirit of enjoyment he felt in just sitting around and sharing with family.

I said, "Larry, when you love this congregation the way you love your family, it will work. If you love this congregation the way you loved all the staff meetings, programs, and activities in your former large church, it will not work. If you lead them in the same informal, people-centered spirit with which you lead a family outing, it will match. If you lead them in the formal, organizational manner to which you grew accustomed in the larger church, it will not work. Fortunately, you can 'bridge' to this congregation through the way you lead in the informal, family experiences with which you have good fun."

We talked at some length.

I said in confirmation: "Larry, your people like you. They respect you. They are almost coming to love you. However, you've been asking them to live life together the way some other church does life. It will not work, especially because you've wanted your congregation to live life the way a large, regional church does life. You will do well here once you and your congregation live together for who you are as a small, strong congregation, not the way some other, larger congregation lives."

Together, we developed a growth plan whereby Larry could learn the qualities of a small, strong congregation. We considered how he, as pastor with his key leaders, could advance some of these qualities with his current congregation. In considerable depth, we discussed possibilities whereby he could bridge with his congregation.

It was not easy. It took about three years. But he began to catch on. He began to think and plan, behave and live as the pastor of a small, strong congregation. He is flourishing. His key leaders are flourishing. The congregation is flourishing. They are discovering the promise of their life together as they live for who they are.

As a small, strong congregation, we live for who we are. We are at peace. We have no pretensions. We put on no airs. We are who we are. We do not try to be something we are not. We have learned that if we try to be something we are not, we lose who we are, and we lose our confidence and assurance in who we are. With integrity, we are a small, strong congregation. This is the promise of our life together.

Further, we live richly and fully for our present, and we look with anticipation to our future. In doing so, we live out

the promise of our life together. We do not live for our past.
We learn from our past. We discover the accomplishments
and achievements in our past. We give thanks to God for
them. We discover the sin and sins in our past. We ask God
for forgiveness. We move beyond our past.

We live in the present. Our life together is our being together, now, this moment. Our life together is more about
being than about doing. We have our share of doings, of
activities, projects, and achievements. Our identity is not in
these. Our identity is in who we are more than in what we
do. The promise we see in our life together is in who we are
together, now.

We live together, here and now, in the present. We are
not striving to be something we are not. We are not living in
some future yet to be. We are not engaged in a flurry of activities, hoping they will help us discover who we are. We have
seen congregations live in the past. We have seen congregations that look to the future and forget the present. They
seem to be always trying to find their identity in the future
time. In doing so, they miss the present moment. They miss
who they are now.

Today is God's present to us. We have today because, with
grace and promise, God gives us this day to live. We discover
the promise of our life together as we live for who we are, as
we live in the present, now. We look to the future so we
know how to live in the present. We do not look to the future
so we can think of how to live in the future. We discover
where we are heading so that we know what to do today.

Our purpose in looking to the future is not to shape the
future. Our purpose is to know what to do today. In sailing,
once we know the destination, we now know how to set the
sails for today. In quilting, once we know what the quilt will
look like, we know which blocks to create today. In construc-

tion, once we know what the finished house will look like, we now know what foundation to lay today.

It is somewhat like a wedding. We love one another. We find fulfillment in our love together, now, in this present moment. Our love is in our being together. Our sense of enjoyment is in sharing this day with one another. We discover confidence and assurance with one another. We cherish each moment together, here, now, today. We look forward.

We set the date for the wedding. We decide what the wedding will look like. Then we work backward from that date. Once we know the wedding date, and our sense of what the wedding will be, we now know when the rehearsal is and when the showers happen. We know when we want to send out the invitations, and when we should arrange for the church. We know when we should visit with our pastor, and when we can informally share the good news with our family and friends. In short, we know what to do today.

People who never set the date for their wedding hardly ever get married. People who set the date for their wedding and picture what the wedding will be like have a high likelihood of getting married because they know what to do today.

We look ahead so we know what to do now. We use well the gift of today with which God blesses us. We enjoy today. We cherish today. We savor today. We do not get so caught up in the future that we miss the enjoyment of this moment. We are not so busy with what can be that we miss what is present, now.

We live in the present. We anticipate the future. When we live well in the present, we will live well in the future. As we anticipate the future, we live richly and fully in the present. Because we have discovered the richness of the present, we can now move forward on the possibilities God gives us for our present. In doing so, we can head to the future God gives us. We share a richness of life together. We live with a spirit of promise.

The Promise of the Possibilities God Gives Us

Our promise is in the possibilities God gives us. The strengths we have are God's gifts to us. God invites us to grow stronger, not bigger. God encourages us to build on the strengths with which God blesses us. God wants for us a strong, promising, present. God leads us to a hopeful, promising future. With the encouragement and blessings of God, we move forward with the possibilities for our present and future. You can move forward as you:

1. Claim your strengths
2. Expand one current strength
3. Add one new strength
4. Act

Look at the possibilities for small, strong congregations that we have discussed. Together, as leaders, grassroots participants, and pastor, discover which of these are lead strengths in your congregation:

- Mission and service
- Compassion and shepherding
- Community and belonging
- Self-reliance and self-sufficiency
- Worship and hope
- Team, leaders, and congregation
- Just enough space and facilities
- Giving and generosity

Claiming Strengths

With grace, God invites us to claim our strengths. When we claim our strengths, we claim God's gifts. When we deny our strengths, we deny God. We deny God's gifts. It is more fun to live this life with God rather than without God. When we claim our strengths, we decide to live this life with God.

We claim the strengths we have, among these eight. We look at the eight qualities present in small, strong congregations. We think. We pray. We study and review the material in each chapter of this book. We visit with friends and family. We discover their wisdom. We gather in a good-fun, good-times planning session. We have fun. We pray. We share together.

Then we decide which of these eight qualities are strengths in our congregation. In effect, on a scale of 1 to 10, we decide which of these are present in our congregation with the energy, the strength, of 8, 9, or 10. On the list of eight qualities, we underline once those that we have discovered are our strengths:

MISSION AND SERVICE
1 2 3 4 5 6 7 8 9 10

WORSHIP AND HOPE
1 2 3 4 5 6 7 8 9 10

COMPASSION AND
SHEPHERDING
1 2 3 4 5 6 7 8 9 10

TEAM, LEADERS,
CONGREGATION
1 2 3 4 5 6 7 8 9 10

COMMUNITY AND BELONGING
1 2 3 4 5 6 7 8 9 10

JUST ENOUGH SPACE
AND FACILITIES
1 2 3 4 5 6 7 8 9 10

SELF-RELIANCE AND
SELF-SUFFICIENCY
1 2 3 4 5 6 7 8 9 10

GIVING AND GENEROSITY
1 2 3 4 5 6 7 8 9 10

Expand a Current Strength

With compassion, God encourages us to expand one or two of our current strengths. We build on our strengths. We do better what we do best. We grow forward our present and our future by beginning with our strengths. We select one current strength that is an 8, and we decide to grow this strength forward to a 9 or a 10.

In our good-fun planning session, we think. We pray. We visit with one another. We gather our best wisdom. Then we decide the one current strength we plan to grow and develop in the coming year, in year one of our congregational plan. Choose a strength to expand that matches your competencies and your community. Importantly, choose one that is fun. Grow forward where you can advance.

On the list of qualities in small, strong congregations, we underline a second time the quality we have decided to expand. We can decide on a second, current strength that we plan to advance in year two of our congregational plan. We can underline this quality a second time as well.

To expand a current strength, we look for two key objectives that advance this present strength. Sometimes, we look for three or four key objectives. We come up with many excellent ideas and good suggestions, and then we select the two to four that expand this current strength. It only takes two objectives (sometimes three or four) to expand a current strength from an 8 to a 9 or 10.

A current strength may be community and belonging. We have many excellent ideas on how we can expand this quality. Among all of them, we look for the two objectives we can accomplish in year one that advance this quality in our congregation. We save the other ideas for a later time. We move on the two that expand this strength *now.* A current strength may be worship and hope. We have many good suggestions on how we can improve this quality. We discover two key objectives that advance and expand this quality in year two of our plan.

We grow forward one or two current strengths. I am not suggesting we ignore our weaknesses. I am not proposing a naïve, Pollyanna, whistling-in-the-dark optimism. I am confirming a God-centered, biblically based understanding of life. We simply begin with the strengths God gives us. When we begin with our weaknesses, we are in the weakest position to deal with our weaknesses. When we begin with our strengths and expand one or two of them, we are now in the strongest position to deal with our weaknesses.

Add a New Strength

With hope, God invites us to add one or two new strengths to help us live well in the present. We look at the list of qualities in small, strong congregations. We look for one new strength to add to overcome a current weakness and shortcoming. We may consider a second new strength as well.

As we expand a current strength, we are in the strongest position to add one new strength. We are at peace. We do not hurry. We are realistic. We focus on what is achievable. In our enthusiasm, we do not try to do too much too soon. We think progress, not perfection. We keep that old friend, a compulsion to perfectionism, at bay.

In our good-times planning session, we think. We visit with one another. We pray. We gather our best wisdom. Then we decide on the one new strength we plan to add in year two or year three of our congregational plan. On the list of qualities in small, strong congregations, we circle this quality. We can decide on a second new strength that we plan to add in year three of our congregational plan. We circle this one as well.

To add a new strength, we look for four key objectives that advance it as a strength. Sometimes, we look for two or three because with just these two or three we achieve this new strength. To add a new strength takes no more than four key objectives. We come up with many good suggestions and excellent ideas, and then we select the two to four that add this new strength. It only takes four objectives (sometimes two or three) to add a new strength so that it is now an 8.

A new strength may be shepherding and compassion. We have many good suggestions on how we add this quality. Among all of them, we look for the four objectives we can accomplish in year two or year three that add this new strength in our congregation. We save the other suggestions for a later time. We move on those that add this new strength now.

A new strength may be self-reliance and self-sufficiency. We have many excellent ideas on how we can add this new quality. We discover four key objectives that advance and expand this quality in year two or year three of our plan.

To add one or two new strengths, we look at the qualities present in our congregation with a midrange level of strength. On a scale of 1 to 10, these are the qualities present with us as a 5, 6, or 7. We select one of these qualities to add as a new strength. We grow this quality forward to an 8.

In seeking to add a new strength, we do not head to our weakest weakness, and decide that somehow we are going to add this weakest of the weak as a new strength. Such an effort takes more energy, time, leadership, and resources than it makes sense to invest. We may want to tackle our weakest weakness at some point in the future. For now, select a quality that is midrange and grow this one forward. We add this one as a newfound strength.

Act
God encourages us to act now, to live the present with which God blesses us, and to move, with the promise of God's grace, toward the future to which God is inviting us. God invites us to act now. God's invitation is to be a small, strong congregation now.

Over time, we find well in place five of the eight qualities of small, strong congregations. We are not trying for all eight. We deliver well five of the eight. One of two things happens with the other three. With excellence we may deliver our five so well that the other three do not matter. Alternatively, spill-over impact may happen. We deliver our five so well that the other three come along.

To act does not mean to grow bigger. Acting means moving forward on these steps: claim, expand, add, act. Our focus is to grow stronger, not bigger. We act on our present and our future whenever we:

- Claim the strengths God gives us
- Expand one of our current strengths
- Add one new strength
- Deliver five of the eight qualities of a small, strong congregation
- Live as a small, strong congregation

We act now. We do not wait. We know God gives us the present so we can act. We are alive. We want our life to count. We act. We move. We head out. We set sail. We do not wait until everything is in perfect order. That day will not come. We do not postpone action. The lives and destinies of too many people are at stake. We act.

We look to the future to know what to do *now*. We know *today* is God's present to us. We sense the leading of the Spirit in our lives. We act with wisdom. We act with encouragement and compassion. We act with hope. God's invitation is before us. God gives us these possibilities. God gives us the freedom to act. God gives us the present. God leads us into the future. We act now.

We build our present, and our future, on who we are, whose we are, and the strengths we now have. To wait would be to lose the moment. To delay would be to lose the privilege of helping people with their lives and destinies. God did not wait on us. God does not wait on us. We are who we are because of God's actions of grace and hope in our lives. We act because God first acted with us.

The Promise of Resurrection and New Life

Our promise is in the new life God gives us. God wants new life for us. The new life we discover is God's gift to us. It is not of our own doing. It is the gift of God. God blesses us with the promise of new life. God encourages us to live as the people of new life. God blesses us with the promise of resurrection. God invites us to live as the people of the resurrection. With the encouragement and blessings of God, we are a small, strong congregation:

- We discover new life together.
- We encourage new disciples.
- We live as the people of the resurrection.

We Discover New Life Together

Small, strong congregations share life together. We do this well. More important, we discover new life together. The key words are *discover, new,* and *together.* We encourage one another toward new life. Life is a search. We do not stay the same. Life is a pilgrimage. We do not simply live a humdrum, boring existence together. We grow and develop as people. We do not stay the same year after year. We advance and build our lives. We discover new life, and we do so together as a small, strong congregation.

With one another, we discover new insights and new understandings for living whole, healthy lives. We discover new possibilities and new encouragement. We make excellent mistakes, and together we learn from our mistakes. We share our new wisdom and our new experience with one another. We mentor one another. We help one another grow. We learn with and from one another. We are constructive influences with each other.

We are sources of health and wholeness with one another. We are not harmful to one another. We encourage constructive living. We do not reinforce poor patterns of behavior with one another. We lift one another up. We do not pull one another down, nor do we put each other down. We share a life of progress, not perfectionism. We do not create codependent-dependent patterns of behavior with each other. We help one another beyond compulsive, addictive tendencies.

We forgive one other. We do not stay angry with one another. We encourage a spirit of compassion with each other. We do not reinforce complaining, lamenting, whining, or bemoaning. We think well of one another. We are grateful God gives us the privilege of sharing this life as God's family. Together, we discover the newness of the grace of God in our lives.

We include the whole family in our new life together. We are generous in our understanding of who is part of our congregation. We include persons connected with us in our discovery of new life. We include those served in mission, constituents, friends of the congregation who live elsewhere, community people, and formal members. We think of the total of all the people our congregation is serving. In our total family, we include everyone associated with our congregation. We are grateful God gives us this remarkable, extended family with which to discover new life.

We think in terms of participation more than formal membership. We include everyone who participates in worship, a group, a program, or an activity connected with our congregation. We include the children in vacation Bible school, the women in the quilting group, the men in the fix-it group, and the people who come on Easter and Christmas. We know they are teaching us that if they have a congregational home, it is with us. Otherwise, they would be somewhere else, in some other church.

In short, we are generous in who we include in our family. We welcome all of the people we are serving and all of those who participate with us. We focus less so on formal membership. We know that many people, in our time, participate in the life and mission of a congregation, and they genuinely sense that they belong—that they are part of the family. They have discovered roots, place, belonging, and friends and family. They have an informal membership with the congregation. We are grateful for the new insights, the wisdom, the experiences they bring, and for what we can learn from them. With gratitude, we welcome them as we discover new life together.

We Encourage New Disciples

You and I are having fun. We discover God is inviting us to begin a new congregation. There are two of us. We look at the strengths God gives us. We look at the community God gives us. We pray. We decide God is inviting us to start a small, strong congregation. From day one, we think, plan, behave, and live the qualities of a small, strong congregation.

We could be in a large city, a good-sized town, or a remote, rural area. Our sense is that God gives us strengths, gifts, and competencies to develop a small, strong congregation. It is not that we start small congregations in areas with small populations and large congregations in areas with large populations. In many metropolitan areas, precisely because of their vastness and bigness, immensity and complexity, a small, strong congregation is the way forward for many people.

We decide we are beginning a small, strong congregation. We look at the eight qualities in this book. We think three years ahead. We decide which qualities to grow forward this year. We consider which ones to advance in our second year. We have a sense of which qualities to develop in our third year. We are on our way to developing a small, strong congregation.

Spirit shapes strengths. Our spirit is to think, plan, behave, and act so we grow forward the qualities present in a small, strong congregation. We plan to become stronger, not bigger. We have no plans to become a middle congregation, or a large, regional congregation. With integrity and wisdom, we look forward to being a healthy small congregation. We have the confidence that, in due course, there will be more than two of us. We have the assurance that, with the grace of God, we will be a solid, small congregation.

In our life and mission together as a small, strong congregation, we look forward to:

- Sharing a joyful invitation with people to become disciples
- Helping people live whole, healthy lives
- Developing the qualities that help us be small and strong
- Helping other congregations be small and strong
- Helping new small, strong congregations come into being

We are grateful God gives us the privilege of encouraging new disciples in these ways.

We encourage new disciples. We live the invitation Jesus shared with the disciples: "Go ye therefore, and teach all nations, baptizing them in the name of the Father, and of the Son, and of the Holy Ghost" (Matthew 28:19 KJV).

We encourage people to discover the grace of God, and to become living disciples of God's promise. With this spirit, we develop the qualities that help us to be small and strong.

We have a sense of joy and wonder about the new life we have found. We feel filled with the good news of the grace of God. For us, Jesus' invitation is not a solemn command, nor a stern challenge. We see it as a joyful invitation to share the amazing grace with which God is blessing our lives.

For us, this good news is like the good news of a drenching rain in a desert, the good news of a newborn babe, the good news of one of the happiest times in our lives. With quiet enthusiasm and humble gratitude, we share the spirit of amazing grace with which God blesses us.

When people discover the good news of the grace of God for their lives, we encourage them to discover the congregation that matches them. We understand that the "great commission" (I think of it as the "great invitation") is to help people become disciples of God's grace, not members of our congregation. We do not exclude them. We are open and inclusive, warm and welcoming. Moreover, we are wise enough to know that our focus is on helping them become disciples.

For them, any one of a number of congregations may be the home where they can live out the newfound grace of God that is blessing their lives. We are not so arrogant to assume that our congregation is the only one where they will find home. We encourage them to explore several possibilities. We want what is best for them. We are interested in disciple growth, not member growth. We are interested in what is helpful for them, not what might help us. Indeed, we feel so overwhelmingly blessed with the grace of God that we are humbly grateful we can simply help them discover the joy of being a disciple.

We encourage new disciples by helping other congregations be small and strong. We discover we have gained wisdom, experience, and strength as we grow forward the qualities of a small, strong congregation. We know that the way forward for us is to become stronger, not bigger. We look forward to sharing what we have discovered with other small congregations. Indeed, we seek out one or two congregations each year with which we can share our mutual learnings and experiences.

We are wise enough to know that each congregation develops these eight qualities in ways that work for them. We do not plan to impose our way of being a small, strong congregation on them. Rather, we look forward to what we can learn from them. We hope we have something they can learn from us. At the least, we know that we can share our story of how we develop these eight qualities, and the wisdom, strength, and experience we have gained in our pilgrimage.

We encourage new disciples as we start new small, strong congregations. We are grateful God has helped us be the healthy congregation we are. From time to time, perhaps, once every three to five years, we help two or more people begin a new congregation. We began this way, whether recently or years ago. We have the confidence that many new small, strong congregations can begin in this same informal, grassroots manner.

It is not that we ask some of our congregation to leave and start a new congregation. Some of our congregation may want to do so, but we do not insist they do so because of some arbitrary mandate that we come up with. That would be law. We are wise enough to know that new congregations beginning with a healthy spirit begin with grace.

It is more as if two or more people discover God is inviting them to start a new congregation. They may be persons we have encouraged to become disciples, recently or in times past. They may be active in our congregation or some other healthy congregation. They may be like Harriet's gardener, who begins a new congregation because he senses this is what God is inviting him to do.

We share our wisdom and experience. We share with them the eight qualities of small, strong congregations. We encourage them to create their own plan as to which ones they plan to develop in year one. We help them look three years ahead and consider which qualities they look forward to advancing in years two and three. We deliver a little help, just enough help that the participants of the congregation can all be on their journey together. We do not deliver too much help, thereby eroding their own emerging self-reliance and self-sufficiency.

We are wise enough to know that small, strong congregations are in the best position to start new small, strong congregations. We have observed that some large, regional congregations know how to do so as well. However, we have noted that a number of large, regional congregations do not do well in starting new *small, strong* congregations.

What they know how to do is large, regional. Therefore, their tendency is to start a new large, regional congregation. In the beginning, the new congregation may be small in numbers, but its way of thinking, planning, behaving, and living is that of a large, regional congregation. In effect, the large, regional congregation starts a new "mini" large, regional congregation.

Such a congregation, over time, may become as large as its sponsoring congregation. However, in its beginning, it is a large, regional congregation. It is this way precisely because of how it thinks, plans, behaves, and acts. To be sure, there is much value in beginning new large, regional congregations. Many people find home in such congregations.

At the same time, it is equally important today to begin many new small, strong congregations. Many people find home in such congregations. This is especially so as they seek to deal with the immensity of the cities, the organizations, and the businesses that have an impact on their lives. Large, regional congregations may provide some modest resources to help, but it is not helpful for them to impart the way of thinking and planning, behaving and living that is present in them. This simply creates a new congregation that is not at peace with itself until it is as large as the congregation that started it. Small, strong congregations know how to do small, strong and are in a healthy position to launch new small, strong congregations.

We are a small, strong congregation. We look forward to developing the qualities that help us be small and strong. We look forward to sharing a joyful invitation with people to become disciples. We look forward to helping other congregations be small and strong, and to starting new small, strong congregations. We are not concerned to become bigger. We have all we can say grace over to become stronger; to encourage people to be disciples; to help other congregations; and to start new small, strong congregations. We are grateful for God's invitation that we live life this richly and fully.

We Live as the People of the Resurrection

We live with the assurance of the promise of resurrection. This is not of our own doing. We live with the confidence that there is new life beyond dying. This is the gift of God. We are amazed at the promise with which God blesses our lives. We are the people of the open tomb, of the Risen Lord, and of new life. We are the people of the promise of resurrection and new life.

When all seems lost, God gives new life. When we despair, God gives signs of new hope. When we waver, God supports us with steadfast grace. When we doubt, God gives us new faith. When we are lost, God shows us a new way. When we are lonely, God sends us new joy. When we think it is over, God gives us a new beginning.

When we are born, we begin living, dying, and discovering new life. We are not who we were. We are who we are.

We will be more than we are. As persons, we are changing and growing, developing and advancing. The rhythms of life, death, and new life are present with us. We find life. We die to that life. We discover new life.

When we focus on living and on new life, we live well and we deal with dying. When we become preoccupied with dying, we do not live well, we do not discover new life, and we do not die well. We do well when we claim the life God gives us and embrace the new life to which God leads us. We experience the death of our old selves and the discovery our new selves, through the grace of God.

It is the same with congregations. When a congregation is born, it begins a dynamic of living, dying, and discovering new life. When our congregation focuses on living, we live well, we discover new life, and we deal with our dying. When our congregation becomes preoccupied with its dying, its survival, it does not live well, it does not discover new life, and it does not deal well with its dying.

People are drawn to a congregation that is living well and discovering new life. They know this grouping helps them with their own living. They have the assurance that this congregation helps them with their own dying. They are confident this congregation helps them discover new life. People are not drawn to a congregation that is focused on its dying, its survival. They know that such a congregation does not help them with their own rhythm of living, dying, and new life.

When we live well, we claim the gift of life God gives us. If we become preoccupied with our dying, we miss our living; we do not claim the gift of life with which God blesses us. The irony is that we might not have been alive to worry about our death. It does not make sense to spend half our lives worrying about our death. We miss our living; we are not prepared for our dying; we miss the new life God gives us.

When we focus on helping others claim their lives and discover the new lives God is giving them, then we discover new life through the grace of God. When a congregation becomes preoccupied with its own dying, its own survival, the congregation denies the resurrection, denies the gift of new life. The congregation seals itself in a tomb. It becomes preoccupied not only with itself but also—what is worse—with its dying. It could at least become preoccupied with its own living and new life. When we help others to discover new life, we discover new life.

Living is being as much as it is doing. We live, move, and have our *being* in the grace of God. It is not so much that we live, move, and have our *doing* in the grace of God. As a small, strong congregation, we have the confidence that we are being the people of God. We are being the people of grace, compassion, and hope. When we, as a congregation, live well together, we sense the grace of God, and we know that at least for this moment we are alive, we have life abundant.

Some of what goes on in the name of helping small congregations is really an effort to help those congregations avoid dying. Moreover, the message that comes across is, "If you do not do such and such, you will not survive, you will die." The effort is then to get more members so the congregation will not die. If a congregation is preoccupied with not dying, it misses living. It also misses the people who are searching for a congregation to help them with their living.

Some congregations have embraced this or that agenda as their way of not dying. For them, the effort is to avoid the declining numbers they hear each year at the annual meeting. Regrettably, whenever the number of members does increase, then they talk about the turnaround in their decline. They miss talking about the people they are encouraging to be disciples. Their preoccupation is, unfortunately, with their own decline and alleged turnaround.

You can see it in the way the numbers are reported at the annual meeting. The people who do the report say, "These are new membership numbers compared to last year. We have had a slight turnaround. Our congregation is no longer declining." They could say, "These are our new numbers compared to last year. We are grateful to God we have been able to help this range of people discover new life in the grace of God." We hardly ever hear such words, and even when we sometimes do, they are quickly followed with the words, "As a result, our congregation is no longer dying." Such congregations are so preoccupied with their own dying that they miss out on their living.

Further, people intuitively sense this is a group of people so preoccupied. They intuitively know this group will not help them with their living, their dying, and their discovery of new life. They are not drawn to the group. They seek out a group whose focus is on living well. They have the confidence that this group instead helps them with their living. They live well. They have the assurance this group helps them with their dying. They will die well. They look forward to new life. They look forward to new life in the grace of God.

Jesus invites the disciples to "go and teach all nations, baptizing them in the name of the Father, and of the Son, and of the Holy Ghost." The focus is on helping the new disciples discover a life more abundant, not on becoming a member of some organization. The focus is not on doing the mission to get more members, and thereby help a congregation avoid its decline. The focus of Christ's "great invitation" is on sharing the mission for the sake of the mission.

We share one excellent mission in the community. We have a spirit of compassion and a sense of community. We have advanced our capacity for self-reliance and self-sufficiency.

We discover hope in our worship. We live well together as teams, leaders, and congregation. We have just enough space and facilities. We are generous in our giving. We are grateful for God's blessings.

Love lasts. We live in love. Hope endures. We live in hope. God's promise is everlasting. We are the Easter people. We are the people of the resurrection. We are the people of hope. We are the people of the promise.

The promise is that God is with us. What more could we ask for? God has not deserted us. God is not remote . . . distant . . . aloof. God is with us! What more could we want? God has not left us. God is not busy somewhere else in the universe. God is not far off . . . alien . . . inaccessible. God visits and redeems us. God is with us now!

Emerging trends come and go, as the wind blows now here, now there. Civilizations rise and fall, as autumn leaves drop from trees. Empires conquer and then are conquered, as the sands of the desert are blown now this way and now that way. Kingdoms overcome and then are overcome, as one wave overcomes another as they wash on a beach and disappear.

Old ways die and new possibilities occur. We do well. We make mistakes. Despair visits us. We share in success. Disappointment comes to us. We move forward. Distractions abound. Defeat and death come our way. We discover new life.

We live in the promise. The promise is not that things will get better and better. The promise is not that things will get bigger and bigger. The promise is that God is with us.

God gives us the gift of the present. We know the present is the moment of hope, the moment of resurrection. It is not that the future is our only source of hope. Yes, some of our deepest yearnings, longings, and hopes will be realized down the road in the immediate future, some in the distant future, and some in the next-life future beyond the river. We know that God goes before us. We know, equally well, that hope happens now. We know that resurrection, new life, happens in the present.

The resurrection happens every time someone wrestling with alcohol becomes sober. Hope happens every time a young couple puts a faltering marriage back together. Resurrection happens every time a youth discovers the purpose for his or her life. It happens every time a child discovers a new insight or discovery. The resurrection happens every time two people, after long resentment and bitterness, forgive one another.

Hope happens every time the hungry are fed, the naked are clothed, the sick are visited, and the gospel is shared with the poor. The resurrection happens whenever a wrong is made right, wherever justice and reconciliation prevail. The resurrection happens whenever people discover new life in the grace of God.

Strong, healthy congregations live on hope, live on new life, live on resurrection. We look to the present and the future, not the past. We look to the mission we are sharing now. We experience the spirit of compassion and sense of community in our congregation. We focus on the people-centered, person-centered lives of our congregation now. We are discovering new life in the grace of God. We share a spirit of promise. We live as a resurrection congregation, a congregation of hope. We live a theology of resurrection, not a theology of retrenchment.

The alarmists do not help us. Their cries of wolf are finally unheeded. Their efforts to frighten and scare are so strident and persistent that we finally quit listening. They are like an obnoxious noise in the background that we simply tune out.

The doomsayers do not advance us. They weigh us down with data and data and data. It is amazing that the early Christian movement flourished without the benefit of computer printouts. Now, I am for data. I do much research. It is helpful. However, data have their proper and rightful place. Data and demographics are the hirelings to the movement, not its master. We are not here to follow the trends. We are here to change the trends.

In our time, the old friends of retrenchment and retreat do not help. People are not drawn to groups that include them. They experience enough of retrenchment and retreat in their day-to-day lives. They do not need the mixed blessing of yet another such group that does the same. Sadly, those old friends lead people to a theology of despair.

People are drawn to a congregation that has a theology of resurrection and new life. We have a theology of incarnation. We discover the grace of God in the manger of Bethlehem. We have a theology of crucifixion. We discover the compassion of Christ, lived out on the cross. But the Christian movement did not end on Golgotha.

We do not hide in an upper room. We do not retreat. We do not bury ourselves in a closed tomb. We do not retrench. We find ourselves in the garden. We discover the open tomb, the Risen Lord, and new life in Christ. Our lives are new and fresh, rich and full.

Regrettably, some congregations are still at the cross. Worse yet, they may be hiding in an upper room, fearful of a knock on the door, afraid to leave the supposed safety of that dim, dark room. They have not yet found their way, on the first day of the week, to the open tomb and the Risen Lord.

The Gospels are written backward from the experience of the resurrection, from the events of new life and hope. Everything the disciples see, they see finally in the light of the Risen Lord and new life in Christ. In a very real way, we are wise to read the passages about the resurrection, and *then* read the passages about the birth of Jesus.

We are in a resurrection time. The first millennium was the millennium of the incarnation. The second millennium was the millennium of the cross. The third millennium is the millennium of the resurrection.

We are a congregation of promise, a resurrection congregation. We have a spirit of wonder and joy, new life and hope. We are the Christmas people. We are the Easter people. We live in the confidence that God goes before us, as a cloud by day and a fire by night. God is leading us to the future God is promising and preparing for us. God prepares the present and the future.

God is the source of our promise. The source of our promise is not in knowing the lessons of history, nor in projecting the newness of the future. Our promise is not in the pedestals and prerogatives of this world. It is not in the perks and prestige of this world. Our promise is the gift of God. We live with humility and gratitude. We are amazed at God's blessings in our lives.

With the grace of God, we discover who we are. We claim our sense of individuality—of identity, integrity, and autonomy. We find a spirit of community—of roots, place, and belonging—of who we share life with in God's family. We develop an understanding of meaning for life—of the value, purpose, and significance of this life. We look to the present and the future—we live, knowing whose we are—and therefore we live with a strong spirit of hope. We internalize a set of values and standards for our lives. We live whole, healthy lives in the grace of God.

We are God's people, fashioned by the steadfast love of God. We are God's people, led by the strong hope of God. We are a small, strong congregation. We live in the grace of God. Love lasts. Hope endures. We live with the assurance of the promise of God. We are the people of promise. We are a small, strong congregation.

The Author

Kennon L. Callahan is the author of many books, including his best known work, the groundbreaking *Twelve Keys to an Effective Church,* which has formed the basis for the widely acclaimed movement of mission growth. He has earned B.A., M.Div., S.T.M., and Ph.D. degrees, has served both rural and urban congregations, and has taught for many years at Emory University. He is the founder of the National Institute for Church Planning. His books are helping thousands of congregations around the globe.

He and Julia, his wife of forty-four years, have two children and three grandchildren. They enjoy the outdoors, hiking, horseback riding, sailing, quilting, and music. They live in Dallas.

Index